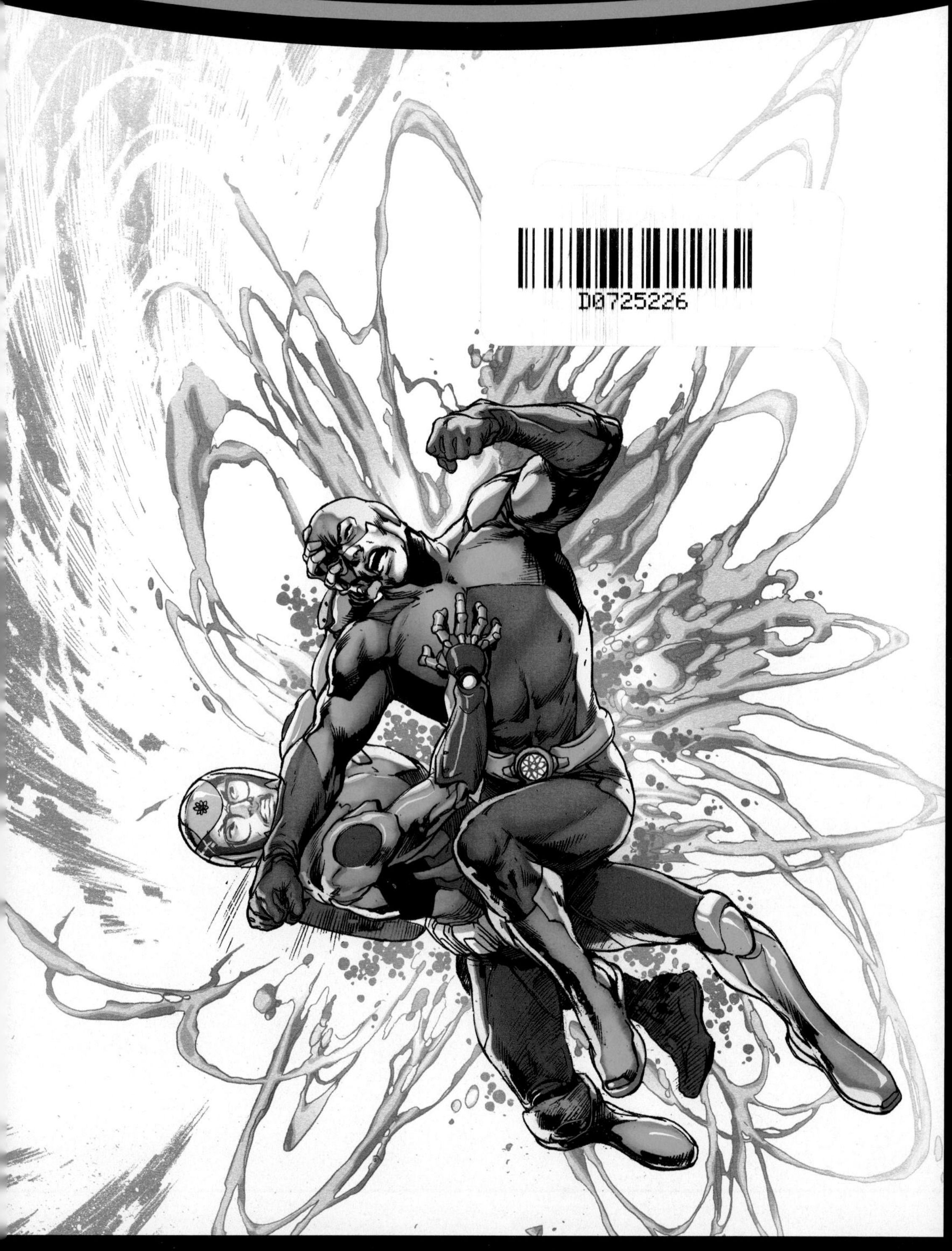

JUSTICE LEAGUE OF AMERICA

VOL.3 PANIC IN THE MICROVERSE

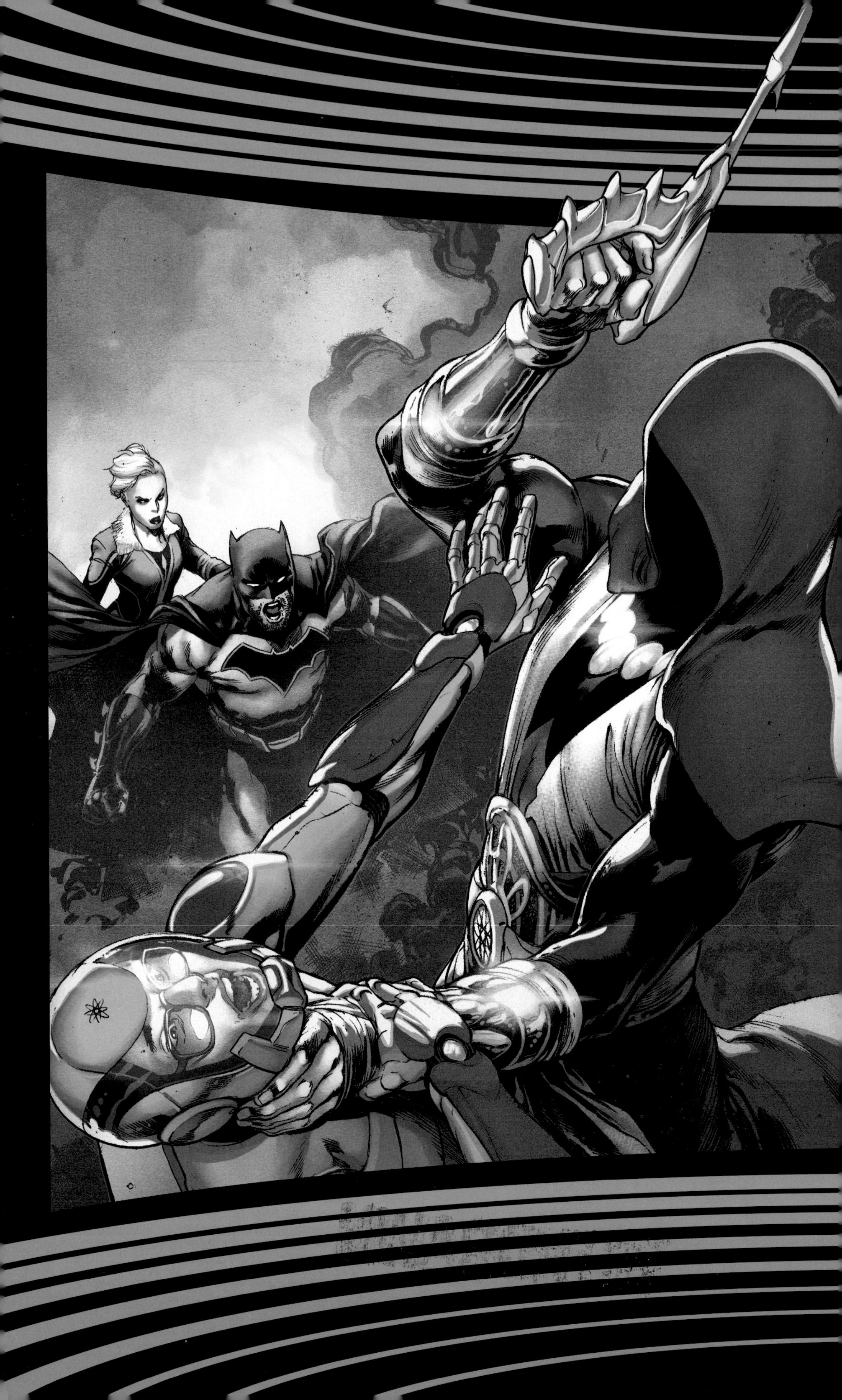

JUSTICE LEAGUE OF AMERICA
VOL.3 PANIC IN THE MICROVERSE

STEVE ORLANDO
writer

IVAN REIS * **FELIPE WATANABE**
pencillers

IVAN REIS * **JULIO FERREIRA** * **RUY JOSE** * **OCLAIR ALBERT**
inkers

MARCELO MAIOLO
colorist

CLAYTON COWLES
letterer

IVAN REIS and MARCELO MAIOLO
collection cover artists

RAY PALMER ATOM created by **GARDNER FOX**

Special thanks to Geoff Johns

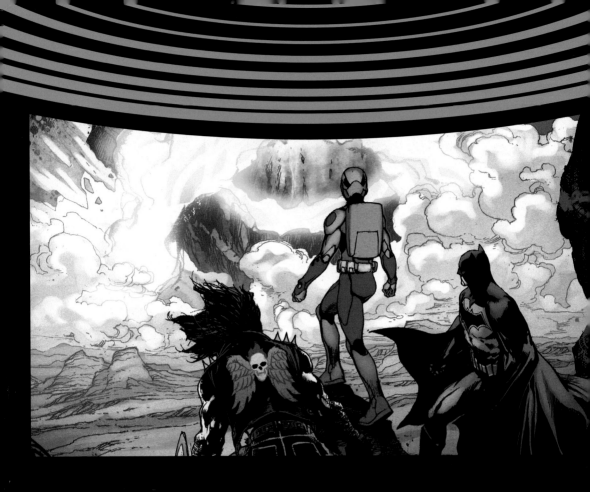

BRIAN CUNNINGHAM Editor - Original Series * **AMEDEO TURTURRO** Associate Editor - Original Series * **DAVE WIELGOSZ** Assistant Editor - Original Series
JEB WOODARD Group Editor - Collected Editions * **ROBIN WILDMAN** Editor - Collected Edition * **STEVE COOK** Design Director - Books * **LOUIS PRANDI** Publication Design

BOB HARRAS Senior VP - Editor-in-Chief, DC Comics * **PAT McCALLUM** Executive Editor, DC Comics

DIANE NELSON President * **DAN DiDIO** Publisher * **JIM LEE** Publisher * **GEOFF JOHNS** President & Chief Creative Officer
AMIT DESAI Executive VP - Business & Marketing Strategy, Direct to Consumer & Global Franchise Management * **SAM ADES** Senior VP & General Manager, Digital Services
BOBBIE CHASE VP & Executive Editor, Young Reader & Talent Development * **MARK CHIARELLO** Senior VP - Art, Design & Collected Editions
JOHN CUNNINGHAM Senior VP - Sales & Trade Marketing * **ANNE DePIES** Senior VP - Business Strategy, Finance & Administration * **DON FALLETTI** VP - Manufacturing Operations
LAWRENCE GANEM VP - Editorial Administration & Talent Relations * **ALISON GILL** Senior VP - Manufacturing & Operations
HANK KANALZ Senior VP - Editorial Strategy & Administration * **JAY KOGAN** VP - Legal Affairs * **JACK MAHAN** VP - Business Affairs
NICK J. NAPOLITANO VP - Manufacturing Administration * **EDDIE SCANNELL** VP - Consumer Marketing
COURTNEY SIMMONS Senior VP - Publicity & Communications * **JIM (SKI) SOKOLOWSKI** VP - Comic Book Specialty Sales & Trade Marketing
NANCY SPEARS VP - Mass, Book, Digital Sales & Trade Marketing * **MICHELE R. WELLS** VP - Content Strategy

JUSTICE LEAGUE OF AMERICA VOL. 3: PANIC IN THE MICROVERSE

DC Comics, 2900 West Alameda Ave., Burbank, CA 91505
Printed by LSC Communications, Kendallville, IN, USA. 2/2/18. First Printing.
ISBN: 978-1-4012-7784-0

Library of Congress Cataloging-in-Publication Data is available.

PEFC Certified
Printed on paper from sustainably managed forests, controlled sources
PEFC
PEFC/29-31-337
www.pefc.org

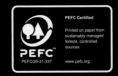

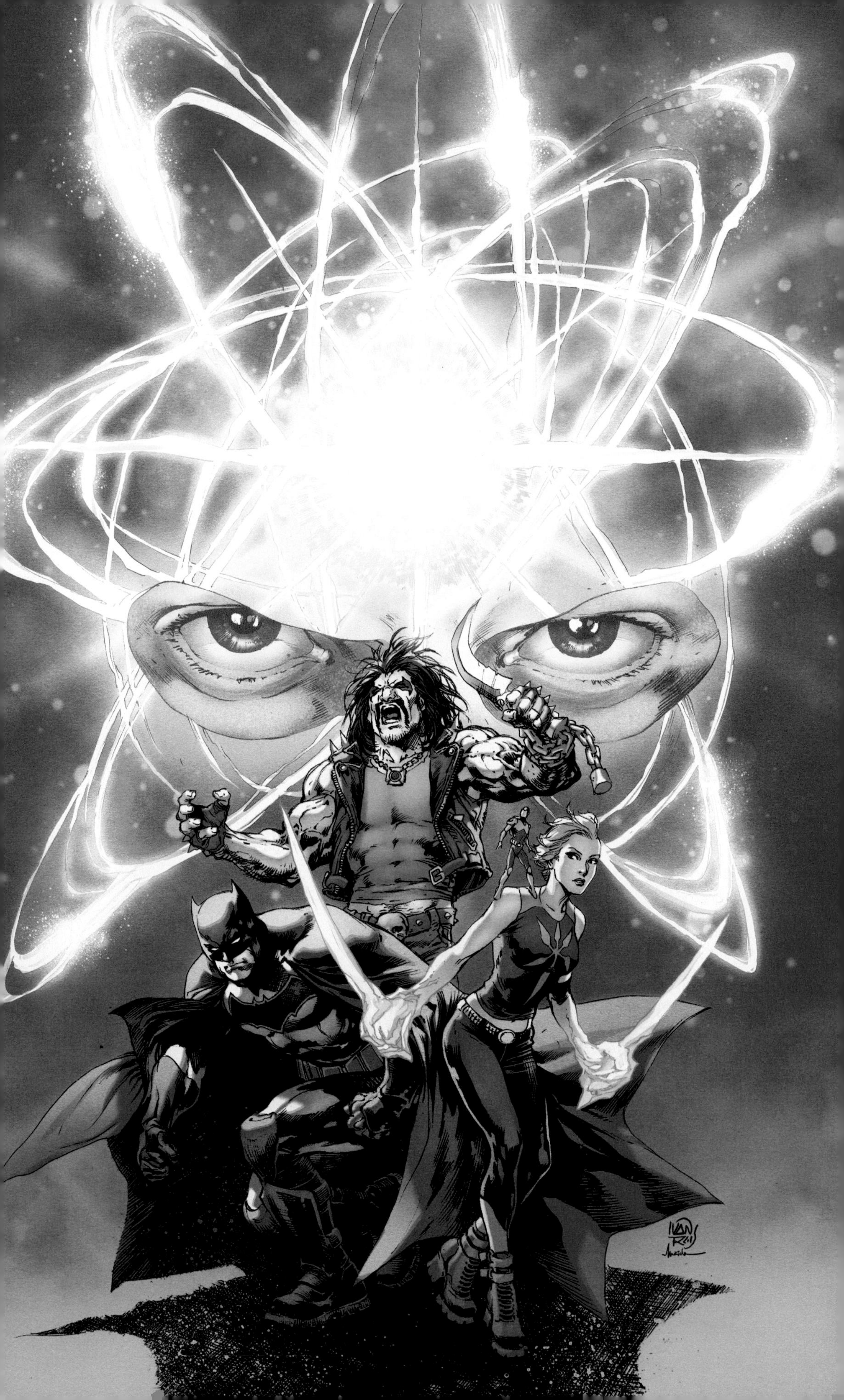

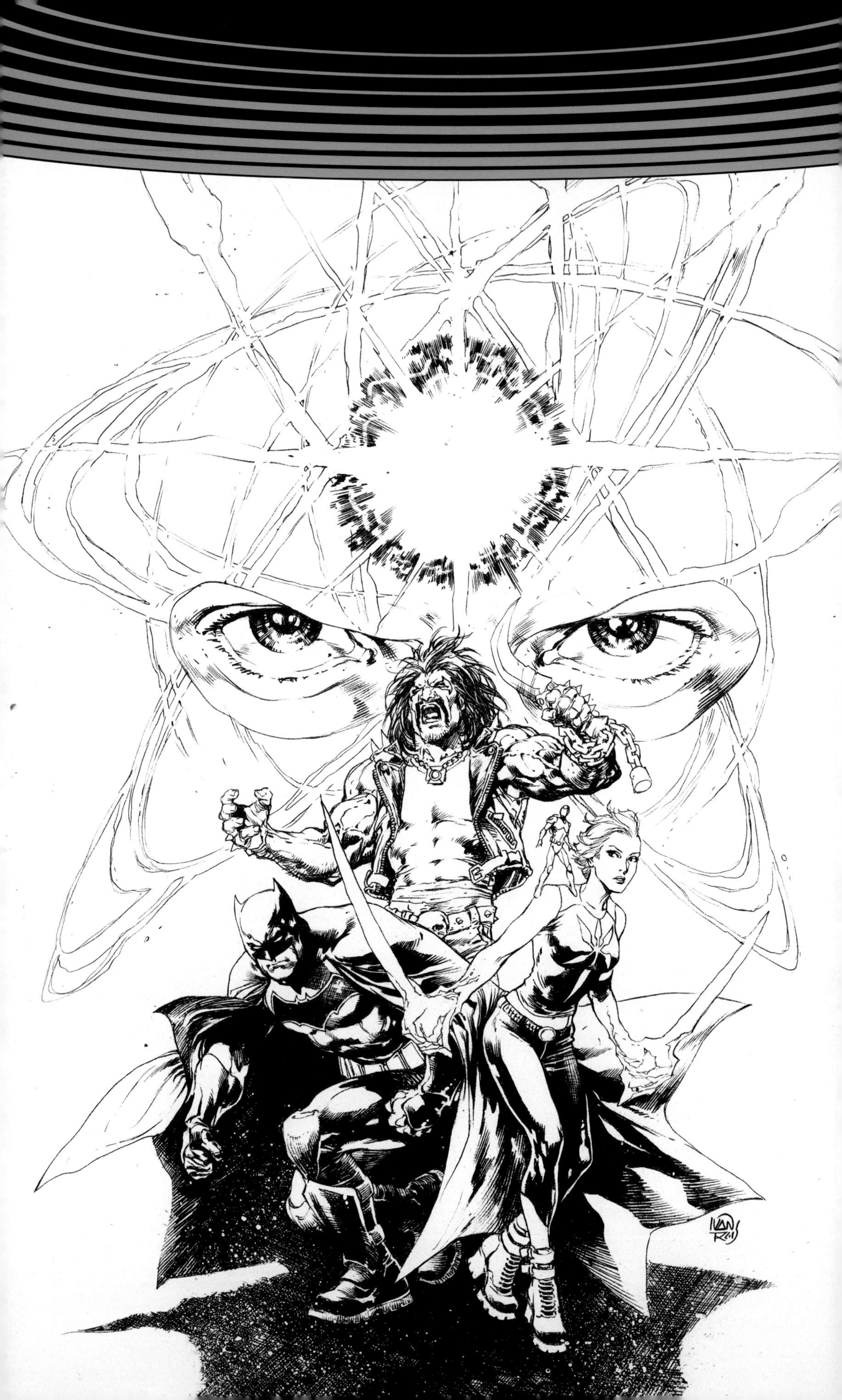

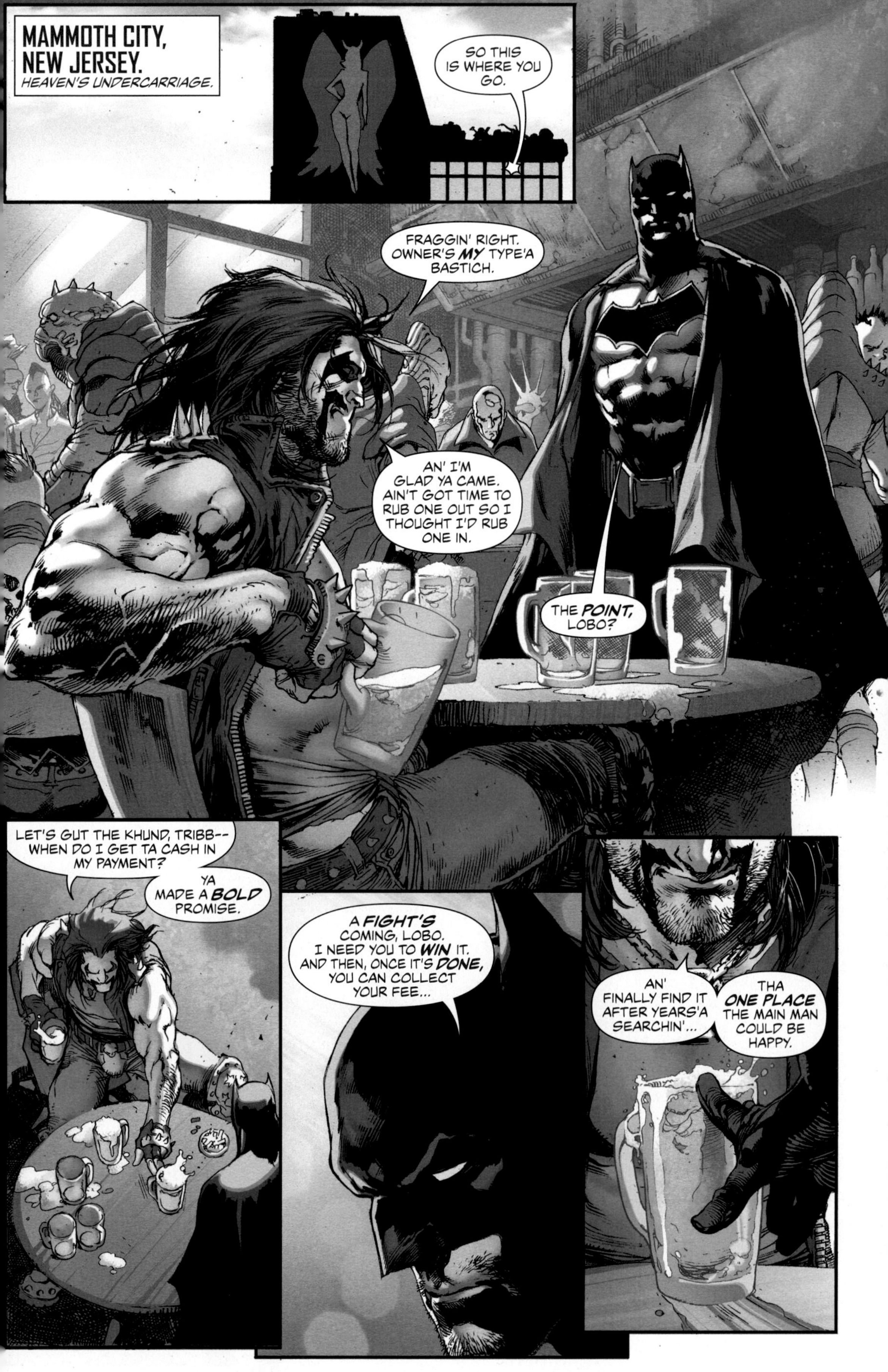
MAMMOTH CITY, NEW JERSEY.
HEAVEN'S UNDERCARRIAGE.
SO THIS IS WHERE YOU GO.
FRAGGIN' RIGHT. OWNER'S MY TYPE'A BASTICH.
AN' I'M GLAD YA CAME. AIN'T GOT TIME TO RUB ONE OUT SO I THOUGHT I'D RUB ONE IN.
THE POINT, LOBO?
LET'S GUT THE KHUND, TRIBB-- WHEN DO I GET TA CASH IN MY PAYMENT?
YA MADE A BOLD PROMISE.
A FIGHT'S COMING, LOBO. I NEED YOU TO WIN IT. AND THEN, ONCE IT'S DONE, YOU CAN COLLECT YOUR FEE...
AN' FINALLY FIND IT AFTER YEARS'A SEARCHIN'...
THA ONE PLACE THE MAIN MAN COULD BE HAPPY.

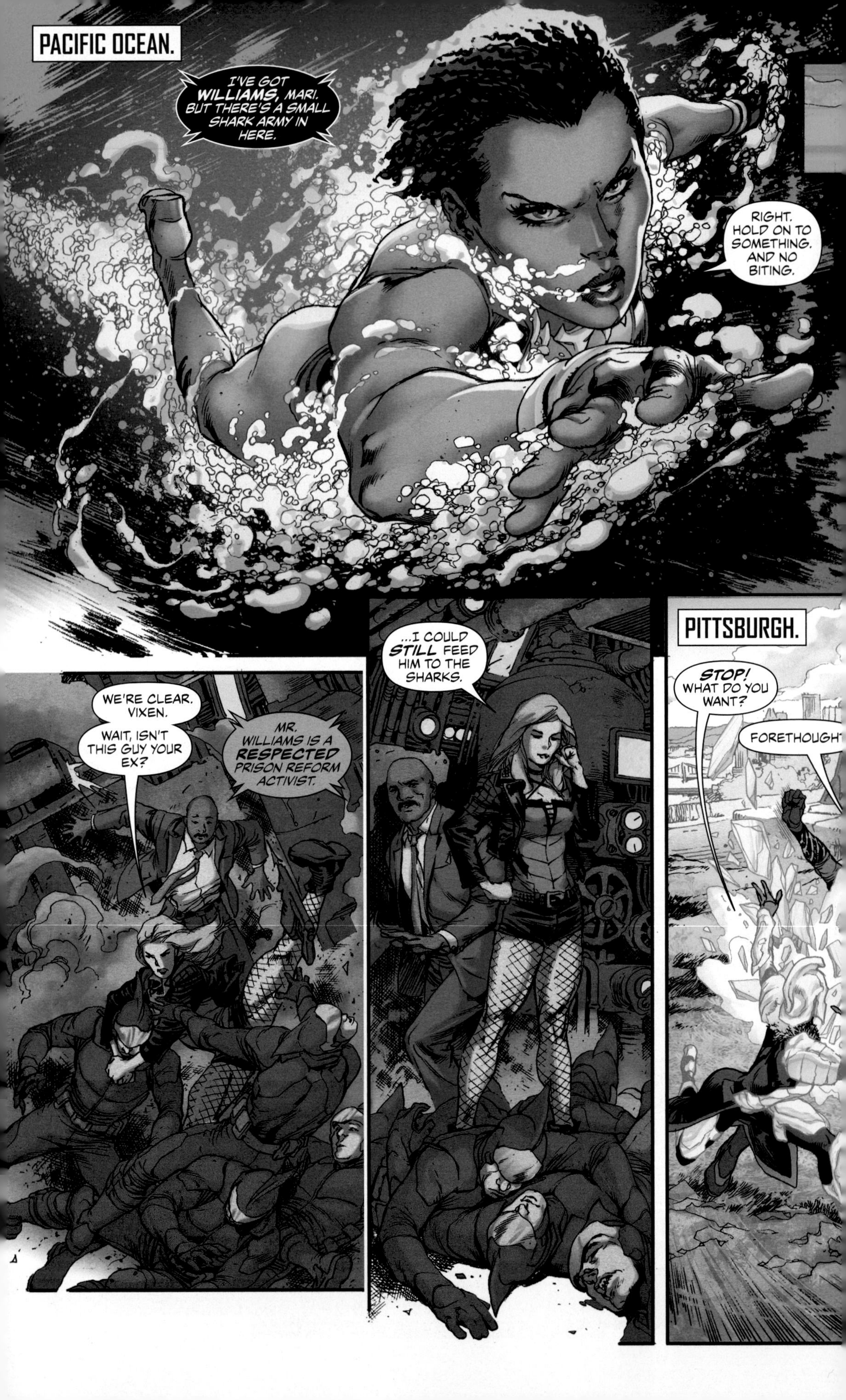
PACIFIC OCEAN.
I'VE GOT WILLIAMS, MARI. BUT THERE'S A SMALL SHARK ARMY IN HERE.
RIGHT. HOLD ON TO SOMETHING. AND NO BITING.
WE'RE CLEAR, VIXEN.
WAIT, ISN'T THIS GUY YOUR EX?
MR. WILLIAMS IS A RESPECTED PRISON REFORM ACTIVIST.
...I COULD STILL FEED HIM TO THE SHARKS.
PITTSBURGH.
STOP! WHAT DO YOU WANT?
FORETHOUGHT

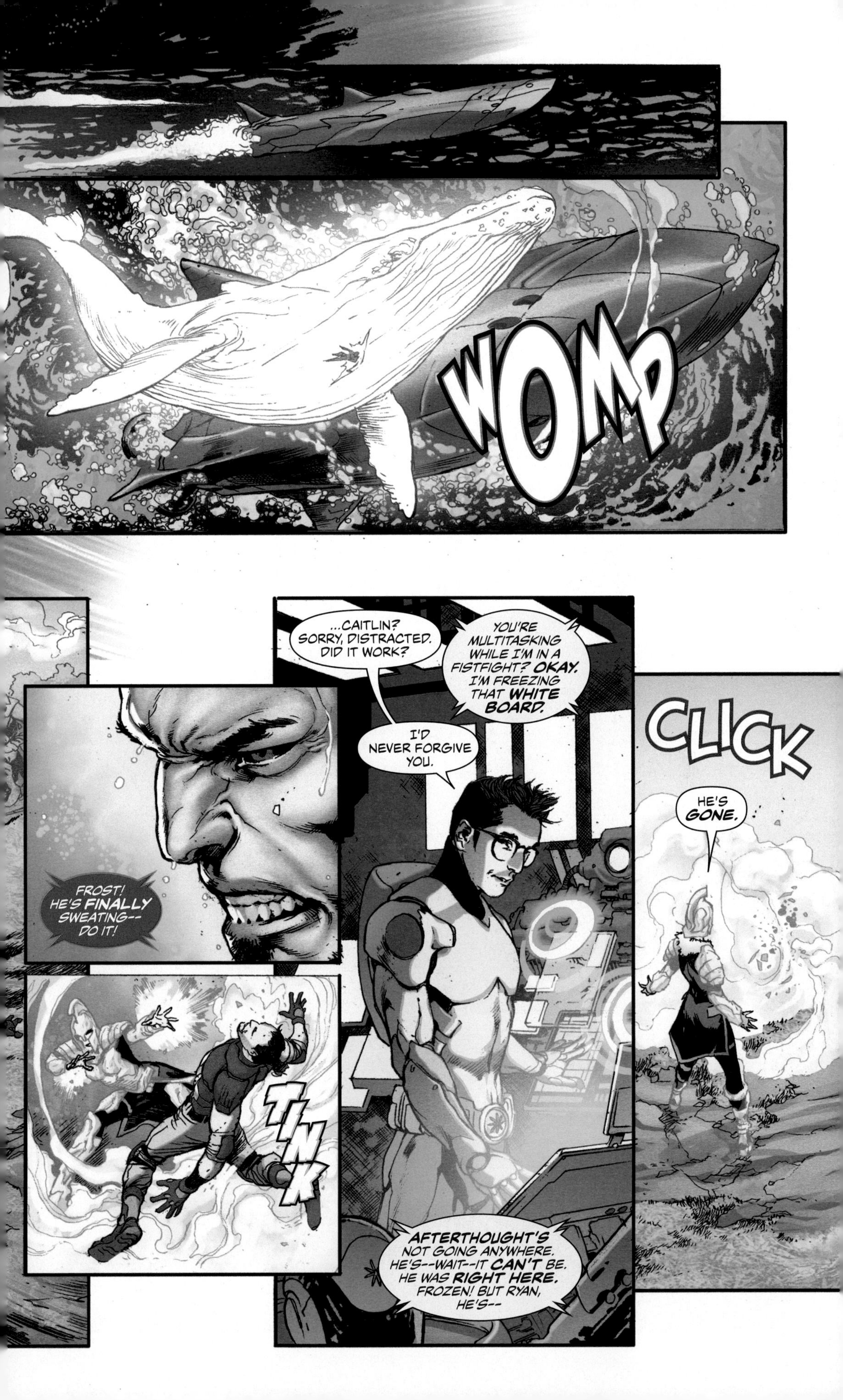
WOMP
FROST! HE'S FINALLY SWEATING-- DO IT!
TINK
...CAITLIN? SORRY, DISTRACTED. DID IT WORK?
YOU'RE MULTITASKING WHILE I'M IN A FISTFIGHT? OKAY. I'M FREEZING THAT WHITE BOARD.
I'D NEVER FORGIVE YOU.
AFTERTHOUGHT'S NOT GOING ANYWHERE. HE'S--WAIT--IT CAN'T BE. HE WAS RIGHT HERE. FROZEN! BUT RYAN, HE'S--
CLICK
HE'S GONE.

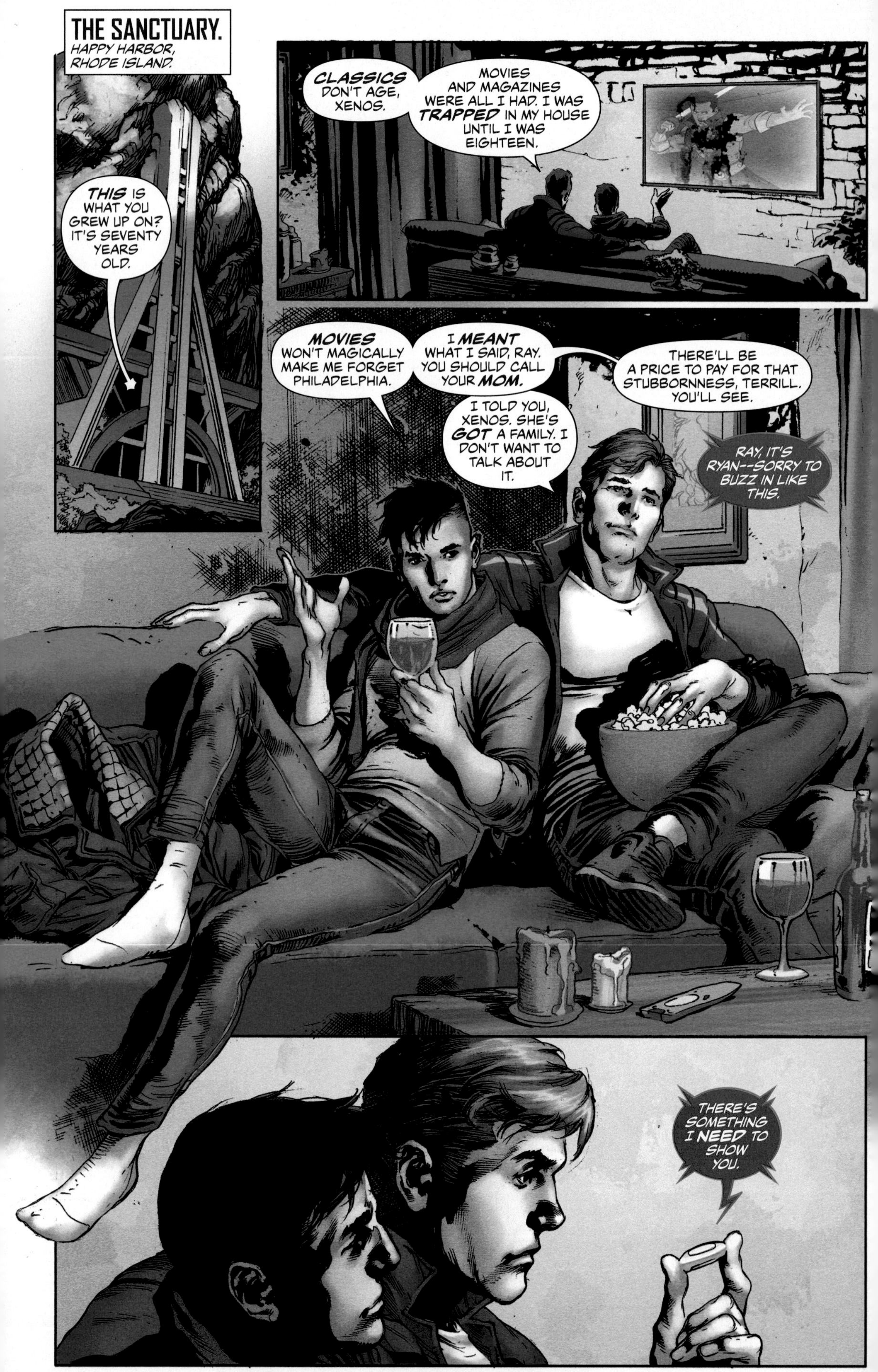
THE SANCTUARY.
HAPPY HARBOR, RHODE ISLAND.
THIS IS WHAT YOU GREW UP ON? IT'S SEVENTY YEARS OLD.
CLASSICS DON'T AGE, XENOS.
MOVIES AND MAGAZINES WERE ALL I HAD. I WAS TRAPPED IN MY HOUSE UNTIL I WAS EIGHTEEN.
MOVIES WON'T MAGICALLY MAKE ME FORGET PHILADELPHIA.
I MEANT WHAT I SAID, RAY. YOU SHOULD CALL YOUR MOM.
I TOLD YOU, XENOS. SHE'S GOT A FAMILY. I DON'T WANT TO TALK ABOUT IT.
THERE'LL BE A PRICE TO PAY FOR THAT STUBBORNNESS, TERRILL. YOU'LL SEE.
RAY, IT'S RYAN--SORRY TO BUZZ IN LIKE THIS.
THERE'S SOMETHING I NEED TO SHOW YOU.

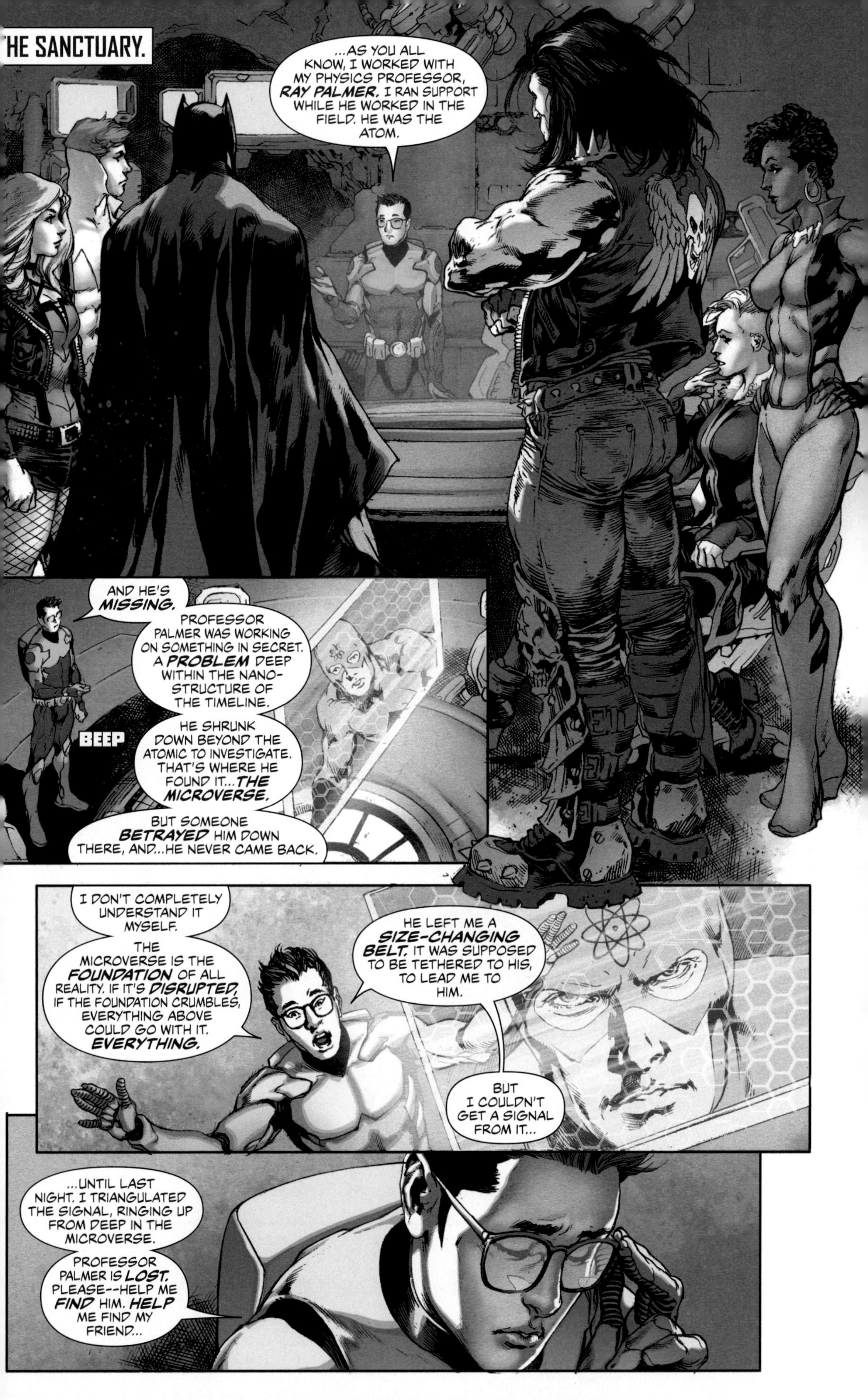
THE SANCTUARY.
...AS YOU ALL KNOW, I WORKED WITH MY PHYSICS PROFESSOR, RAY PALMER. I RAN SUPPORT WHILE HE WORKED IN THE FIELD. HE WAS THE ATOM.
AND HE'S MISSING.
PROFESSOR PALMER WAS WORKING ON SOMETHING IN SECRET. A PROBLEM DEEP WITHIN THE NANO-STRUCTURE OF THE TIMELINE.
HE SHRUNK DOWN BEYOND THE ATOMIC TO INVESTIGATE. THAT'S WHERE HE FOUND IT...THE MICROVERSE.
BEEP
BUT SOMEONE BETRAYED HIM DOWN THERE, AND...HE NEVER CAME BACK.
I DON'T COMPLETELY UNDERSTAND IT MYSELF.
THE MICROVERSE IS THE FOUNDATION OF ALL REALITY. IF IT'S DISRUPTED, IF THE FOUNDATION CRUMBLES, EVERYTHING ABOVE COULD GO WITH IT. EVERYTHING.
HE LEFT ME A SIZE-CHANGING BELT. IT WAS SUPPOSED TO BE TETHERED TO HIS, TO LEAD ME TO HIM.
BUT I COULDN'T GET A SIGNAL FROM IT...
...UNTIL LAST NIGHT. I TRIANGULATED THE SIGNAL, RINGING UP FROM DEEP IN THE MICROVERSE.
PROFESSOR PALMER IS LOST. PLEASE--HELP ME FIND HIM. HELP ME FIND MY FRIEND...

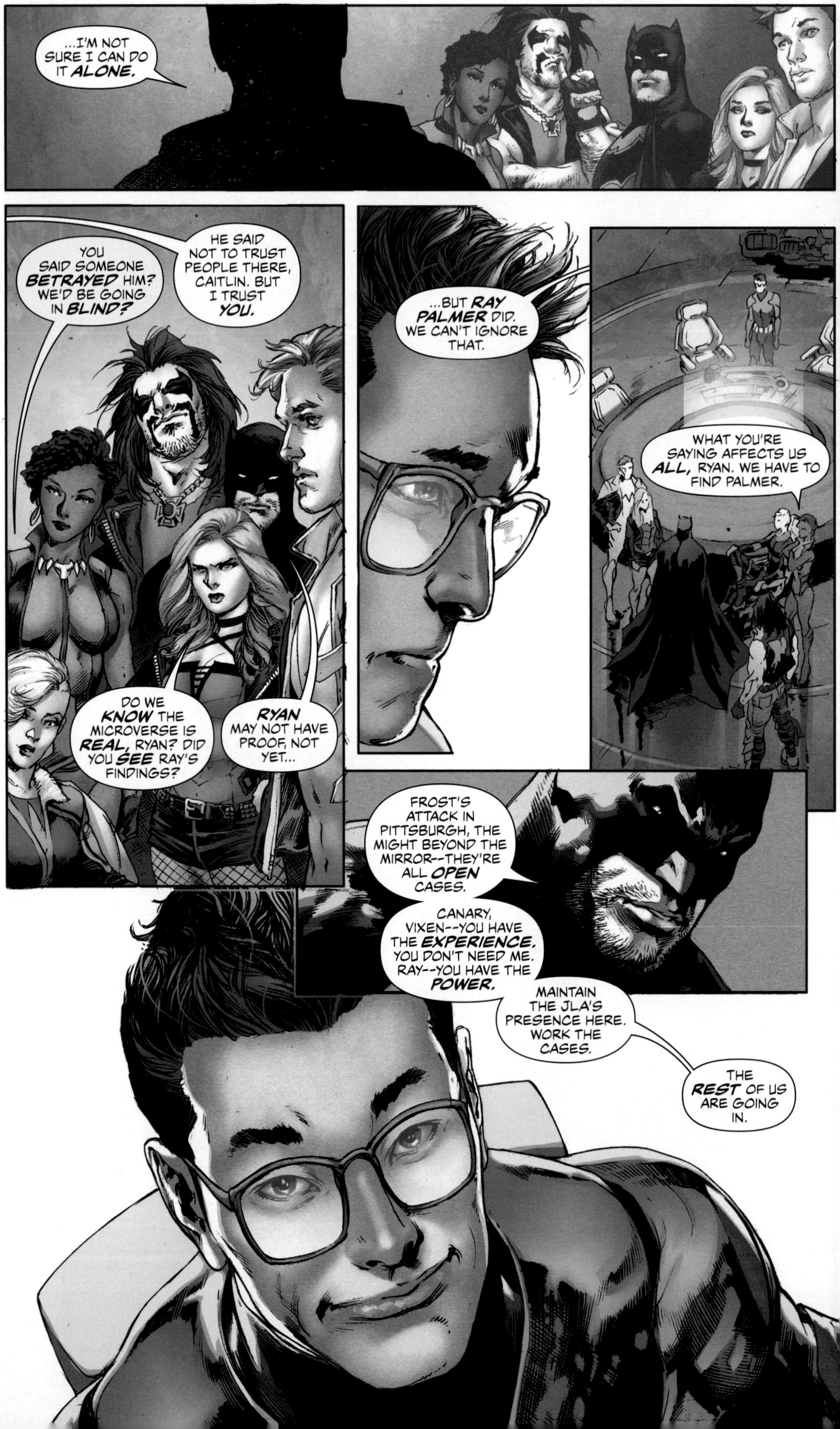
...I'M NOT SURE I CAN DO IT ALONE.
YOU SAID SOMEONE BETRAYED HIM? WE'D BE GOING IN BLIND?
HE SAID NOT TO TRUST PEOPLE THERE, CAITLIN. BUT I TRUST YOU.
DO WE KNOW THE MICROVERSE IS REAL, RYAN? DID YOU SEE RAY'S FINDINGS?
RYAN MAY NOT HAVE PROOF, NOT YET...
...BUT RAY PALMER DID. WE CAN'T IGNORE THAT.
WHAT YOU'RE SAYING AFFECTS US ALL, RYAN. WE HAVE TO FIND PALMER.
FROST'S ATTACK IN PITTSBURGH, THE MIGHT BEYOND THE MIRROR--THEY'RE ALL OPEN CASES.
CANARY, VIXEN--YOU HAVE THE EXPERIENCE. YOU DON'T NEED ME. RAY--YOU HAVE THE POWER.
MAINTAIN THE JLA'S PRESENCE HERE. WORK THE CASES.
THE REST OF US ARE GOING IN.

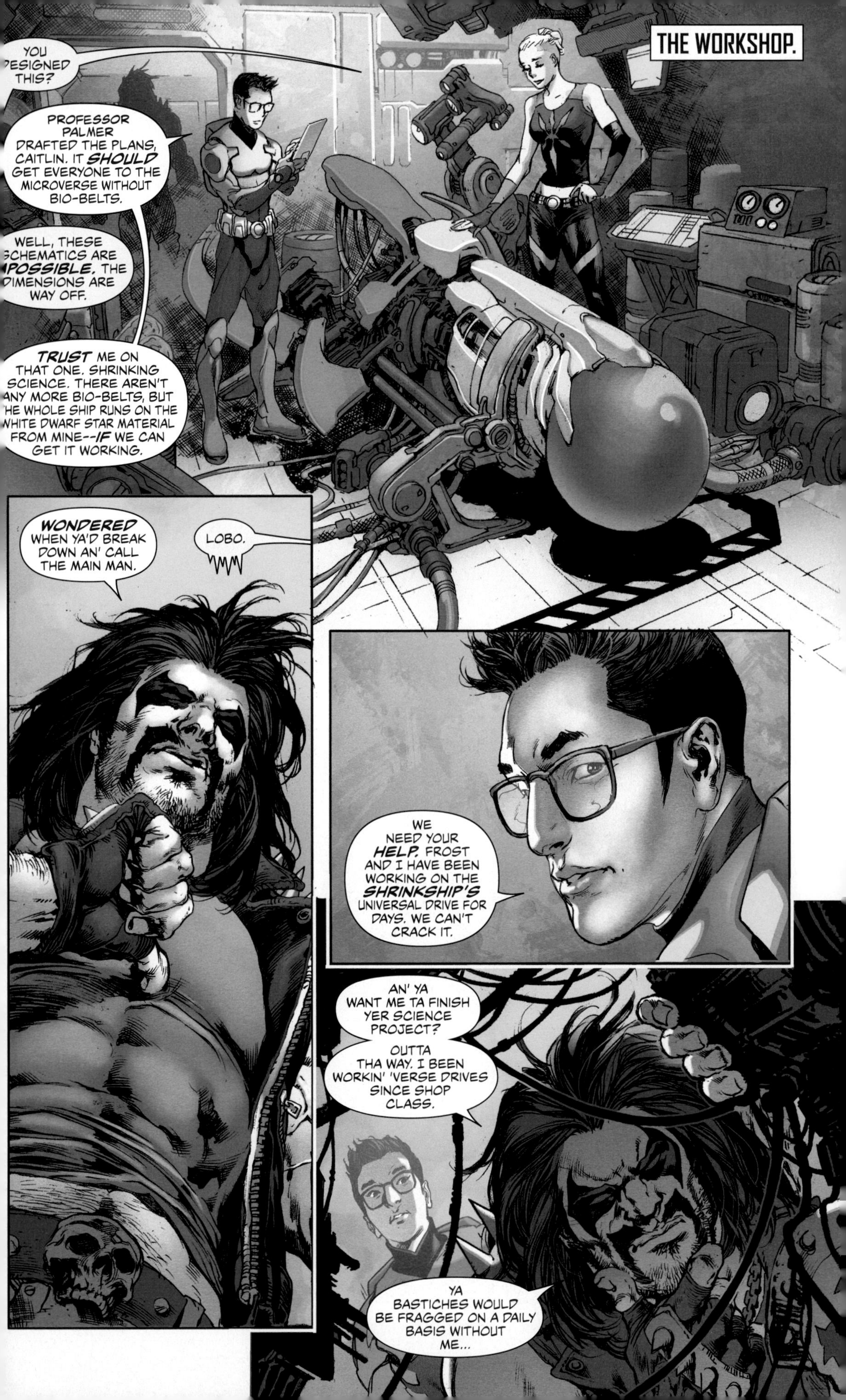
THE WORKSHOP.
YOU DESIGNED THIS?
PROFESSOR PALMER DRAFTED THE PLANS, CAITLIN. IT SHOULD GET EVERYONE TO THE MICROVERSE WITHOUT BIO-BELTS.
WELL, THESE SCHEMATICS ARE IMPOSSIBLE. THE DIMENSIONS ARE WAY OFF.
TRUST ME ON THAT ONE. SHRINKING SCIENCE. THERE AREN'T ANY MORE BIO-BELTS, BUT THE WHOLE SHIP RUNS ON THE WHITE DWARF STAR MATERIAL FROM MINE--IF WE CAN GET IT WORKING.
WONDERED WHEN YA'D BREAK DOWN AN' CALL THE MAIN MAN.
LOBO.
WE NEED YOUR HELP. FROST AND I HAVE BEEN WORKING ON THE SHRINKSHIP'S UNIVERSAL DRIVE FOR DAYS. WE CAN'T CRACK IT.
AN' YA WANT ME TA FINISH YER SCIENCE PROJECT?
OUTTA THA WAY. I BEEN WORKIN' 'VERSE DRIVES SINCE SHOP CLASS.
YA BASTICHES WOULD BE FRAGGED ON A DAILY BASIS WITHOUT ME...

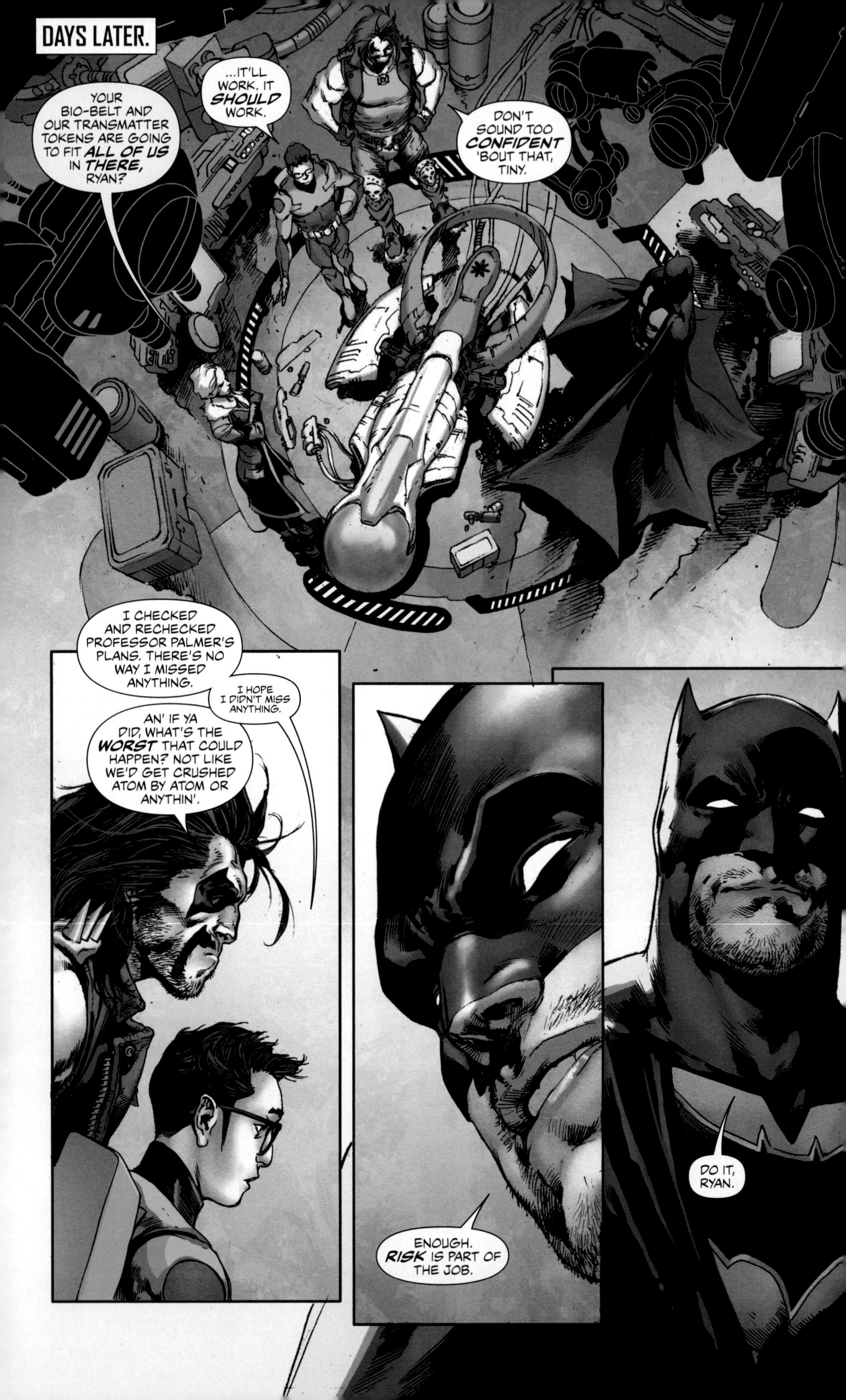
DAYS LATER.
YOUR BIO-BELT AND OUR TRANSMATTER TOKENS ARE GOING TO FIT ALL OF US IN THERE, RYAN?
...IT'LL WORK. IT SHOULD WORK.
DON'T SOUND TOO CONFIDENT 'BOUT THAT, TINY.
I CHECKED AND RECHECKED PROFESSOR PALMER'S PLANS. THERE'S NO WAY I MISSED ANYTHING.
I HOPE I DIDN'T MISS ANYTHING.
AN' IF YA DID, WHAT'S THE WORST THAT COULD HAPPEN? NOT LIKE WE'D GET CRUSHED ATOM BY ATOM OR ANYTHIN'.
ENOUGH. RISK IS PART OF THE JOB.
DO IT, RYAN.

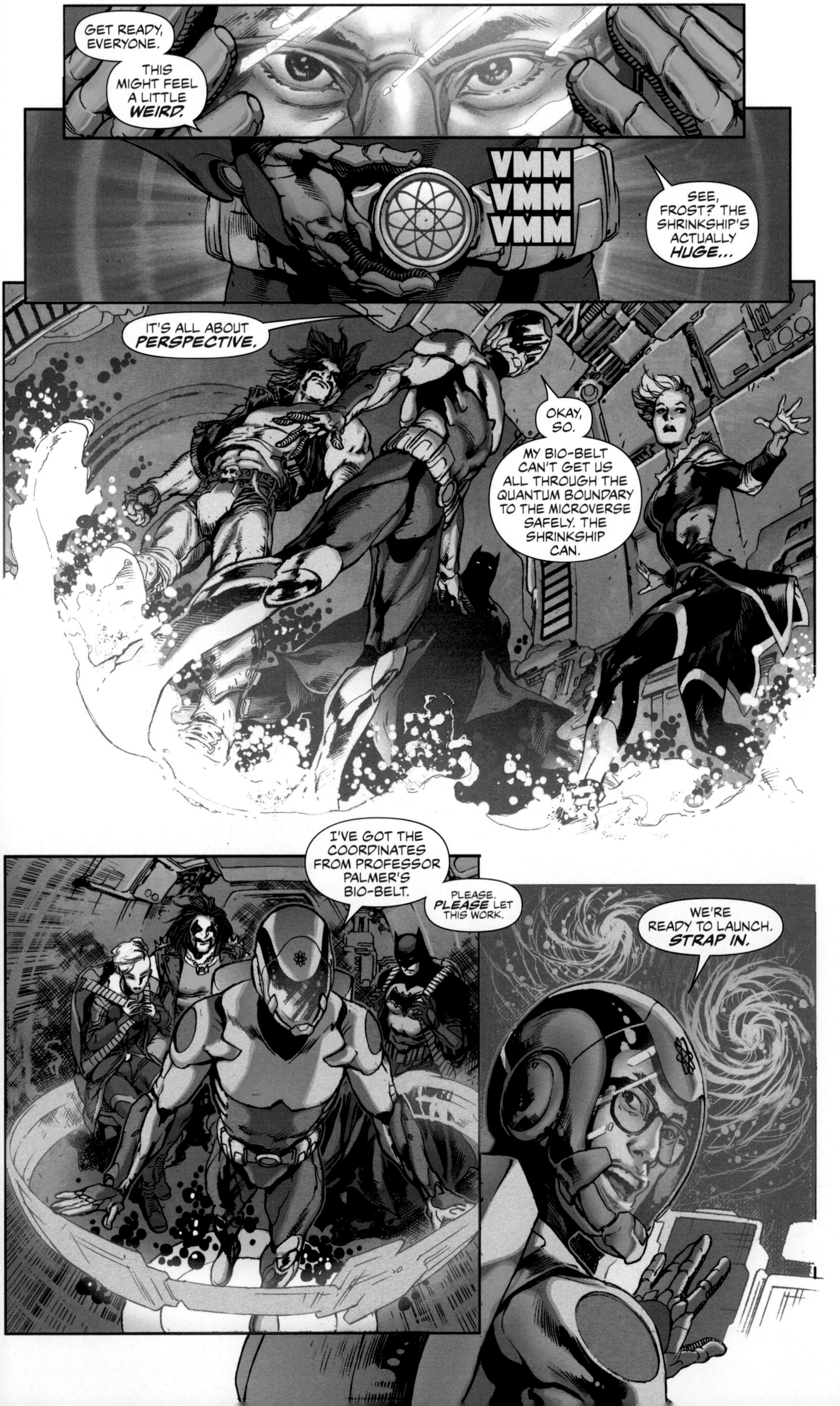
GET READY, EVERYONE.
THIS MIGHT FEEL A LITTLE WEIRD.
VMM VMM VMM
SEE, FROST? THE SHRINKSHIP'S ACTUALLY HUGE...
IT'S ALL ABOUT PERSPECTIVE.
OKAY, SO.
MY BIO-BELT CAN'T GET US ALL THROUGH THE QUANTUM BOUNDARY TO THE MICROVERSE SAFELY. THE SHRINKSHIP CAN.
I'VE GOT THE COORDINATES FROM PROFESSOR PALMER'S BIO-BELT.
PLEASE. PLEASE LET THIS WORK.
WE'RE READY TO LAUNCH. STRAP IN.

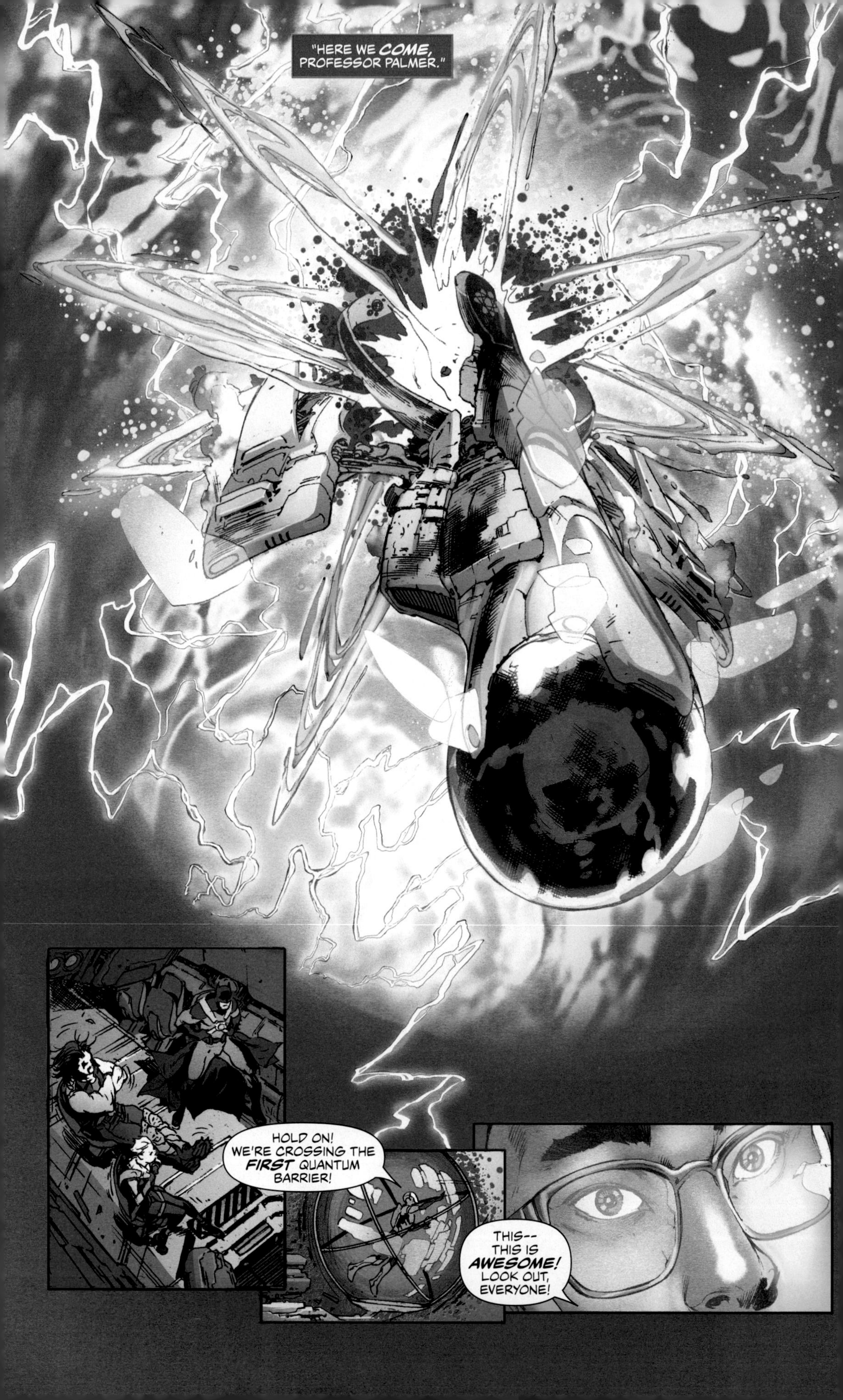
"HERE WE *COME*, PROFESSOR PALMER."
HOLD ON! WE'RE CROSSING THE *FIRST* QUANTUM BARRIER!
THIS-- THIS IS *AWESOME!* LOOK OUT, EVERYONE!

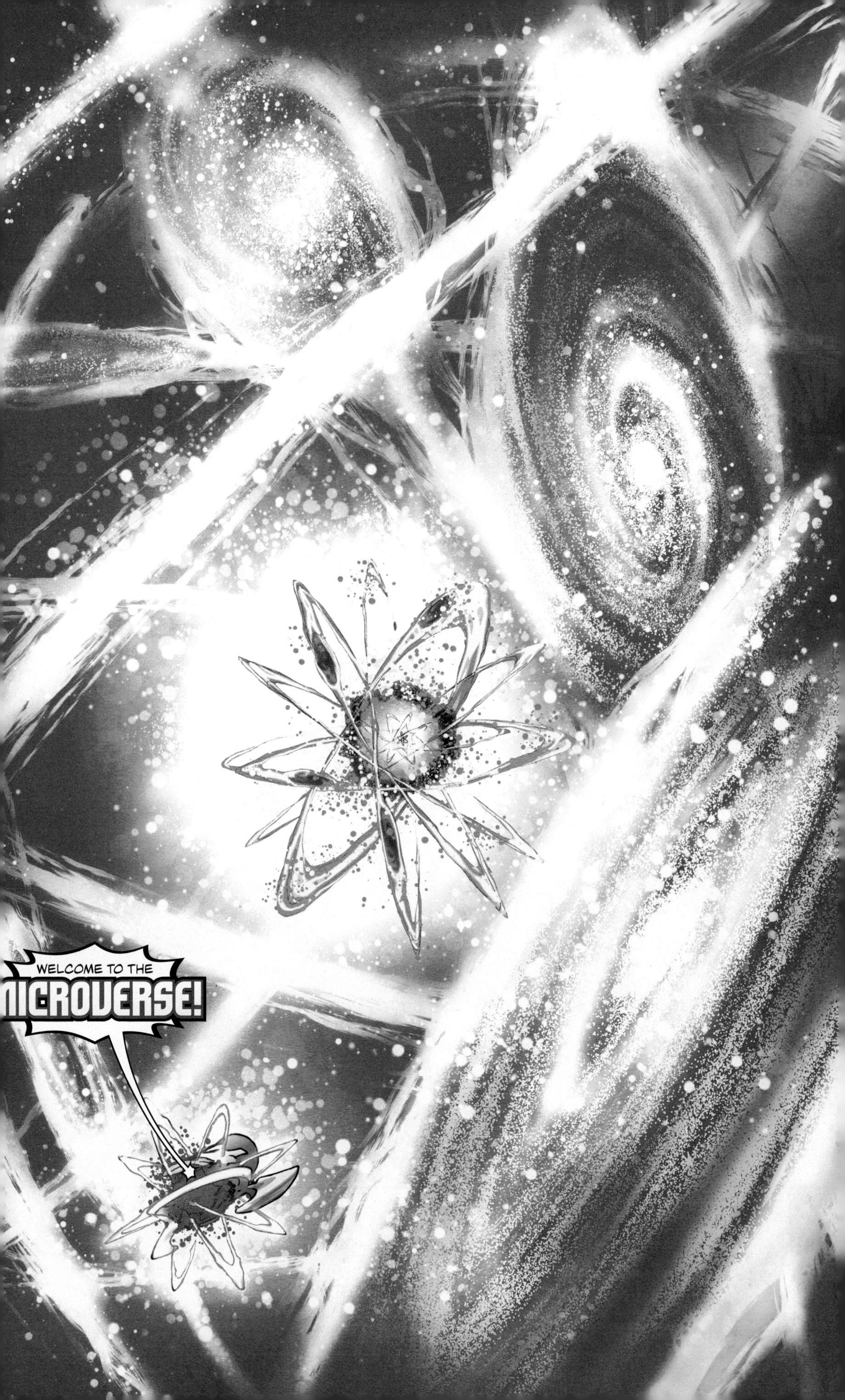
WELCOME TO THE
ICROVERSE!

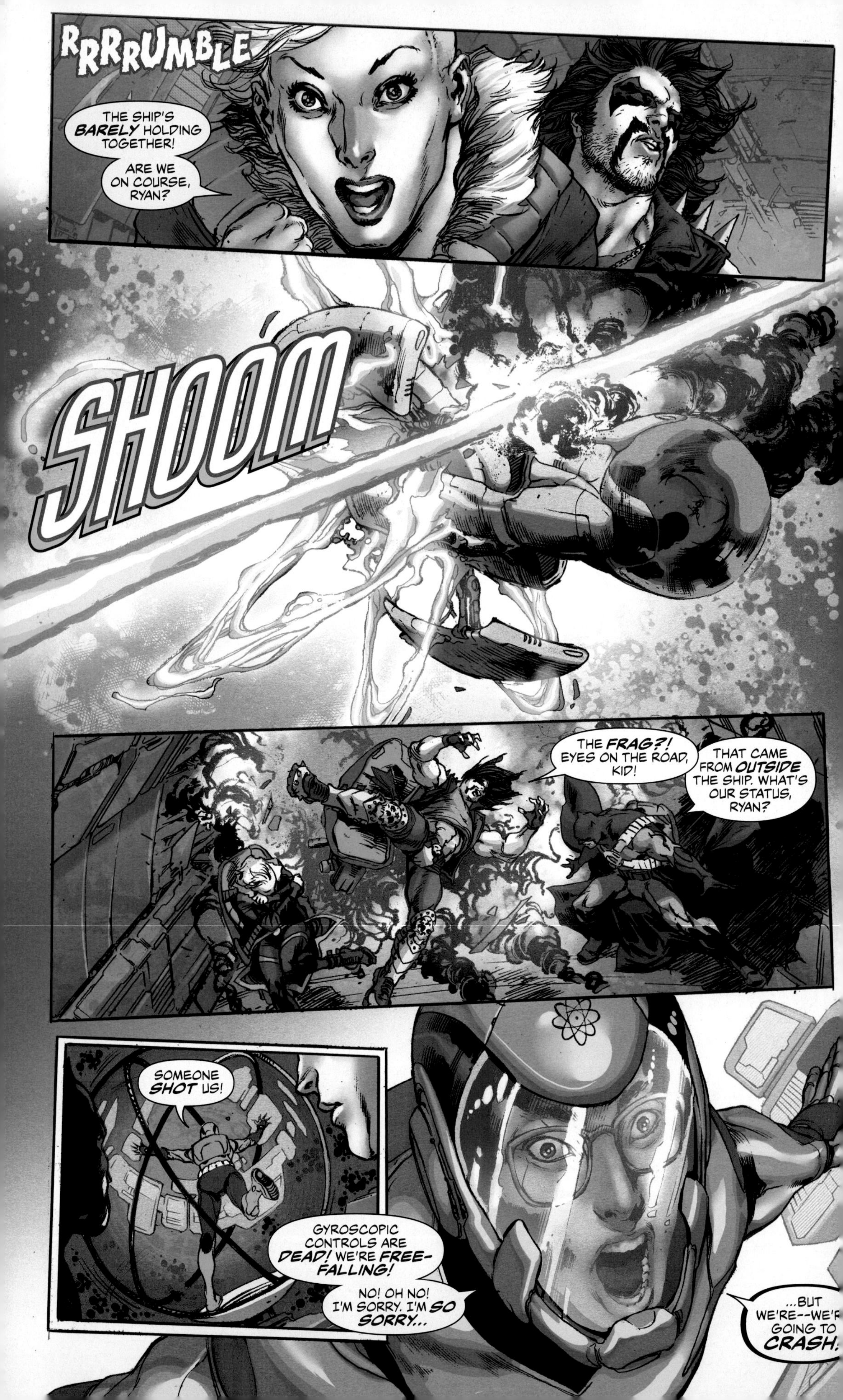
RRRRUMBLE
THE SHIP'S BARELY HOLDING TOGETHER!
ARE WE ON COURSE, RYAN?
SHOOM
THE FRAG?! EYES ON THE ROAD, KID!
THAT CAME FROM OUTSIDE THE SHIP. WHAT'S OUR STATUS, RYAN?
SOMEONE SHOT US!
GYROSCOPIC CONTROLS ARE DEAD! WE'RE FREE-FALLING!
NO! OH NO! I'M SORRY. I'M SO SORRY...
...BUT WE'RE--WE'RE GOING TO CRASH.

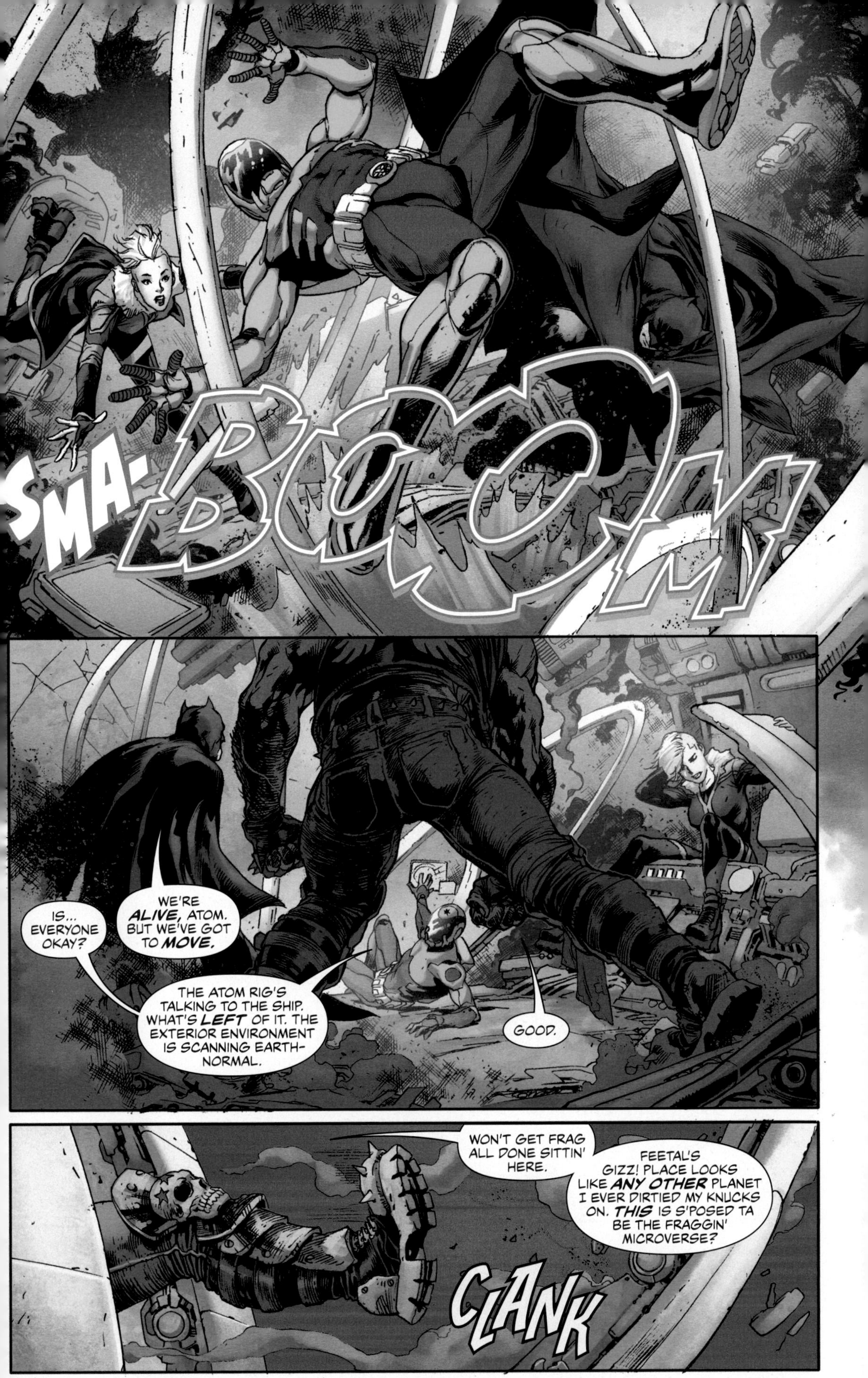
SMA-BOOM
IS... EVERYONE OKAY?
WE'RE ALIVE, ATOM. BUT WE'VE GOT TO MOVE.
THE ATOM RIG'S TALKING TO THE SHIP. WHAT'S LEFT OF IT. THE EXTERIOR ENVIRONMENT IS SCANNING EARTH-NORMAL.
GOOD.
WON'T GET FRAG ALL DONE SITTIN' HERE.
FEETAL'S GIZZ! PLACE LOOKS LIKE ANY OTHER PLANET I EVER DIRTIED MY KNUCKS ON. THIS IS S'POSED TA BE THE FRAGGIN' MICROVERSE?
CLANK

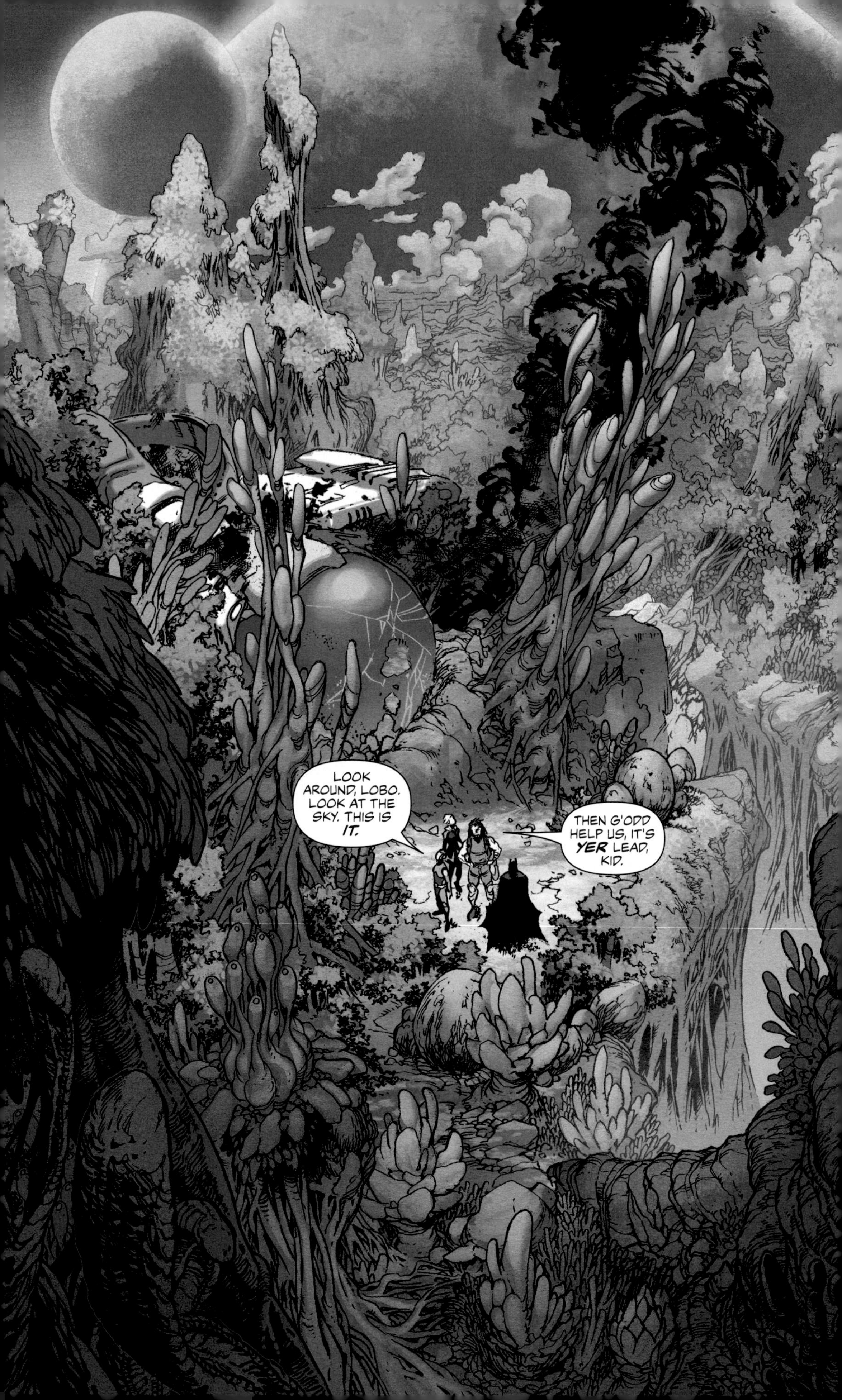
LOOK AROUND, LOBO. LOOK AT THE SKY. THIS IS *IT.*
THEN G'ODD HELP US, IT'S *YER* LEAD, KID.

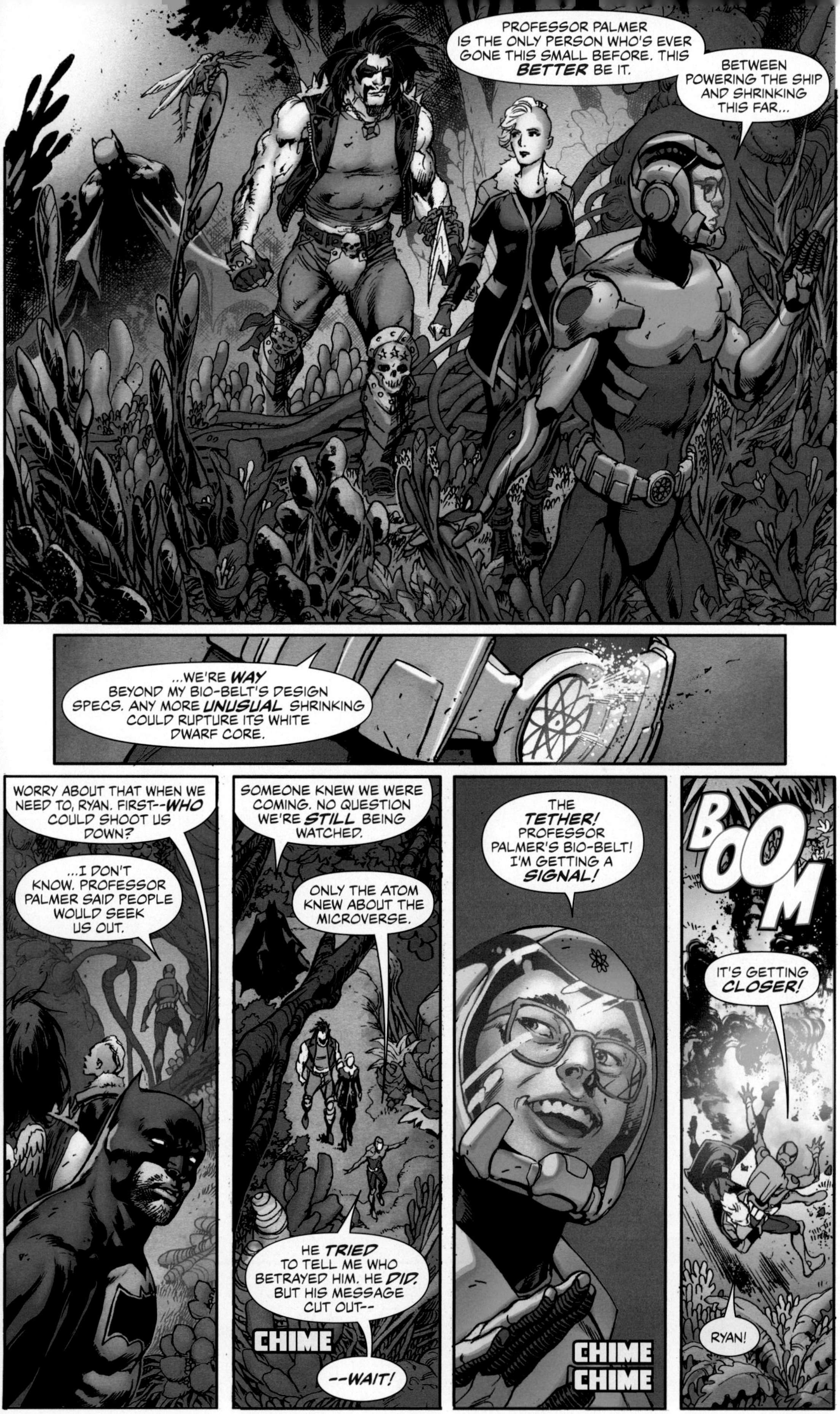
PROFESSOR PALMER IS THE ONLY PERSON WHO'S EVER GONE THIS SMALL BEFORE. THIS BETTER BE IT.
BETWEEN POWERING THE SHIP AND SHRINKING THIS FAR...
...WE'RE WAY BEYOND MY BIO-BELT'S DESIGN SPECS. ANY MORE UNUSUAL SHRINKING COULD RUPTURE ITS WHITE DWARF CORE.
WORRY ABOUT THAT WHEN WE NEED TO, RYAN. FIRST--WHO COULD SHOOT US DOWN?
...I DON'T KNOW. PROFESSOR PALMER SAID PEOPLE WOULD SEEK US OUT.
SOMEONE KNEW WE WERE COMING. NO QUESTION WE'RE STILL BEING WATCHED.
ONLY THE ATOM KNEW ABOUT THE MICROVERSE.
HE TRIED TO TELL ME WHO BETRAYED HIM. HE DID. BUT HIS MESSAGE CUT OUT--
CHIME
--WAIT!
THE TETHER! PROFESSOR PALMER'S BIO-BELT! I'M GETTING A SIGNAL!
CHIME
CHIME
BOOM
IT'S GETTING CLOSER!
RYAN!

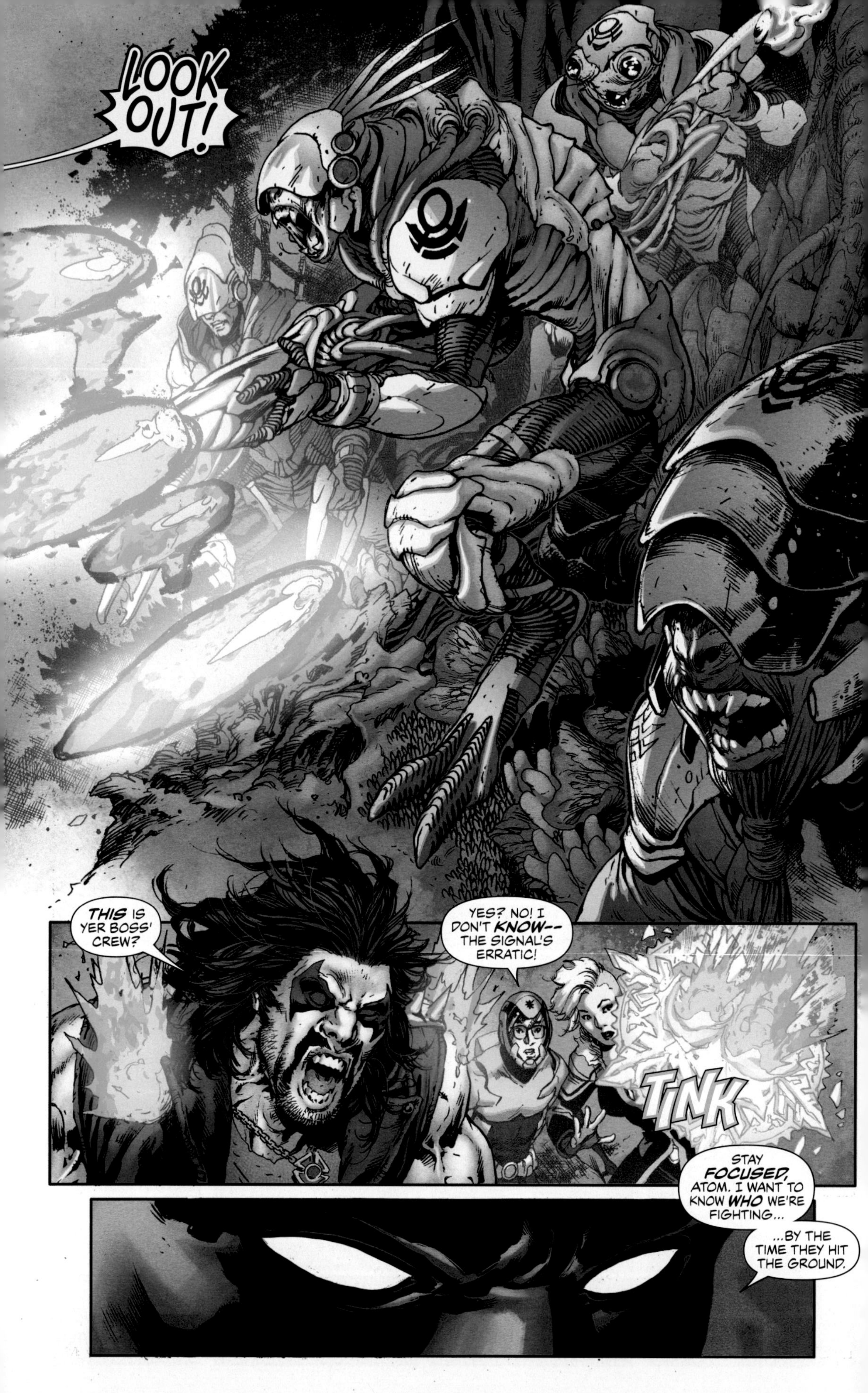
LOOK OUT!
THIS IS YER BOSS' CREW?
YES? NO! I DON'T KNOW-- THE SIGNAL'S ERRATIC!
TINK
STAY FOCUSED, ATOM. I WANT TO KNOW WHO WE'RE FIGHTING...
...BY THE TIME THEY HIT THE GROUND.

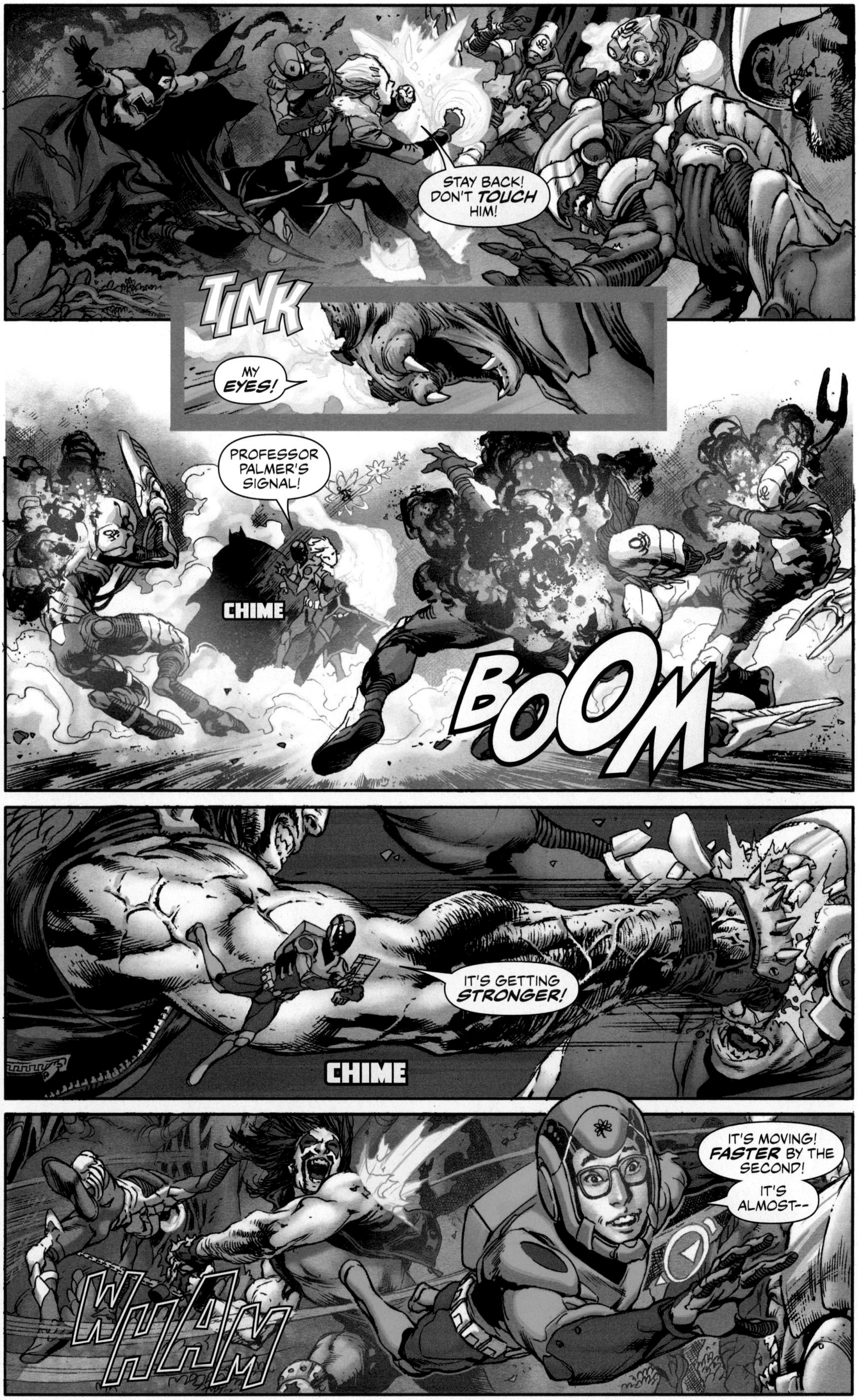
STAY BACK! DON'T TOUCH HIM!
TINK
MY EYES!
PROFESSOR PALMER'S SIGNAL!
CHIME
BOOM
IT'S GETTING STRONGER!
CHIME
IT'S MOVING! FASTER BY THE SECOND!
IT'S ALMOST--
WHAM

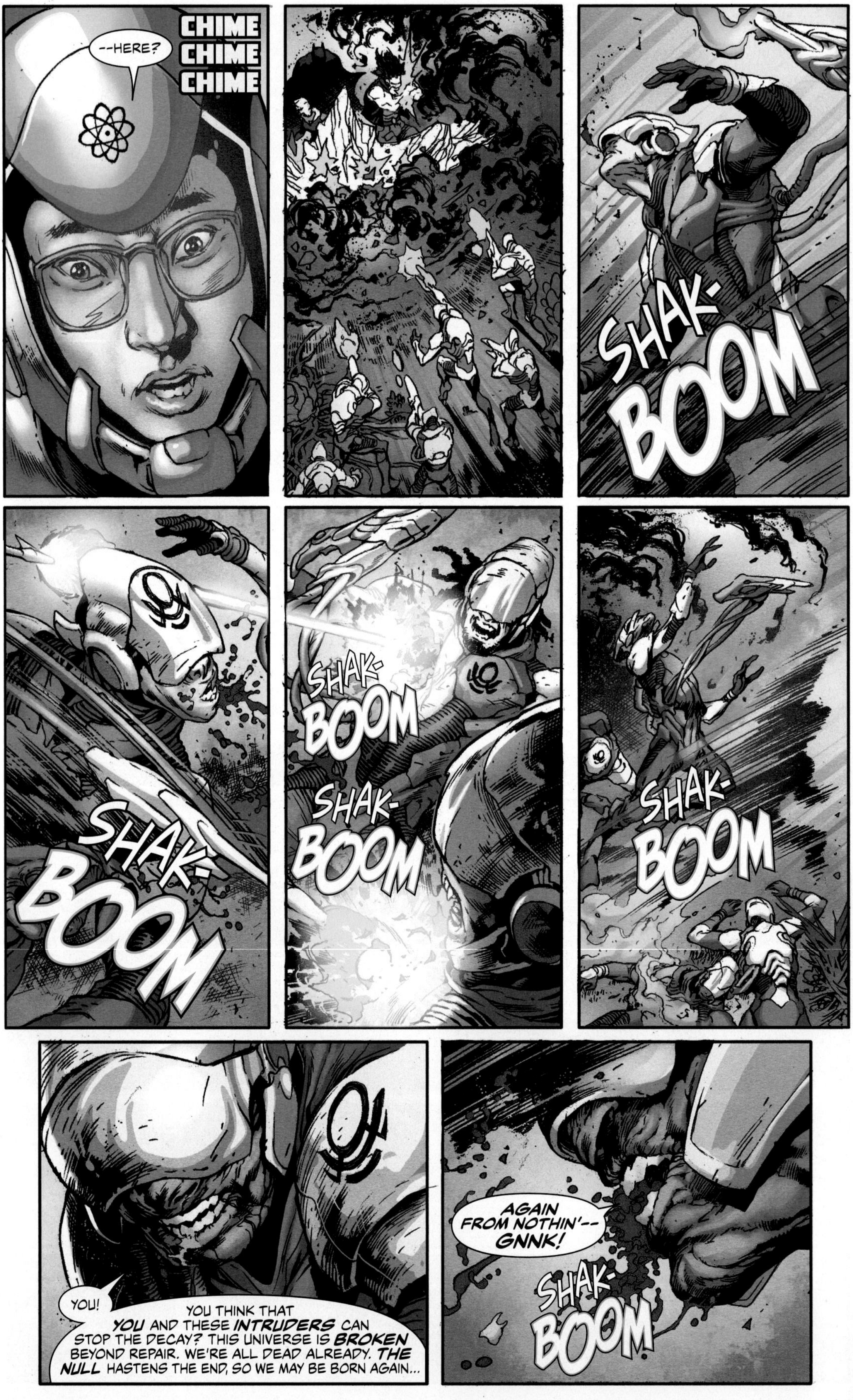

CHIME
CHIME
CHIME
--HERE?
SHAK-BOOM
SHAK-BOOM
SHAK-BOOM
SHAK-BOOM
SHAK-BOOM
YOU!
YOU THINK THAT YOU AND THESE INTRUDERS CAN STOP THE DECAY? THIS UNIVERSE IS BROKEN BEYOND REPAIR. WE'RE ALL DEAD ALREADY. THE NULL HASTENS THE END, SO WE MAY BE BORN AGAIN...
AGAIN FROM NOTHIN'-- GNNK!
SHAK-BOOM

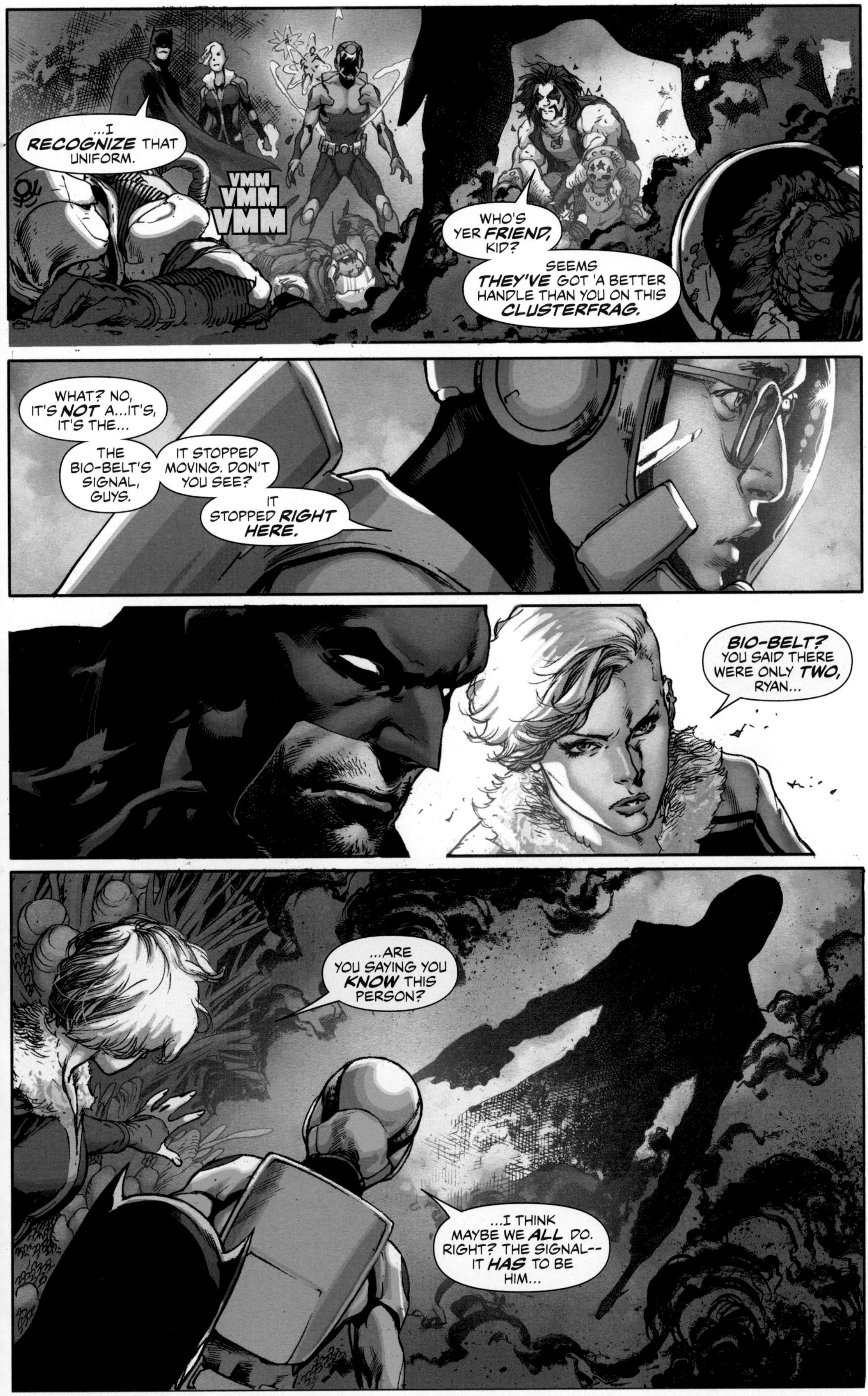
...I RECOGNIZE THAT UNIFORM.
VMM VMM VMM
WHO'S YER FRIEND, KID?
SEEMS THEY'VE GOT 'A BETTER HANDLE THAN YOU ON THIS CLUSTERFRAG.
WHAT? NO, IT'S NOT A...IT'S, IT'S THE...
THE BIO-BELT'S SIGNAL, GUYS.
IT STOPPED MOVING. DON'T YOU SEE?
IT STOPPED RIGHT HERE.
BIO-BELT? YOU SAID THERE WERE ONLY TWO, RYAN...
...ARE YOU SAYING YOU KNOW THIS PERSON?
...I THINK MAYBE WE ALL DO. RIGHT? THE SIGNAL-- IT HAS TO BE HIM...

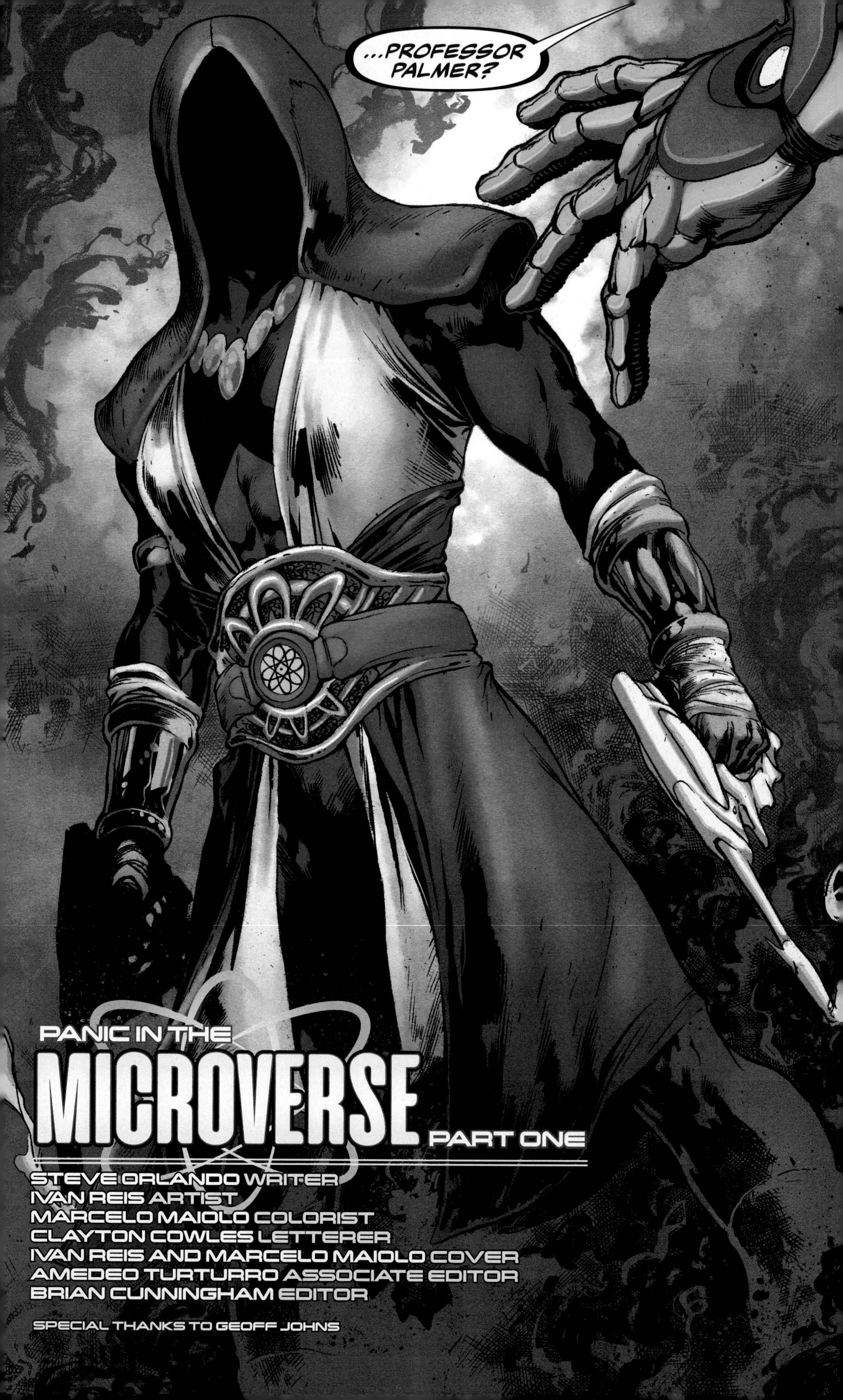
...PROFESSOR PALMER?
PANIC IN THE
MICROVERSE
PART ONE
STEVE ORLANDO WRITER
IVAN REIS ARTIST
MARCELO MAIOLO COLORIST
CLAYTON COWLES LETTERER
IVAN REIS AND MARCELO MAIOLO COVER
AMEDEO TURTURRO ASSOCIATE EDITOR
BRIAN CUNNINGHAM EDITOR
SPECIAL THANKS TO GEOFF JOHNS

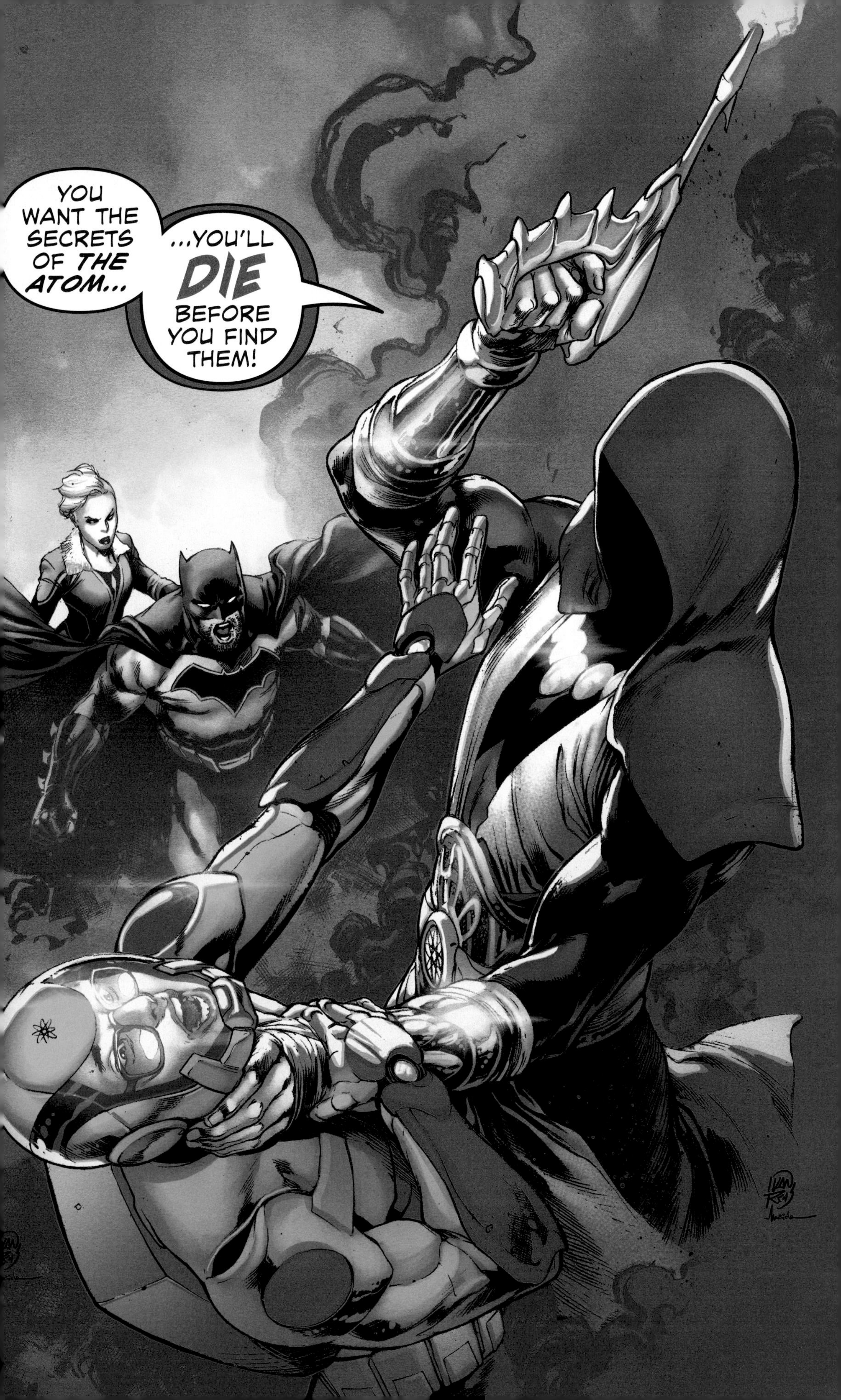

YOU WANT THE SECRETS OF *THE ATOM*...
...YOU'LL **DIE** BEFORE YOU FIND THEM!

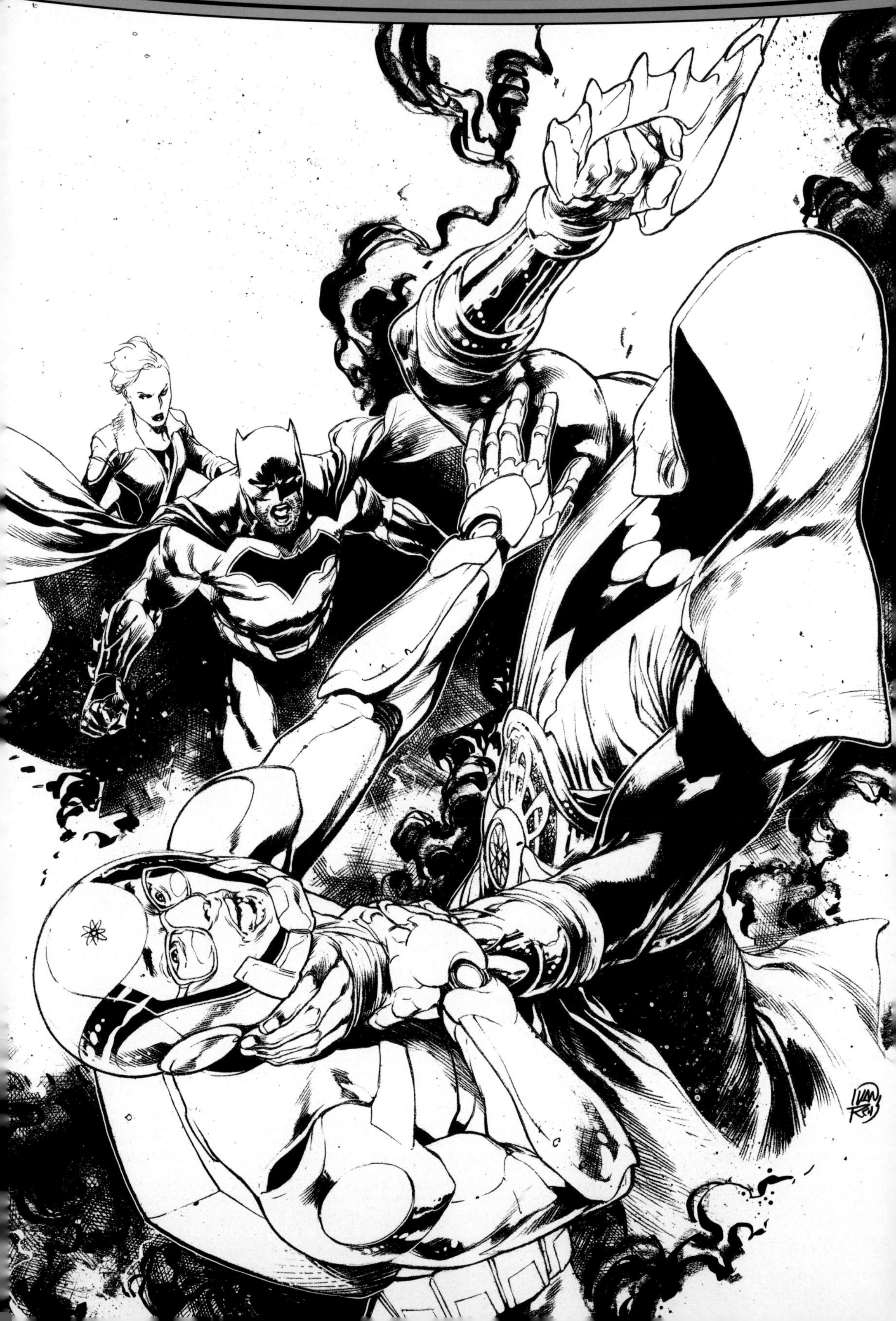

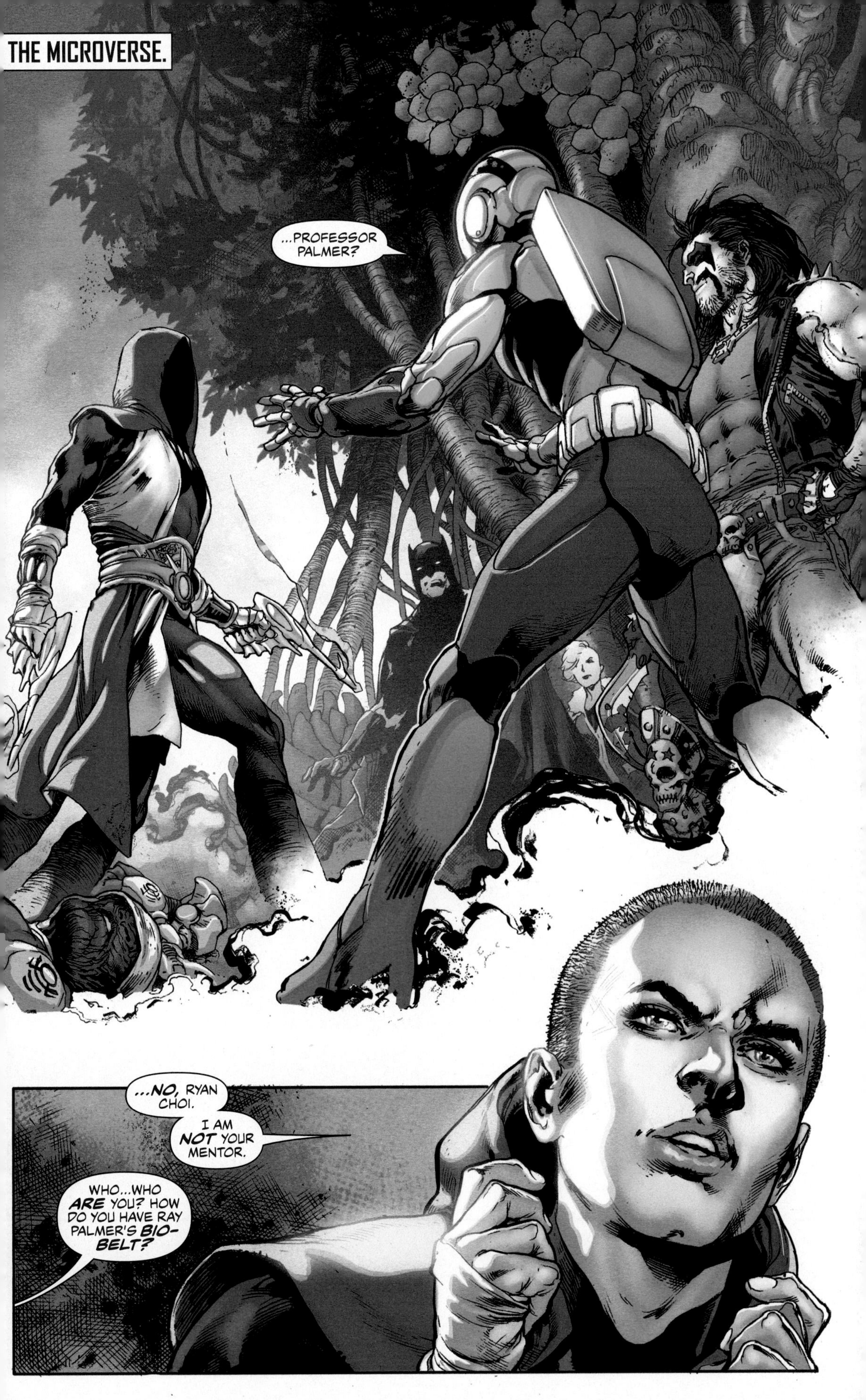
THE MICROVERSE.
...PROFESSOR PALMER?
...NO, RYAN CHOI.
I AM NOT YOUR MENTOR.
WHO...WHO ARE YOU? HOW DO YOU HAVE RAY PALMER'S BIO-BELT?

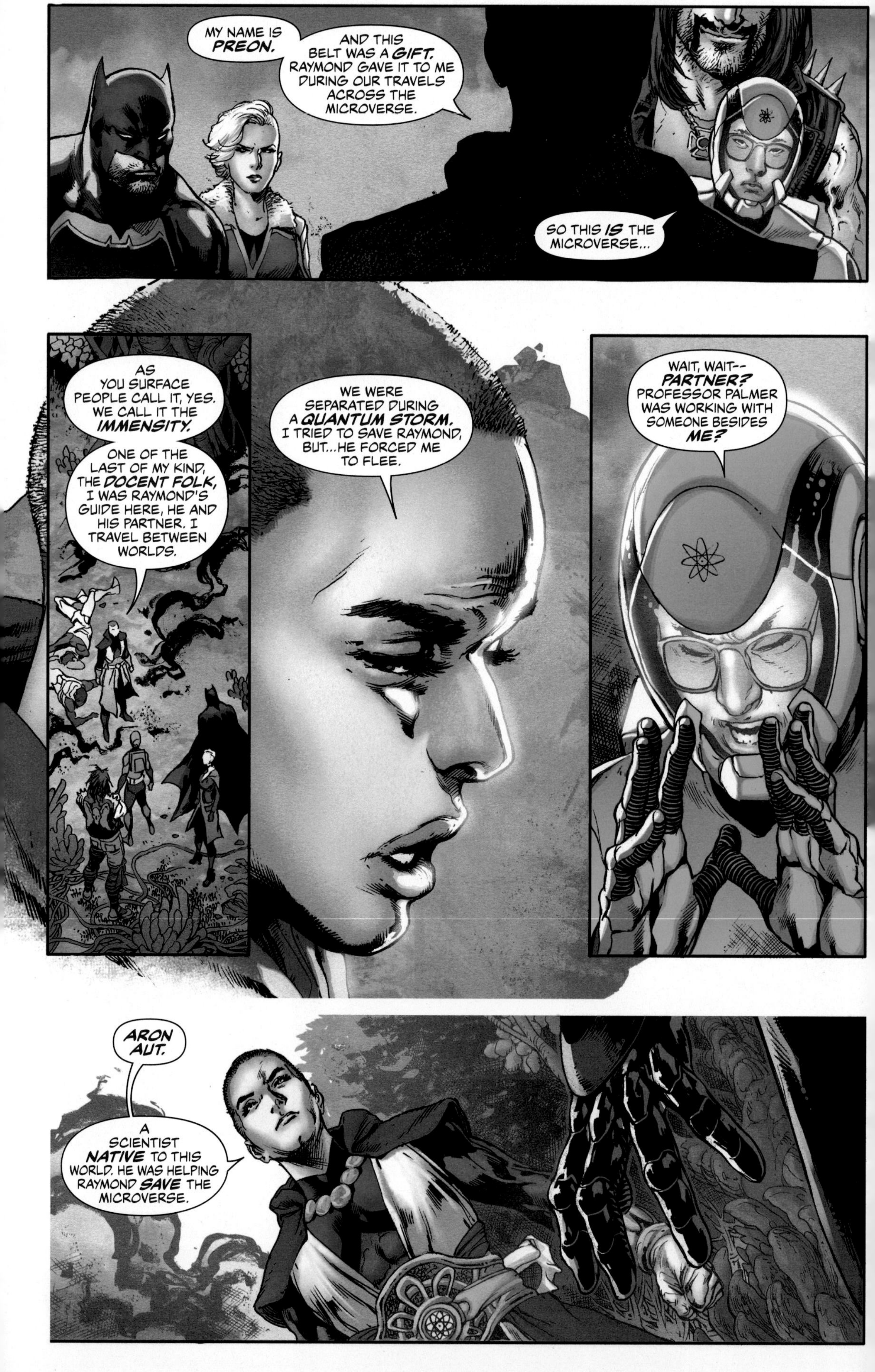
MY NAME IS PREON.
AND THIS BELT WAS A GIFT. RAYMOND GAVE IT TO ME DURING OUR TRAVELS ACROSS THE MICROVERSE.
SO THIS IS THE MICROVERSE...
AS YOU SURFACE PEOPLE CALL IT, YES. WE CALL IT THE IMMENSITY.
ONE OF THE LAST OF MY KIND, THE DOCENT FOLK, I WAS RAYMOND'S GUIDE HERE, HE AND HIS PARTNER. I TRAVEL BETWEEN WORLDS.
WE WERE SEPARATED DURING A QUANTUM STORM. I TRIED TO SAVE RAYMOND, BUT...HE FORCED ME TO FLEE.
WAIT, WAIT-- PARTNER? PROFESSOR PALMER WAS WORKING WITH SOMEONE BESIDES ME?
ARON AUT.
A SCIENTIST NATIVE TO THIS WORLD. HE WAS HELPING RAYMOND SAVE THE MICROVERSE.

I...I DIDN'T *KNOW.* HE NEVER TOLD ME. *WHY* WOULDN'T HE TELL ME?

MUST BE *A LOT* YER BOSS DIDN'T TELL YA, KID.

SHUT UP, LOBO. YOU'RE NOT HELPING.

DID I *ASK* YA, POPSICLE HANDS?

RYAN'S *TRYING.* YOU SHOULD *THINK* ABOUT IT.

HA. OR *WHAT?* YOU'LL GET *HOT?*

YOU *REALLY* WANT TO PUSH ME RIGHT NOW?

STOP! *BOTH* OF YOU.

PREON...WHAT WAS PROFESSOR PALMER *LOOKING* FOR?

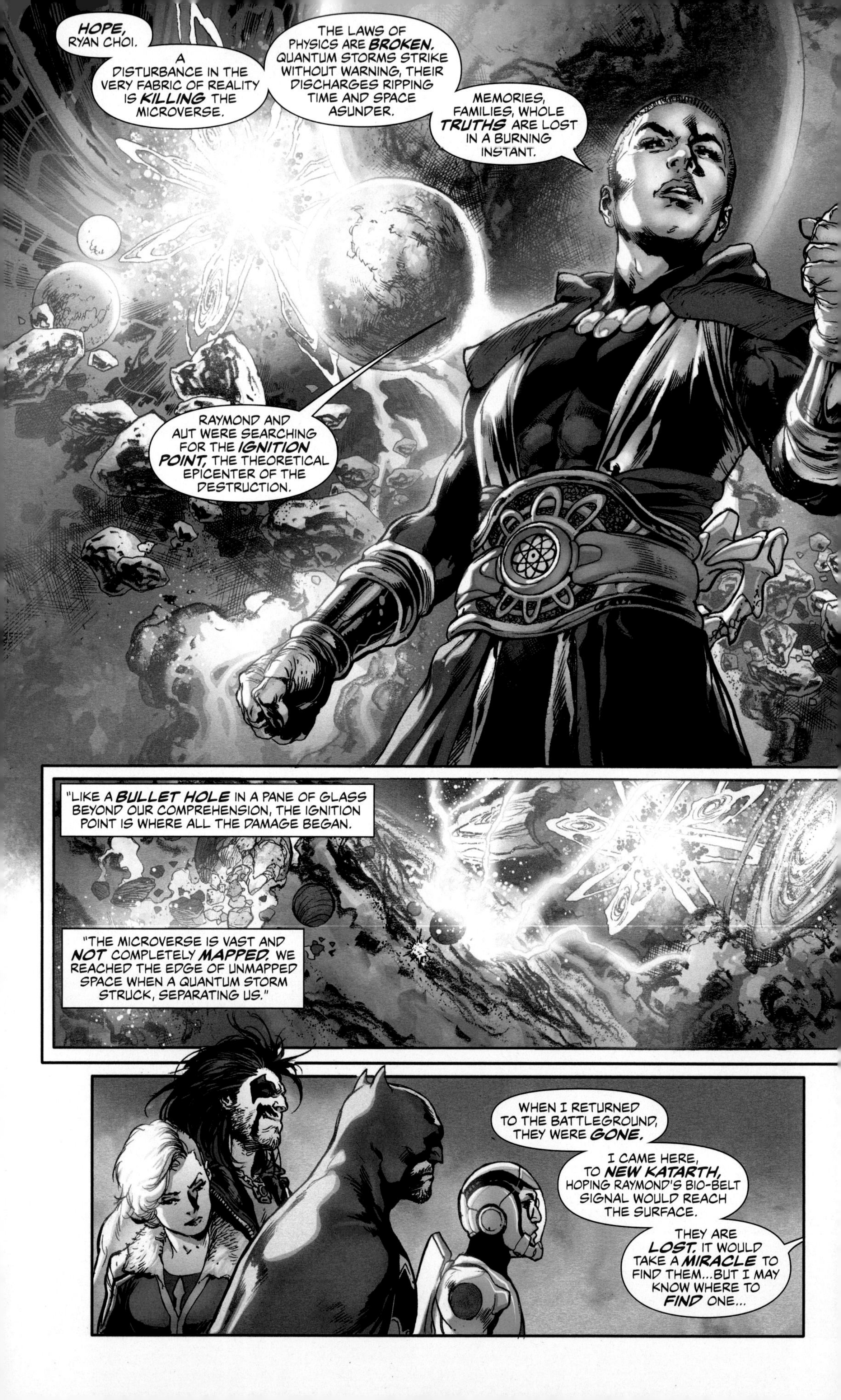
HOPE, RYAN CHOI.
A DISTURBANCE IN THE VERY FABRIC OF REALITY IS KILLING THE MICROVERSE.
THE LAWS OF PHYSICS ARE BROKEN. QUANTUM STORMS STRIKE WITHOUT WARNING, THEIR DISCHARGES RIPPING TIME AND SPACE ASUNDER.
MEMORIES, FAMILIES, WHOLE TRUTHS ARE LOST IN A BURNING INSTANT.
RAYMOND AND AUT WERE SEARCHING FOR THE IGNITION POINT, THE THEORETICAL EPICENTER OF THE DESTRUCTION.
"LIKE A BULLET HOLE IN A PANE OF GLASS BEYOND OUR COMPREHENSION, THE IGNITION POINT IS WHERE ALL THE DAMAGE BEGAN.
"THE MICROVERSE IS VAST AND NOT COMPLETELY MAPPED. WE REACHED THE EDGE OF UNMAPPED SPACE WHEN A QUANTUM STORM STRUCK, SEPARATING US."
WHEN I RETURNED TO THE BATTLEGROUND, THEY WERE GONE.
I CAME HERE, TO NEW KATARTH, HOPING RAYMOND'S BIO-BELT SIGNAL WOULD REACH THE SURFACE.
THEY ARE LOST. IT WOULD TAKE A MIRACLE TO FIND THEM...BUT I MAY KNOW WHERE TO FIND ONE...

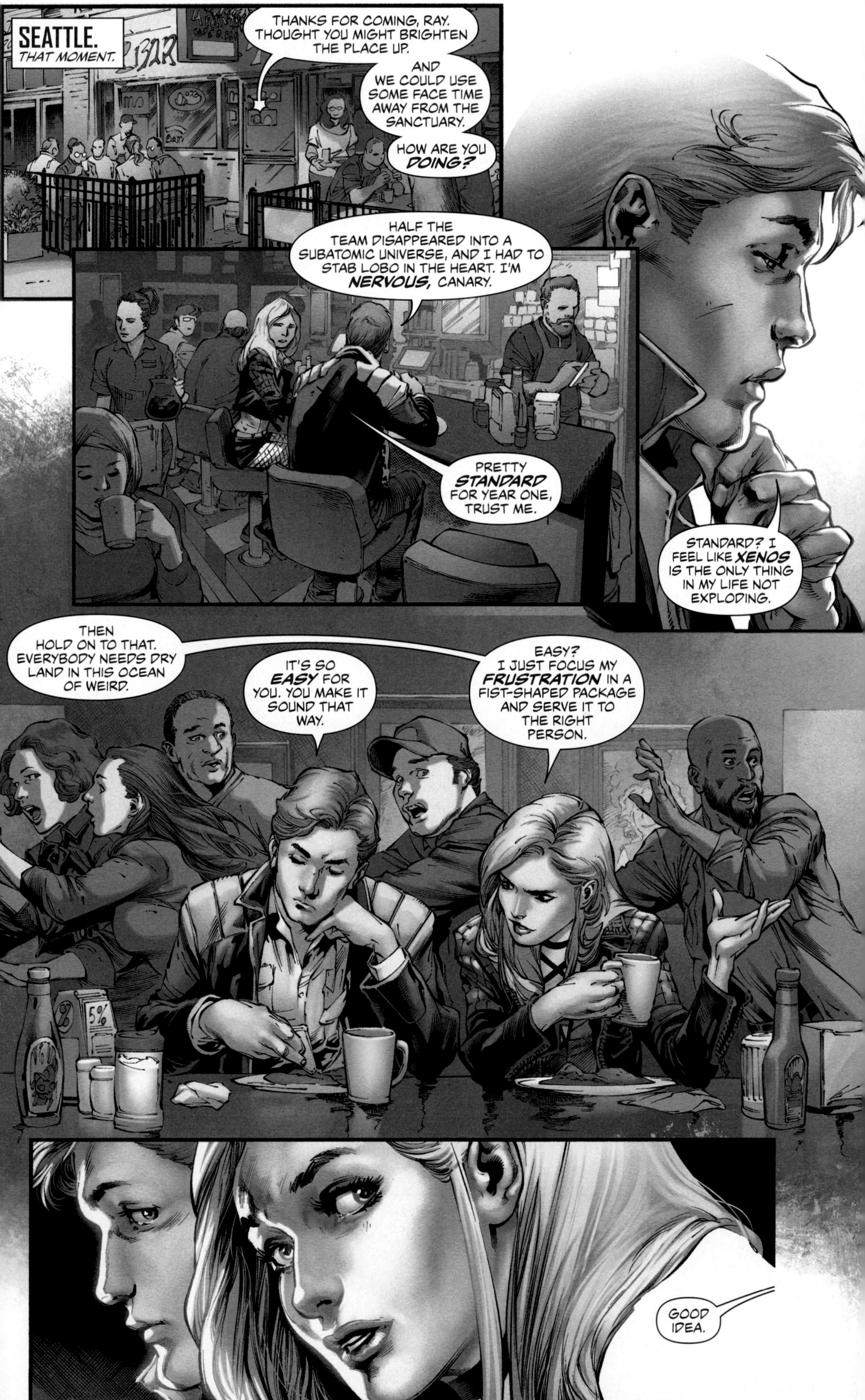
SEATTLE.
THAT MOMENT.
THANKS FOR COMING, RAY. THOUGHT YOU MIGHT BRIGHTEN THE PLACE UP.
AND WE COULD USE SOME FACE TIME AWAY FROM THE SANCTUARY.
HOW ARE YOU DOING?
HALF THE TEAM DISAPPEARED INTO A SUBATOMIC UNIVERSE, AND I HAD TO STAB LOBO IN THE HEART. I'M NERVOUS, CANARY.
PRETTY STANDARD FOR YEAR ONE, TRUST ME.
STANDARD? I FEEL LIKE XENOS IS THE ONLY THING IN MY LIFE NOT EXPLODING.
THEN HOLD ON TO THAT. EVERYBODY NEEDS DRY LAND IN THIS OCEAN OF WEIRD.
IT'S SO EASY FOR YOU. YOU MAKE IT SOUND THAT WAY.
EASY? I JUST FOCUS MY FRUSTRATION IN A FIST-SHAPED PACKAGE AND SERVE IT TO THE RIGHT PERSON.
GOOD IDEA.

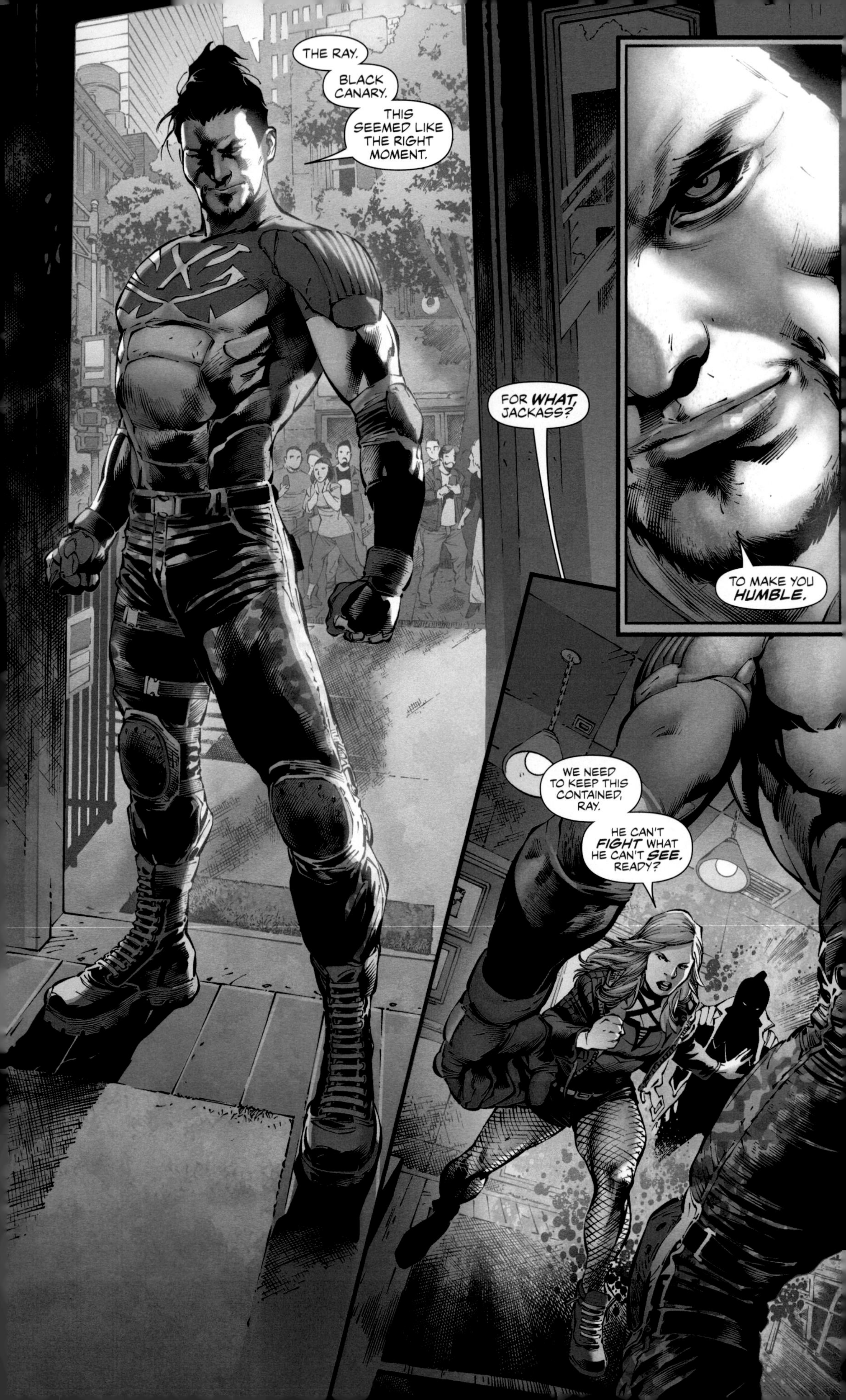
THE RAY.
BLACK CANARY.
THIS SEEMED LIKE THE RIGHT MOMENT.
FOR WHAT, JACKASS?
TO MAKE YOU HUMBLE.
WE NEED TO KEEP THIS CONTAINED, RAY.
HE CAN'T FIGHT WHAT HE CAN'T SEE. READY?

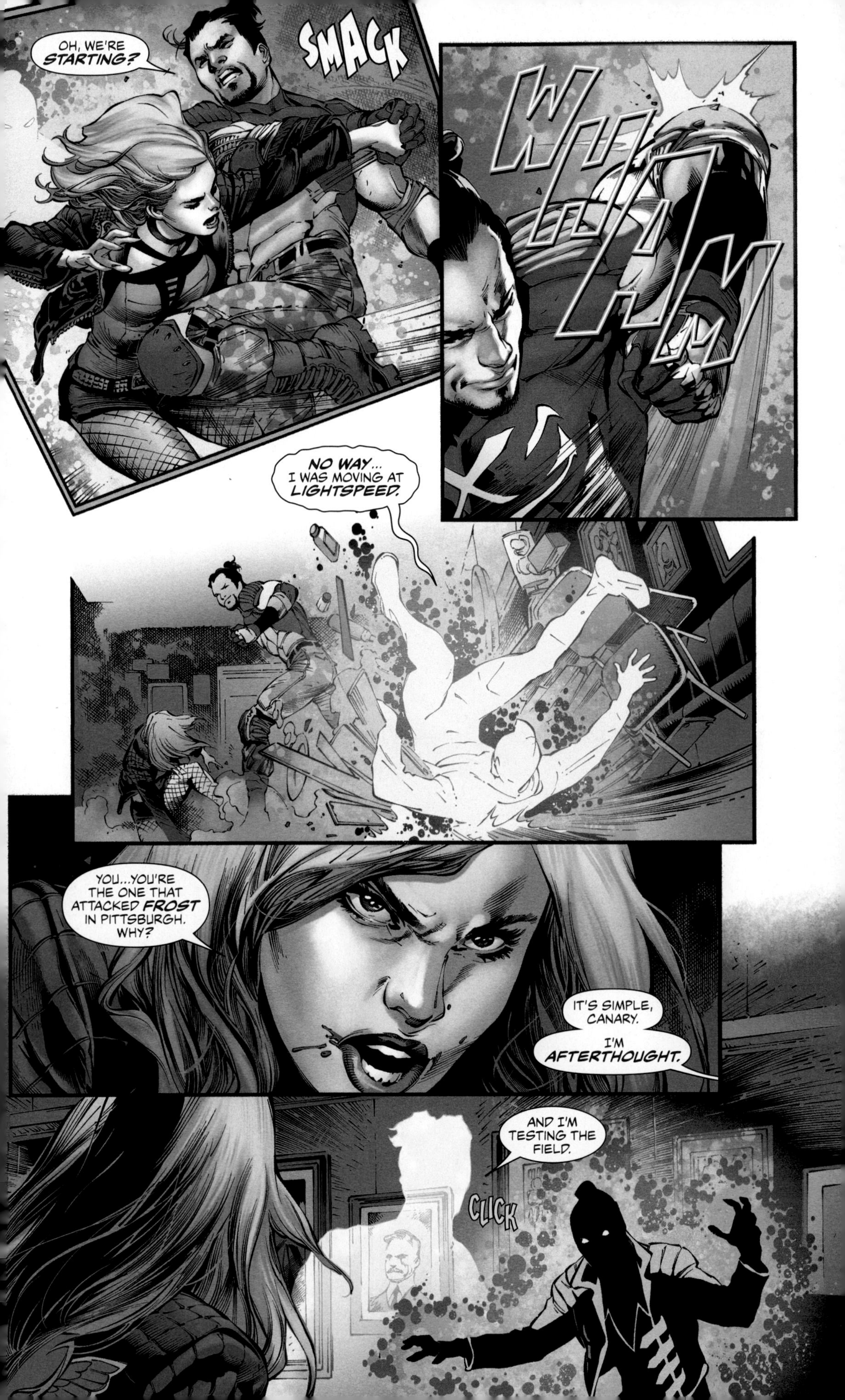
OH, WE'RE STARTING?
SMACK
WHAM
NO WAY... I WAS MOVING AT LIGHTSPEED.
YOU...YOU'RE THE ONE THAT ATTACKED FROST IN PITTSBURGH. WHY?
IT'S SIMPLE, CANARY.
I'M AFTERTHOUGHT.
AND I'M TESTING THE FIELD.
CLICK

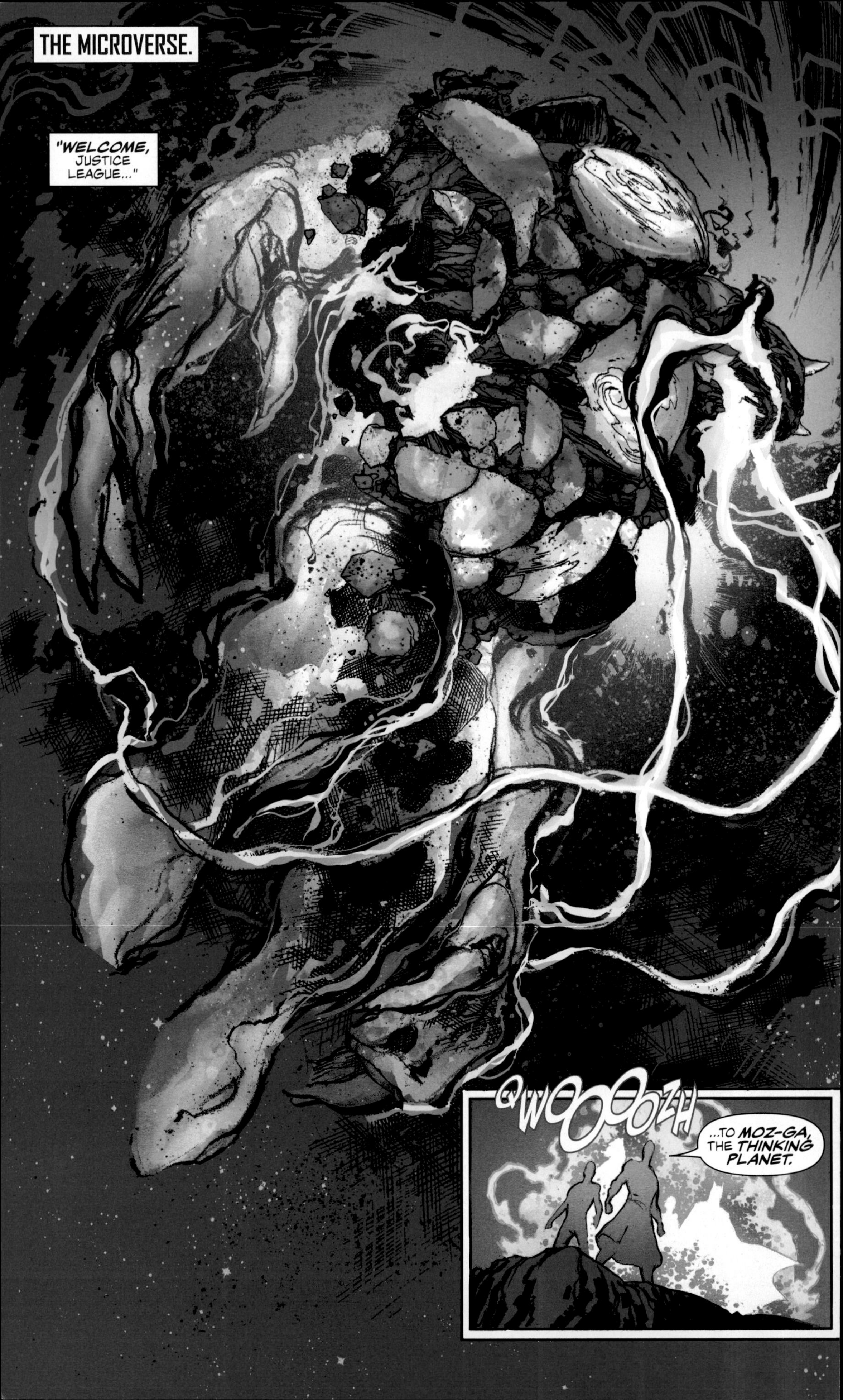
THE MICROVERSE.
"WELCOME, JUSTICE LEAGUE..."
QWOOOOZH
...TO MOZ-GA, THE THINKING PLANET.

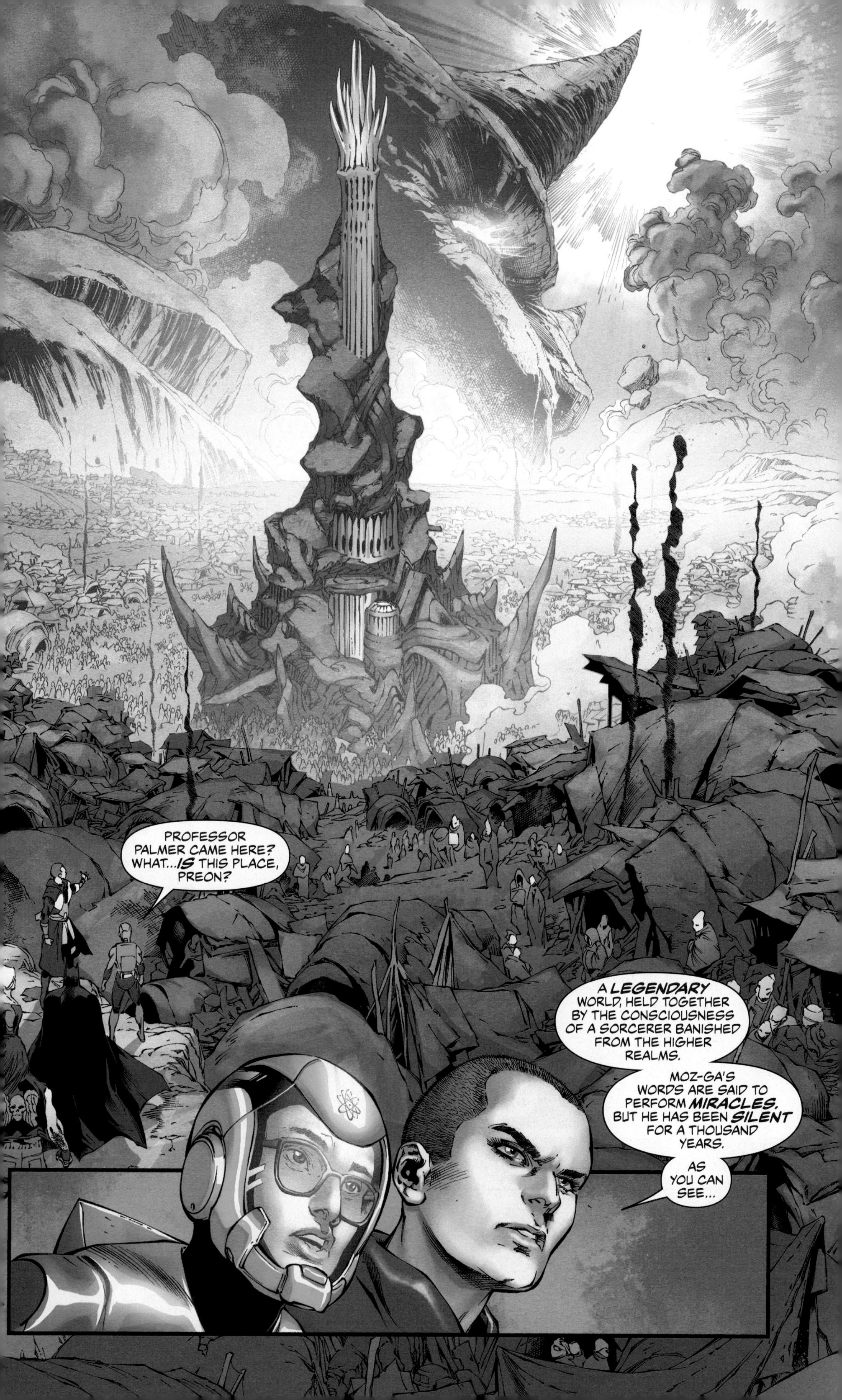
PROFESSOR PALMER CAME HERE? WHAT...IS THIS PLACE, PREON?
A LEGENDARY WORLD, HELD TOGETHER BY THE CONSCIOUSNESS OF A SORCERER BANISHED FROM THE HIGHER REALMS.
MOZ-GA'S WORDS ARE SAID TO PERFORM MIRACLES, BUT HE HAS BEEN SILENT FOR A THOUSAND YEARS.
AS YOU CAN SEE...

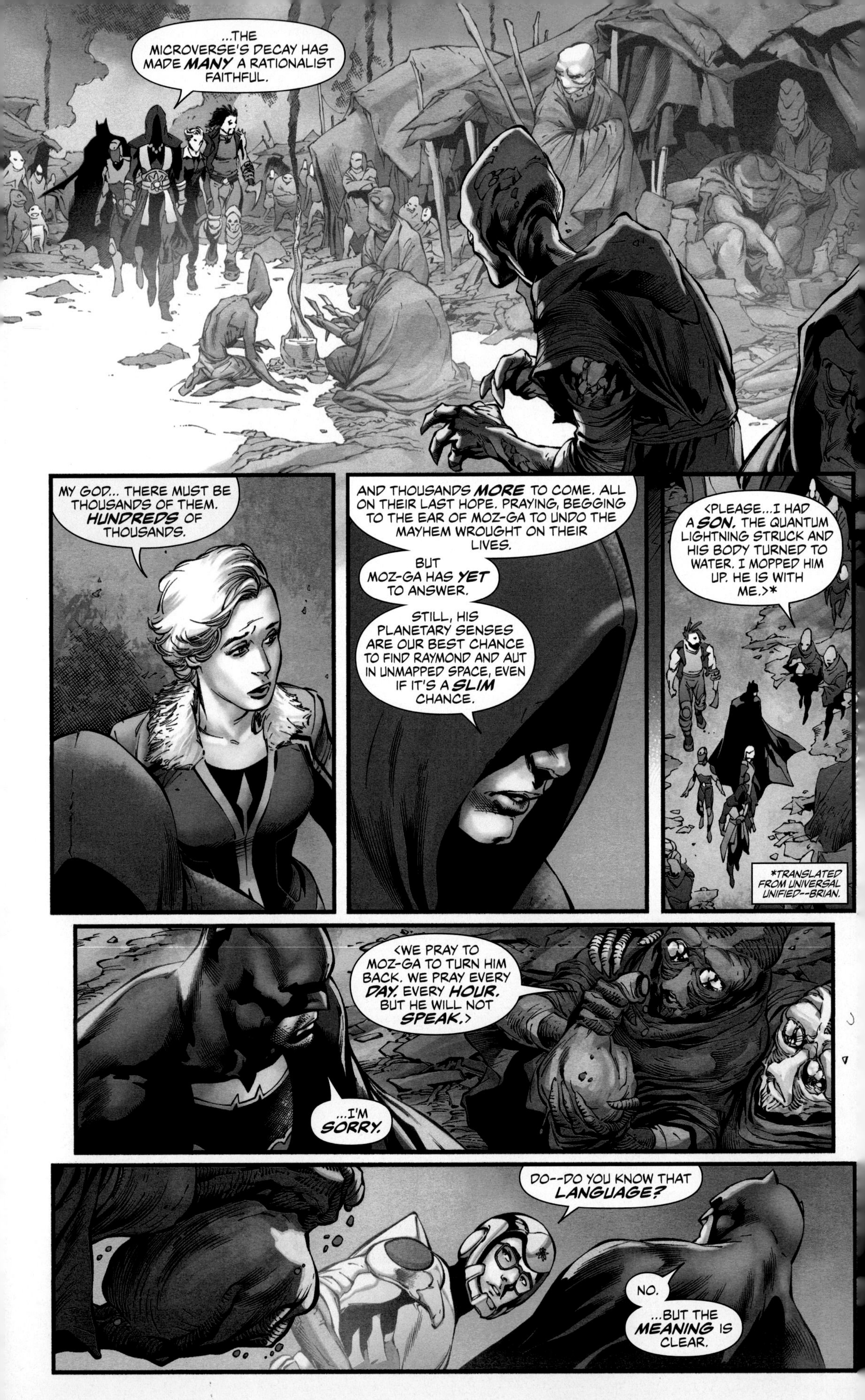
...THE MICROVERSE'S DECAY HAS MADE MANY A RATIONALIST FAITHFUL.
MY GOD... THERE MUST BE THOUSANDS OF THEM. HUNDREDS OF THOUSANDS.
AND THOUSANDS MORE TO COME. ALL ON THEIR LAST HOPE. PRAYING, BEGGING TO THE EAR OF MOZ-GA TO UNDO THE MAYHEM WROUGHT ON THEIR LIVES.
BUT MOZ-GA HAS YET TO ANSWER.
STILL, HIS PLANETARY SENSES ARE OUR BEST CHANCE TO FIND RAYMOND AND AUT IN UNMAPPED SPACE, EVEN IF IT'S A SLIM CHANCE.
<PLEASE...I HAD A SON. THE QUANTUM LIGHTNING STRUCK AND HIS BODY TURNED TO WATER. I MOPPED HIM UP. HE IS WITH ME.>*
*TRANSLATED FROM UNIVERSAL UNIFIED--BRIAN.
<WE PRAY TO MOZ-GA TO TURN HIM BACK. WE PRAY EVERY DAY. EVERY HOUR. BUT HE WILL NOT SPEAK.>
...I'M SORRY.
DO--DO YOU KNOW THAT LANGUAGE?
NO.
...BUT THE MEANING IS CLEAR.

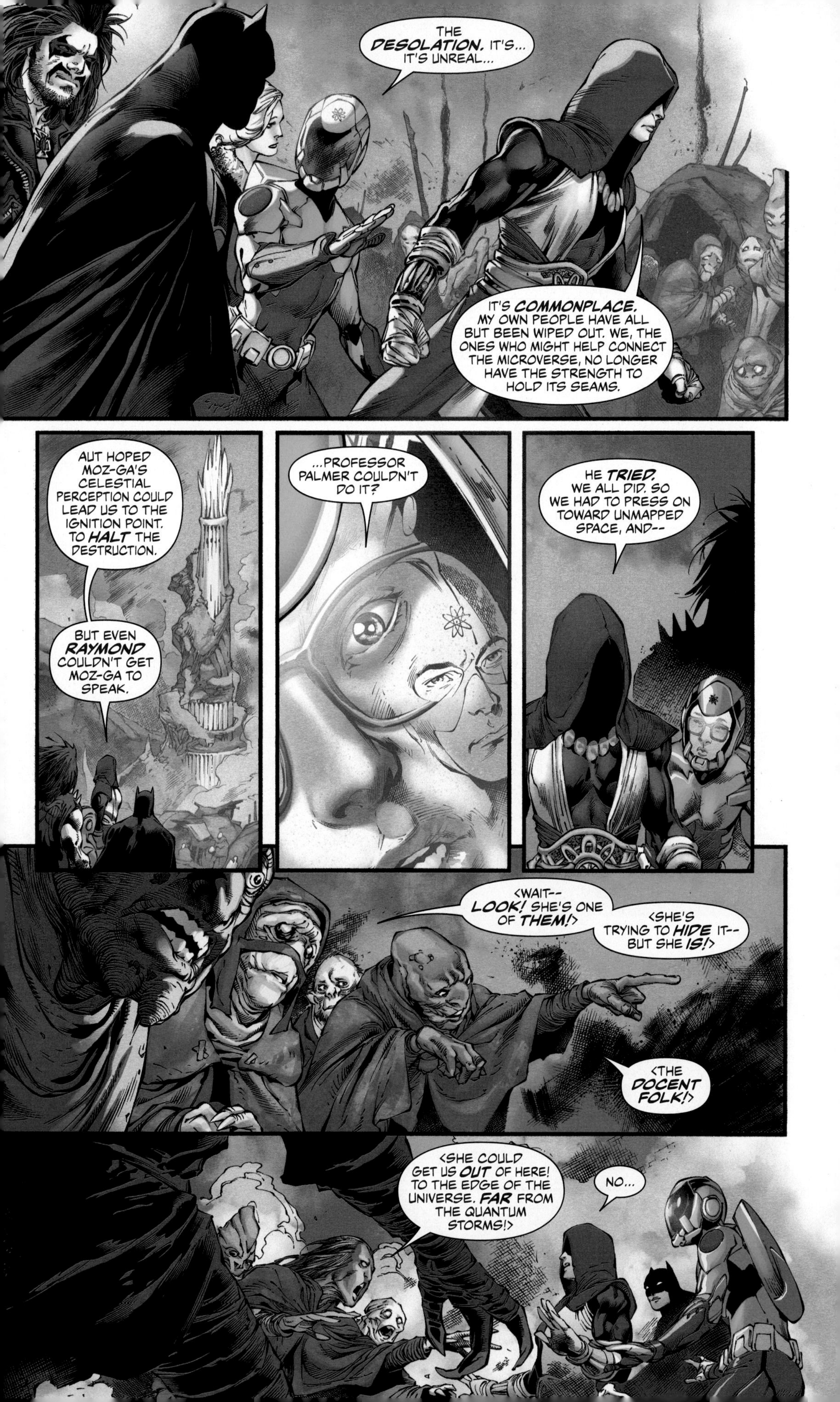
THE DESOLATION. IT'S... IT'S UNREAL...
IT'S COMMONPLACE. MY OWN PEOPLE HAVE ALL BUT BEEN WIPED OUT. WE, THE ONES WHO MIGHT HELP CONNECT THE MICROVERSE, NO LONGER HAVE THE STRENGTH TO HOLD ITS SEAMS.
AUT HOPED MOZ-GA'S CELESTIAL PERCEPTION COULD LEAD US TO THE IGNITION POINT. TO HALT THE DESTRUCTION.
BUT EVEN RAYMOND COULDN'T GET MOZ-GA TO SPEAK.
...PROFESSOR PALMER COULDN'T DO IT?
HE TRIED. WE ALL DID. SO WE HAD TO PRESS ON TOWARD UNMAPPED SPACE, AND--
<WAIT-- LOOK! SHE'S ONE OF THEM!>
<SHE'S TRYING TO HIDE IT-- BUT SHE IS!>
<THE DOCENT FOLK!>
<SHE COULD GET US OUT OF HERE! TO THE EDGE OF THE UNIVERSE. FAR FROM THE QUANTUM STORMS!>
NO...

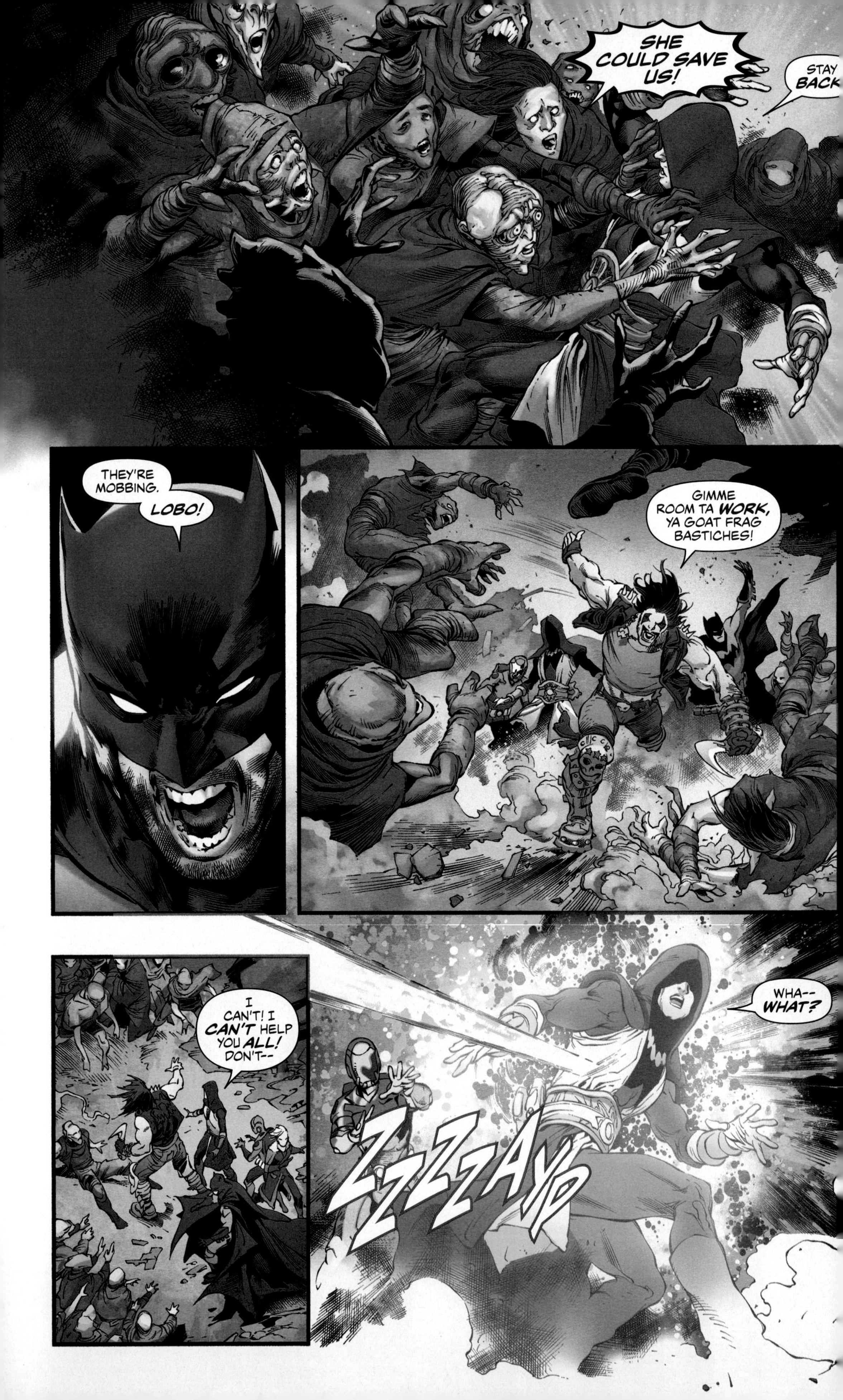
SHE COULD SAVE US!
STAY BACK
THEY'RE MOBBING. LOBO!
GIMME ROOM TA WORK, YA GOAT FRAG BASTICHES!
I CAN'T! I CAN'T HELP YOU ALL! DON'T--
WHA-- WHAT?
ZZZZAYD

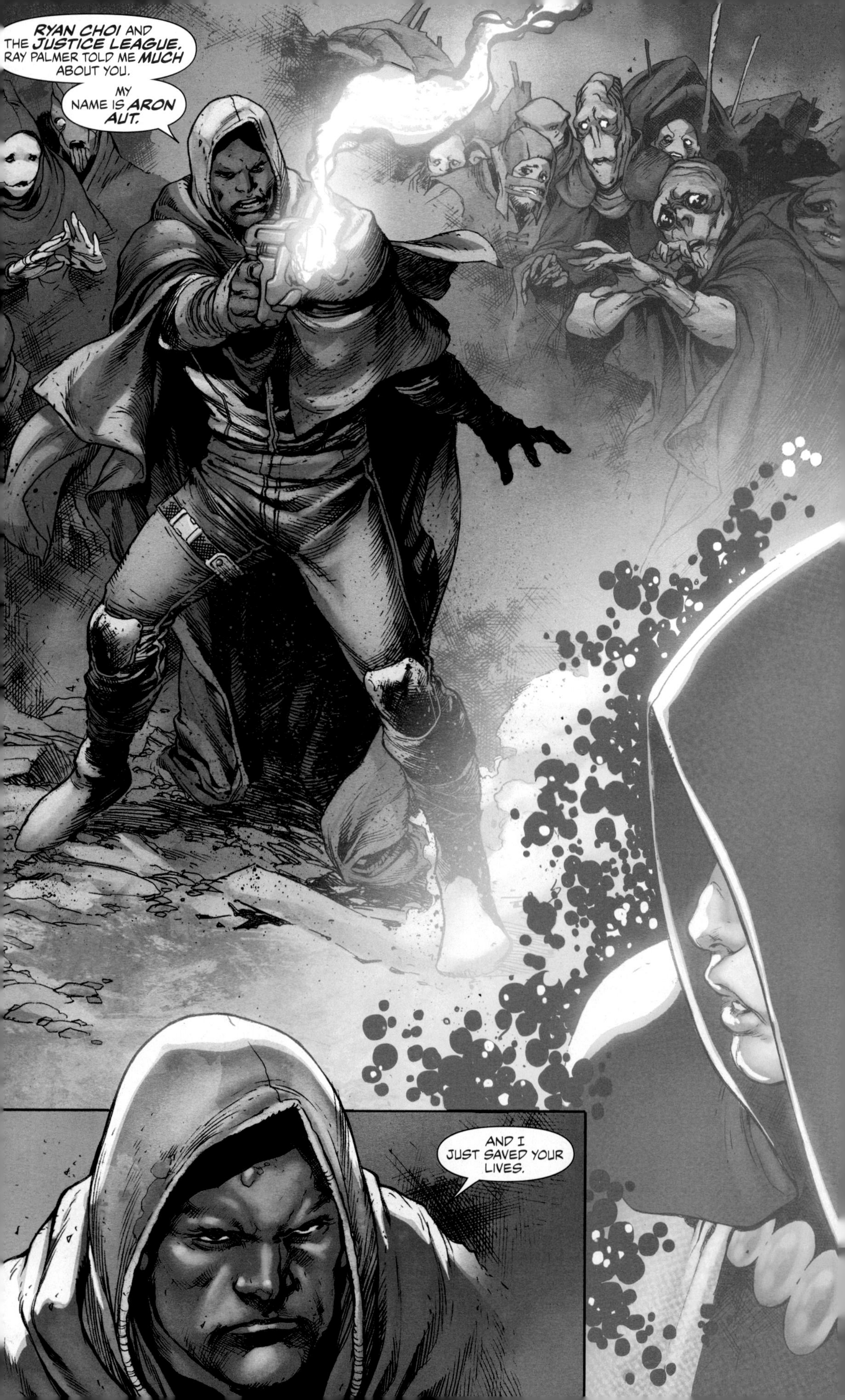
RYAN CHOI AND THE JUSTICE LEAGUE. RAY PALMER TOLD ME MUCH ABOUT YOU.
MY NAME IS ARON AUT.
AND I JUST SAVED YOUR LIVES.

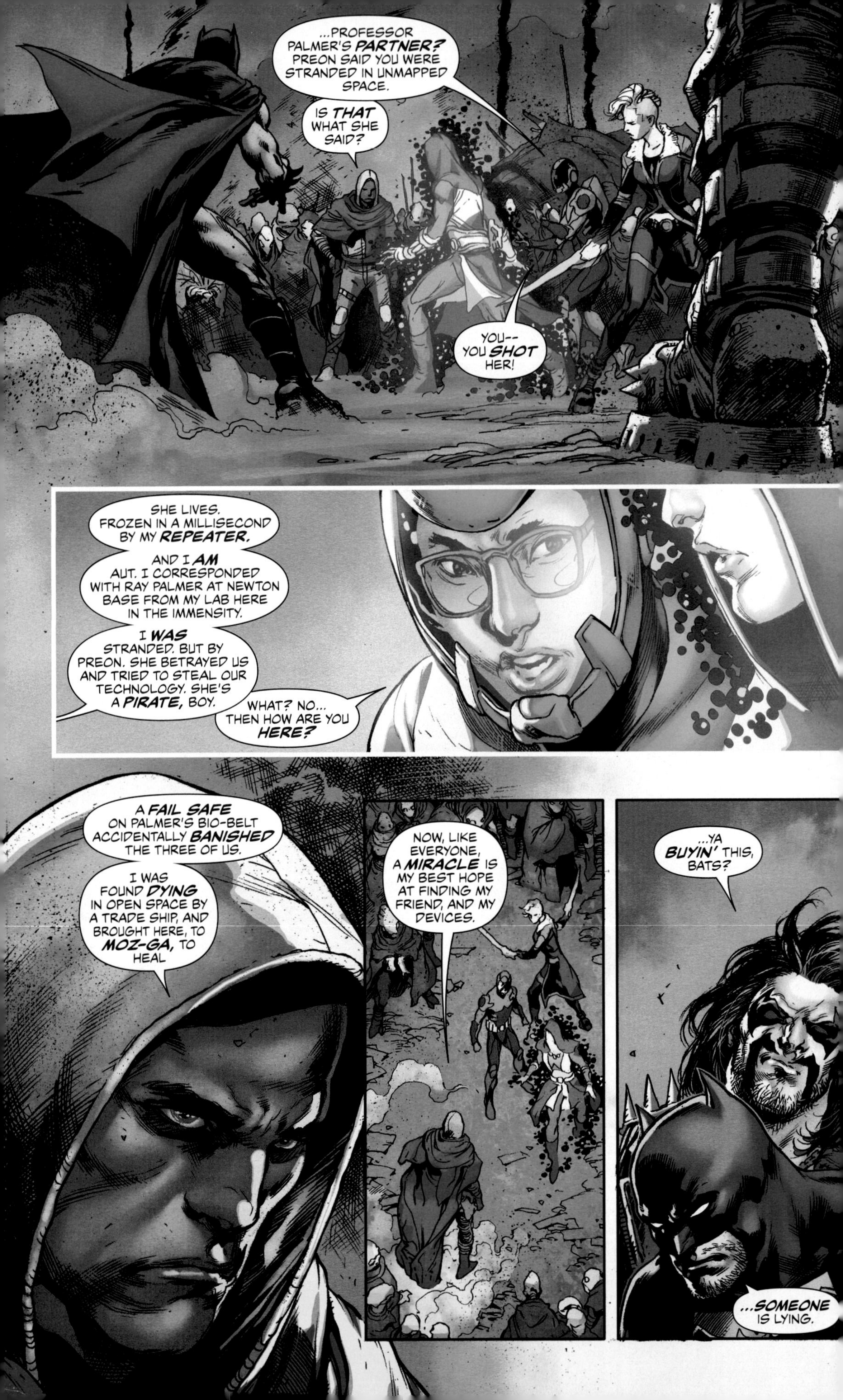
...PROFESSOR PALMER'S PARTNER? PREON SAID YOU WERE STRANDED IN UNMAPPED SPACE.
IS THAT WHAT SHE SAID?
YOU-- YOU SHOT HER!
SHE LIVES. FROZEN IN A MILLISECOND BY MY REPEATER.
AND I AM AUT. I CORRESPONDED WITH RAY PALMER AT NEWTON BASE FROM MY LAB HERE IN THE IMMENSITY.
I WAS STRANDED. BUT BY PREON. SHE BETRAYED US AND TRIED TO STEAL OUR TECHNOLOGY. SHE'S A PIRATE, BOY.
WHAT? NO... THEN HOW ARE YOU HERE?
A FAIL SAFE ON PALMER'S BIO-BELT ACCIDENTALLY BANISHED THE THREE OF US.
I WAS FOUND DYING IN OPEN SPACE BY A TRADE SHIP, AND BROUGHT HERE, TO MOZ-GA, TO HEAL
NOW, LIKE EVERYONE, A MIRACLE IS MY BEST HOPE AT FINDING MY FRIEND, AND MY DEVICES.
...YA BUYIN' THIS, BATS?
...SOMEONE IS LYING.

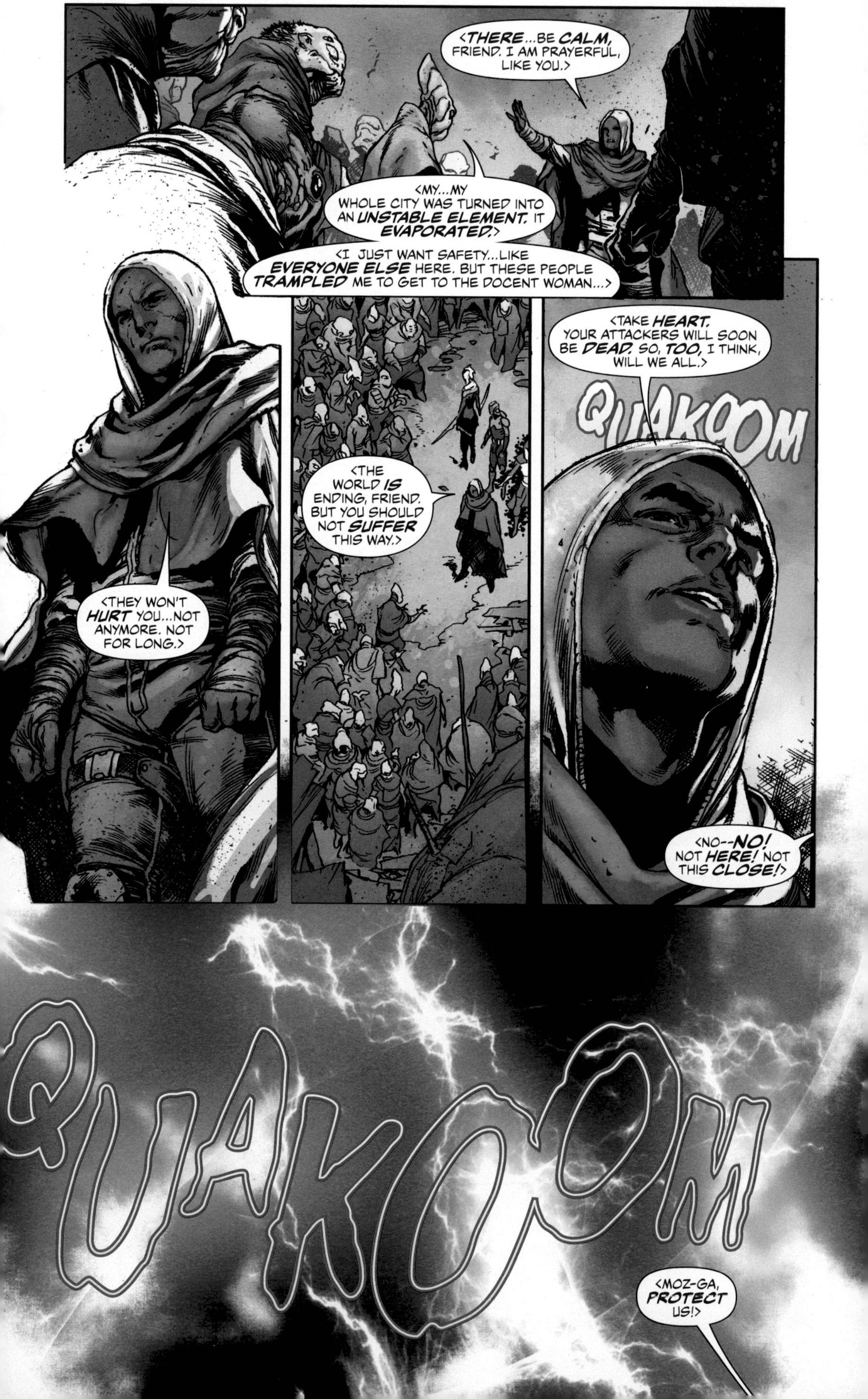

<THERE...BE CALM, FRIEND. I AM PRAYERFUL, LIKE YOU.>
<MY...MY WHOLE CITY WAS TURNED INTO AN UNSTABLE ELEMENT. IT EVAPORATED.>
<I JUST WANT SAFETY...LIKE EVERYONE ELSE HERE. BUT THESE PEOPLE TRAMPLED ME TO GET TO THE DOCENT WOMAN...>
<THEY WON'T HURT YOU...NOT ANYMORE. NOT FOR LONG.>
<THE WORLD IS ENDING, FRIEND. BUT YOU SHOULD NOT SUFFER THIS WAY.>
<TAKE HEART. YOUR ATTACKERS WILL SOON BE DEAD. SO, TOO, I THINK, WILL WE ALL.>
QUAKOOM
<NO--NO! NOT HERE! NOT THIS CLOSE!>
QUAKOOM
<MOZ-GA, PROTECT US!>

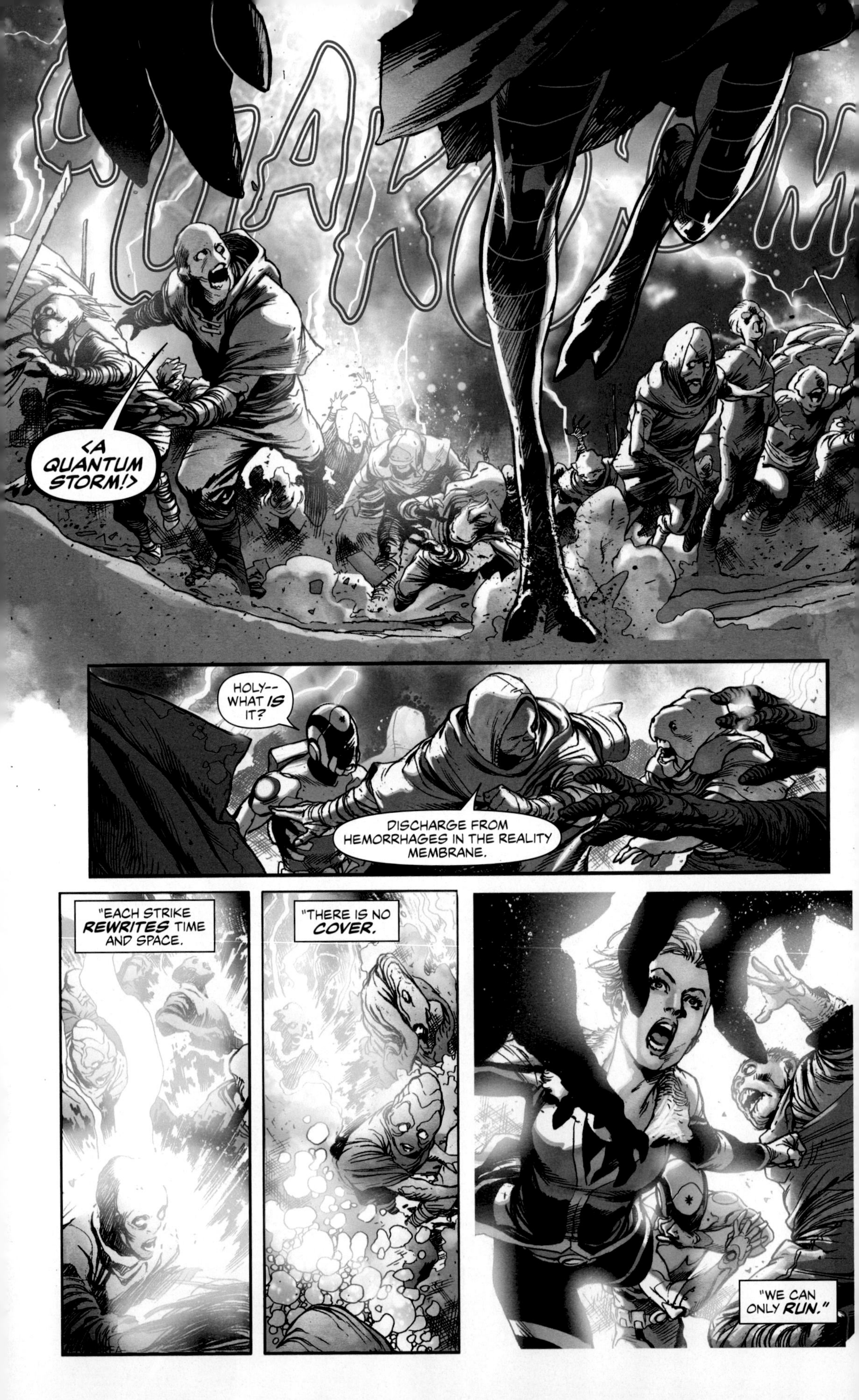
<A QUANTUM STORM!>
HOLY-- WHAT IS IT?
DISCHARGE FROM HEMORRHAGES IN THE REALITY MEMBRANE.
"EACH STRIKE REWRITES TIME AND SPACE.
"THERE IS NO COVER.
"WE CAN ONLY RUN."

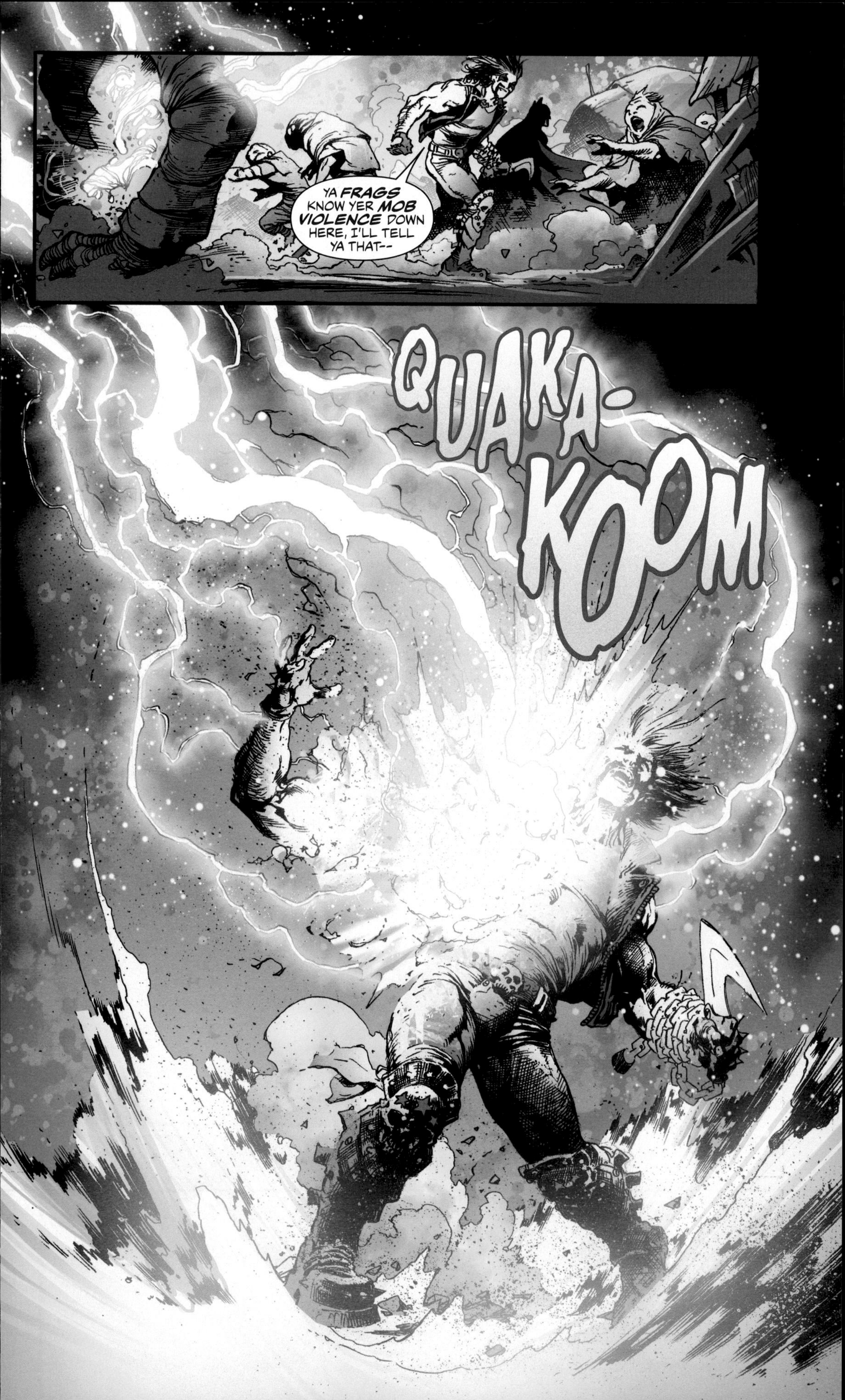
YA FRAGS KNOW YER MOB VIOLENCE DOWN HERE, I'LL TELL YA THAT--
QUAKA-KOOM

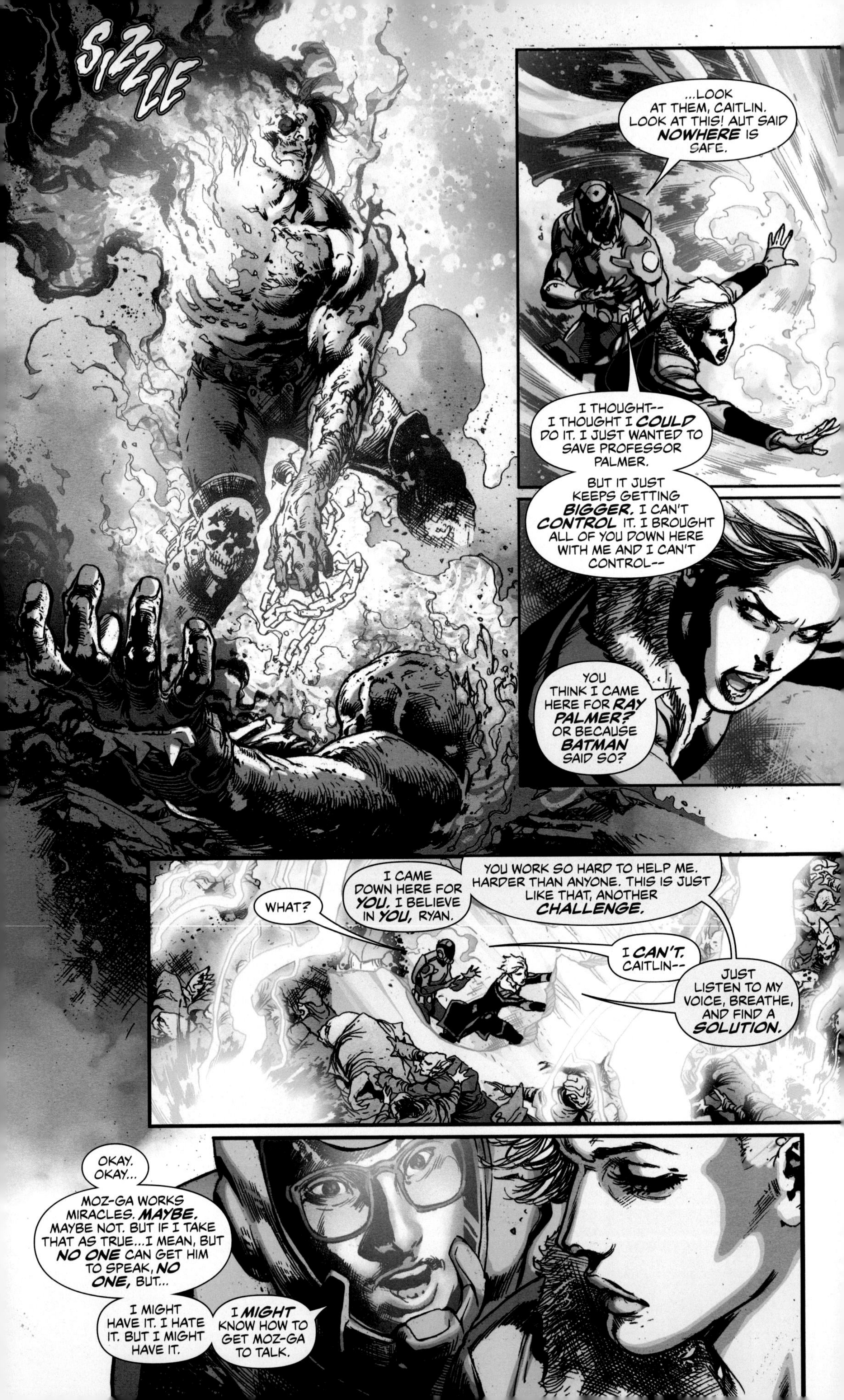
SIZZLE
...LOOK AT THEM, CAITLIN. LOOK AT THIS! AUT SAID NOWHERE IS SAFE.
I THOUGHT-- I THOUGHT I COULD DO IT. I JUST WANTED TO SAVE PROFESSOR PALMER.
BUT IT JUST KEEPS GETTING BIGGER. I CAN'T CONTROL IT. I BROUGHT ALL OF YOU DOWN HERE WITH ME AND I CAN'T CONTROL--
YOU THINK I CAME HERE FOR RAY PALMER? OR BECAUSE BATMAN SAID SO?
WHAT?
I CAME DOWN HERE FOR YOU. I BELIEVE IN YOU, RYAN.
YOU WORK SO HARD TO HELP ME. HARDER THAN ANYONE. THIS IS JUST LIKE THAT, ANOTHER CHALLENGE.
I CAN'T. CAITLIN--
JUST LISTEN TO MY VOICE, BREATHE, AND FIND A SOLUTION.
OKAY. OKAY...
MOZ-GA WORKS MIRACLES. MAYBE. MAYBE NOT. BUT IF I TAKE THAT AS TRUE...I MEAN, BUT NO ONE CAN GET HIM TO SPEAK, NO ONE, BUT...
I MIGHT HAVE IT. I HATE IT. BUT I MIGHT HAVE IT.
I MIGHT KNOW HOW TO GET MOZ-GA TO TALK.

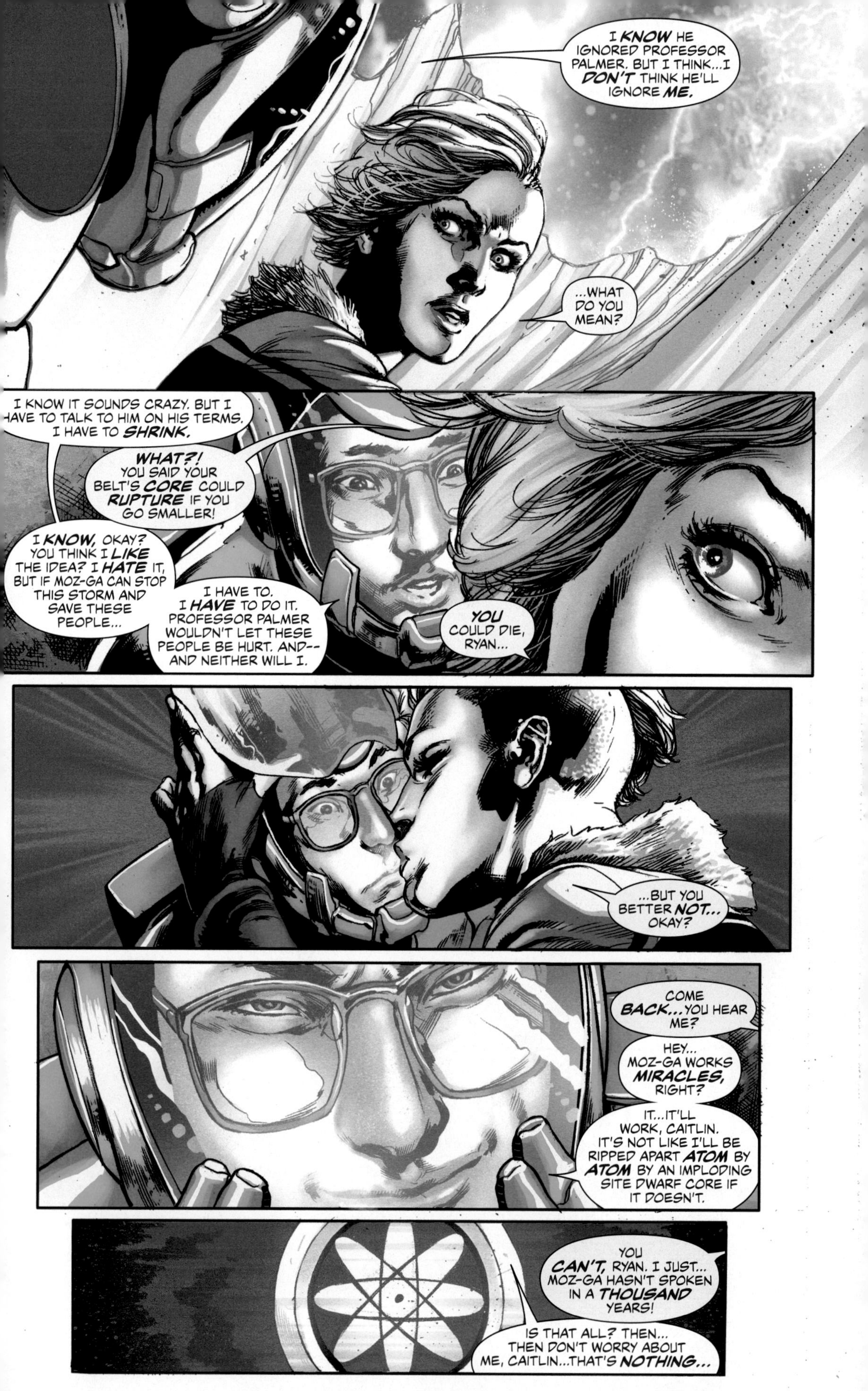
I KNOW HE IGNORED PROFESSOR PALMER. BUT I THINK...I DON'T THINK HE'LL IGNORE ME.
...WHAT DO YOU MEAN?
I KNOW IT SOUNDS CRAZY. BUT I HAVE TO TALK TO HIM ON HIS TERMS. I HAVE TO SHRINK.
WHAT?! YOU SAID YOUR BELT'S CORE COULD RUPTURE IF YOU GO SMALLER!
I KNOW, OKAY? YOU THINK I LIKE THE IDEA? I HATE IT, BUT IF MOZ-GA CAN STOP THIS STORM AND SAVE THESE PEOPLE...
I HAVE TO. I HAVE TO DO IT. PROFESSOR PALMER WOULDN'T LET THESE PEOPLE BE HURT. AND-- AND NEITHER WILL I.
YOU COULD DIE, RYAN...
...BUT YOU BETTER NOT... OKAY?
COME BACK...YOU HEAR ME?
HEY... MOZ-GA WORKS MIRACLES, RIGHT?
IT...IT'LL WORK, CAITLIN. IT'S NOT LIKE I'LL BE RIPPED APART ATOM BY ATOM BY AN IMPLODING SITE DWARF CORE IF IT DOESN'T.
YOU CAN'T, RYAN. I JUST... MOZ-GA HASN'T SPOKEN IN A THOUSAND YEARS!
IS THAT ALL? THEN... THEN DON'T WORRY ABOUT ME, CAITLIN...THAT'S NOTHING...

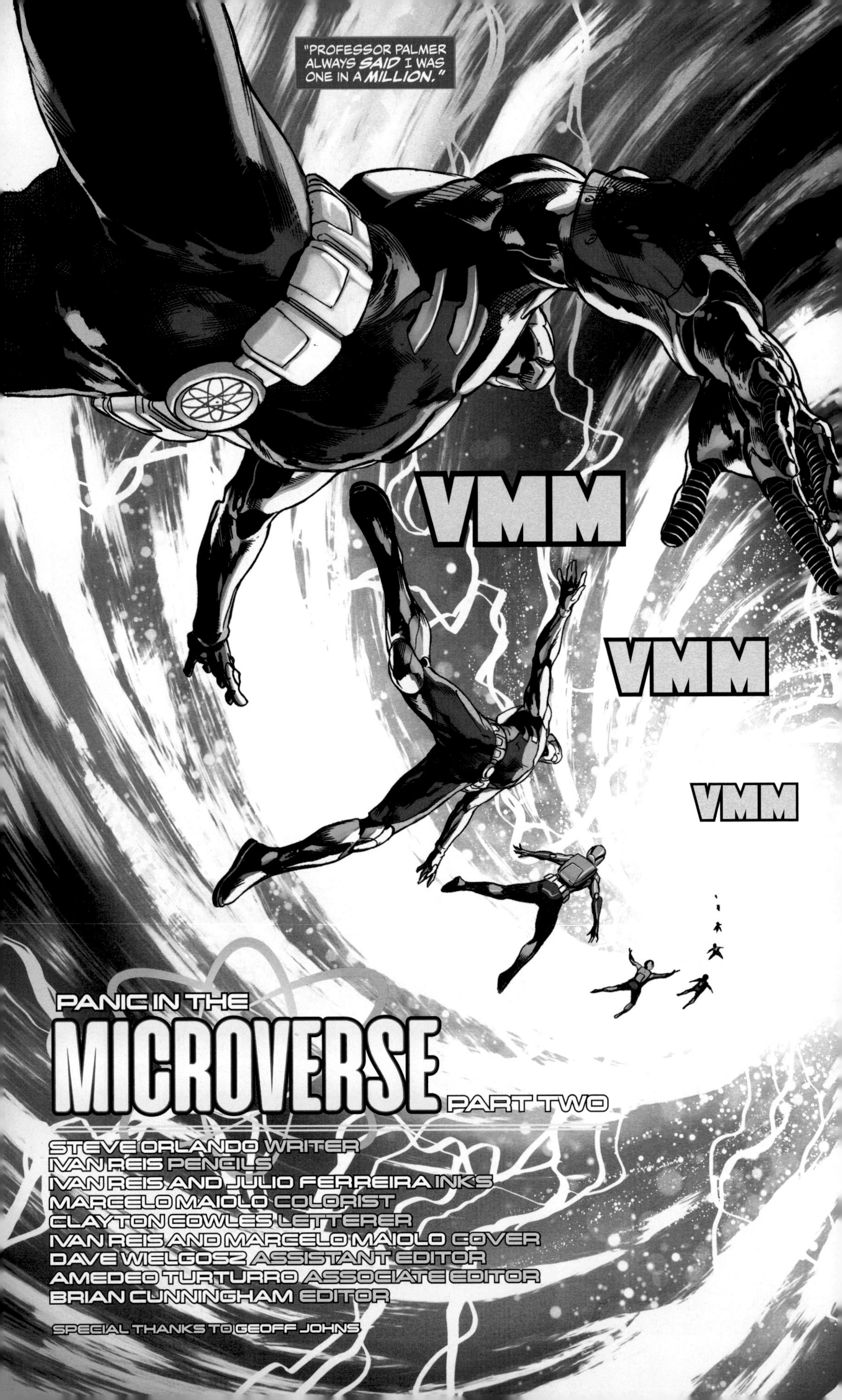
"PROFESSOR PALMER ALWAYS SAID I WAS ONE IN A MILLION."
VMM
VMM
VMM
PANIC IN THE
MICROVERSE
PART TWO
STEVE ORLANDO WRITER
IVAN REIS PENCILS
IVAN REIS AND JULIO FERREIRA INKS
MARCELO MAIOLO COLORIST
CLAYTON COWLES LETTERER
IVAN REIS AND MARCELO MAIOLO COVER
DAVE WIELGOSZ ASSISTANT EDITOR
AMEDEO TURTURRO ASSOCIATE EDITOR
BRIAN CUNNINGHAM EDITOR
SPECIAL THANKS TO GEOFF JOHNS

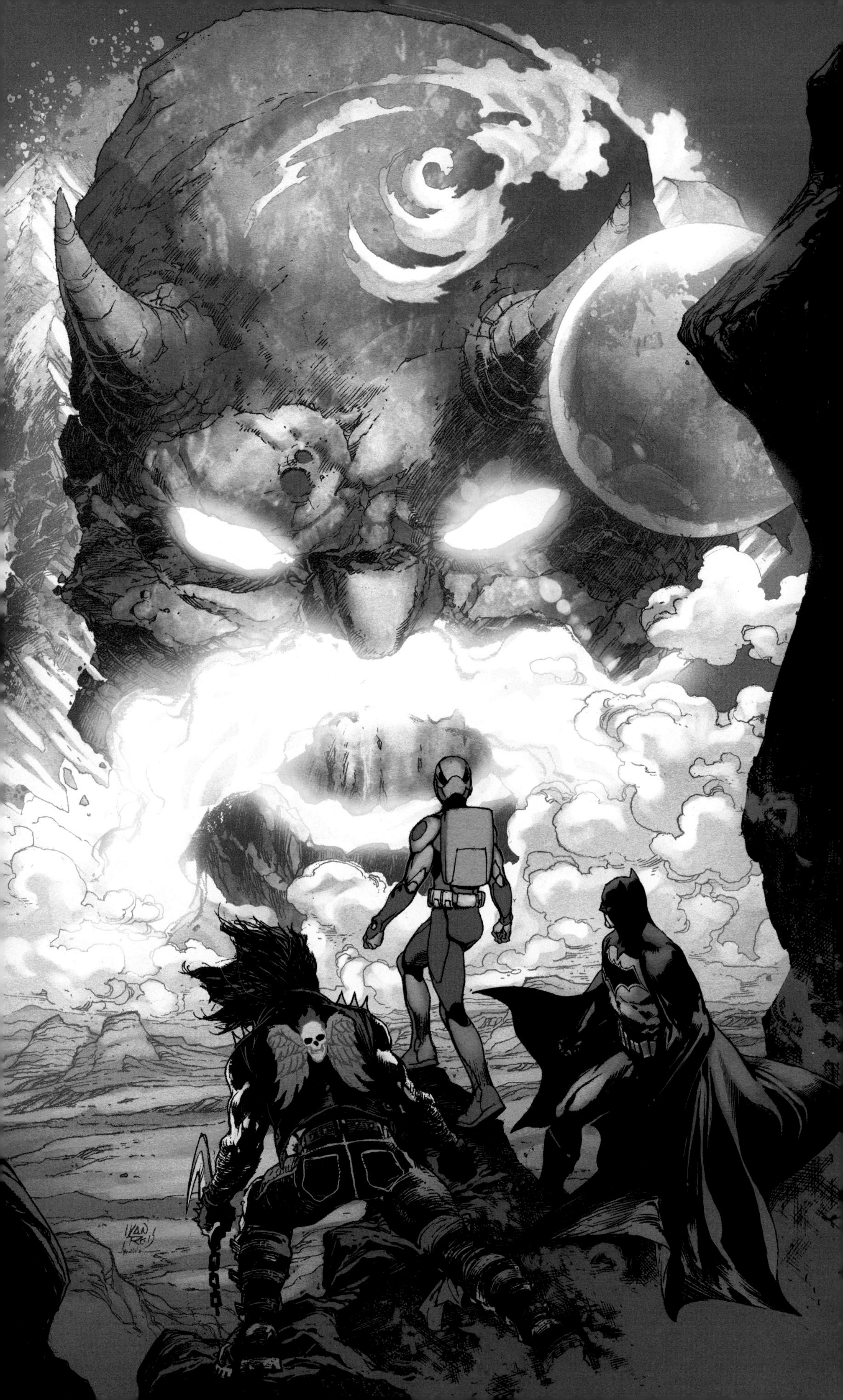

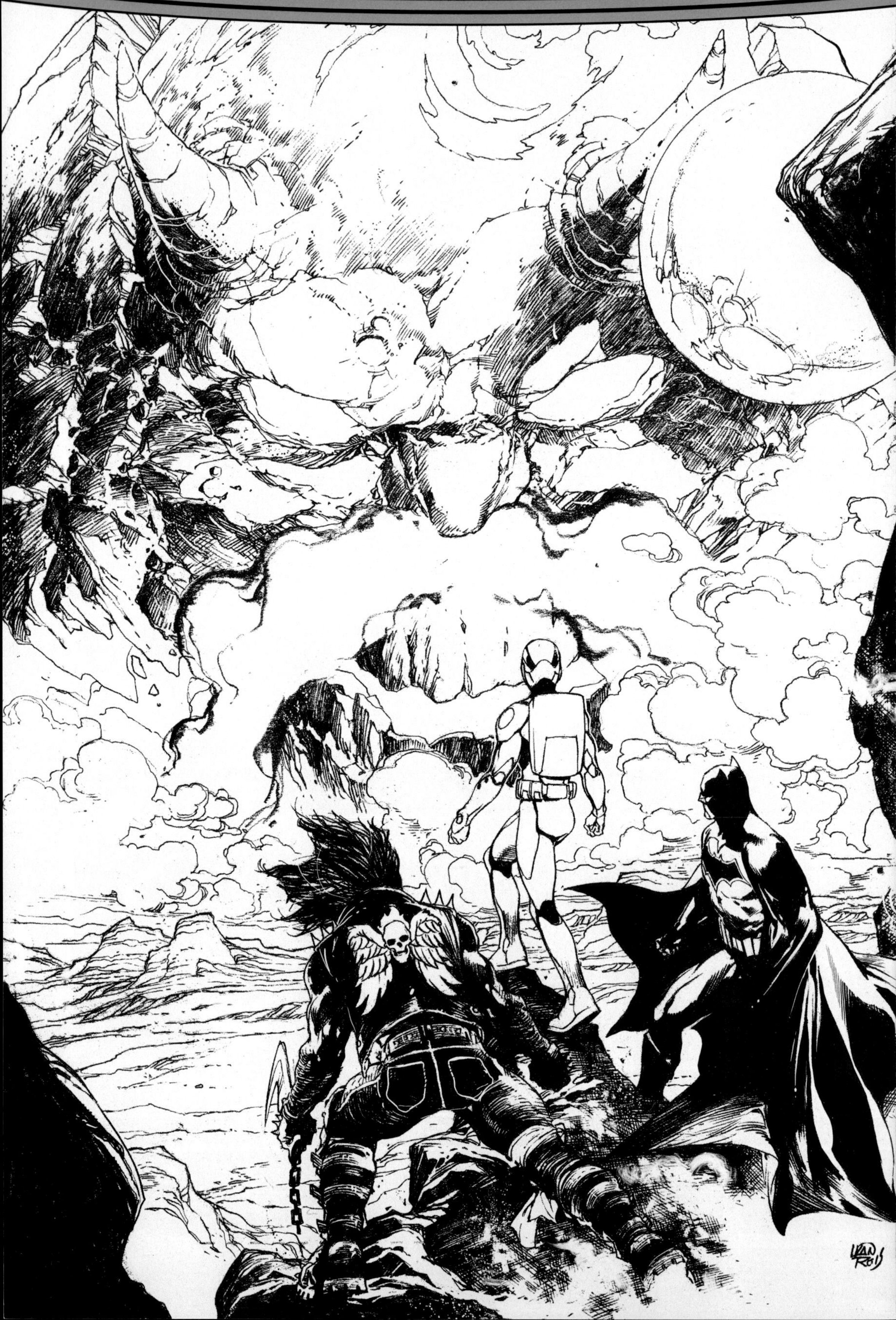

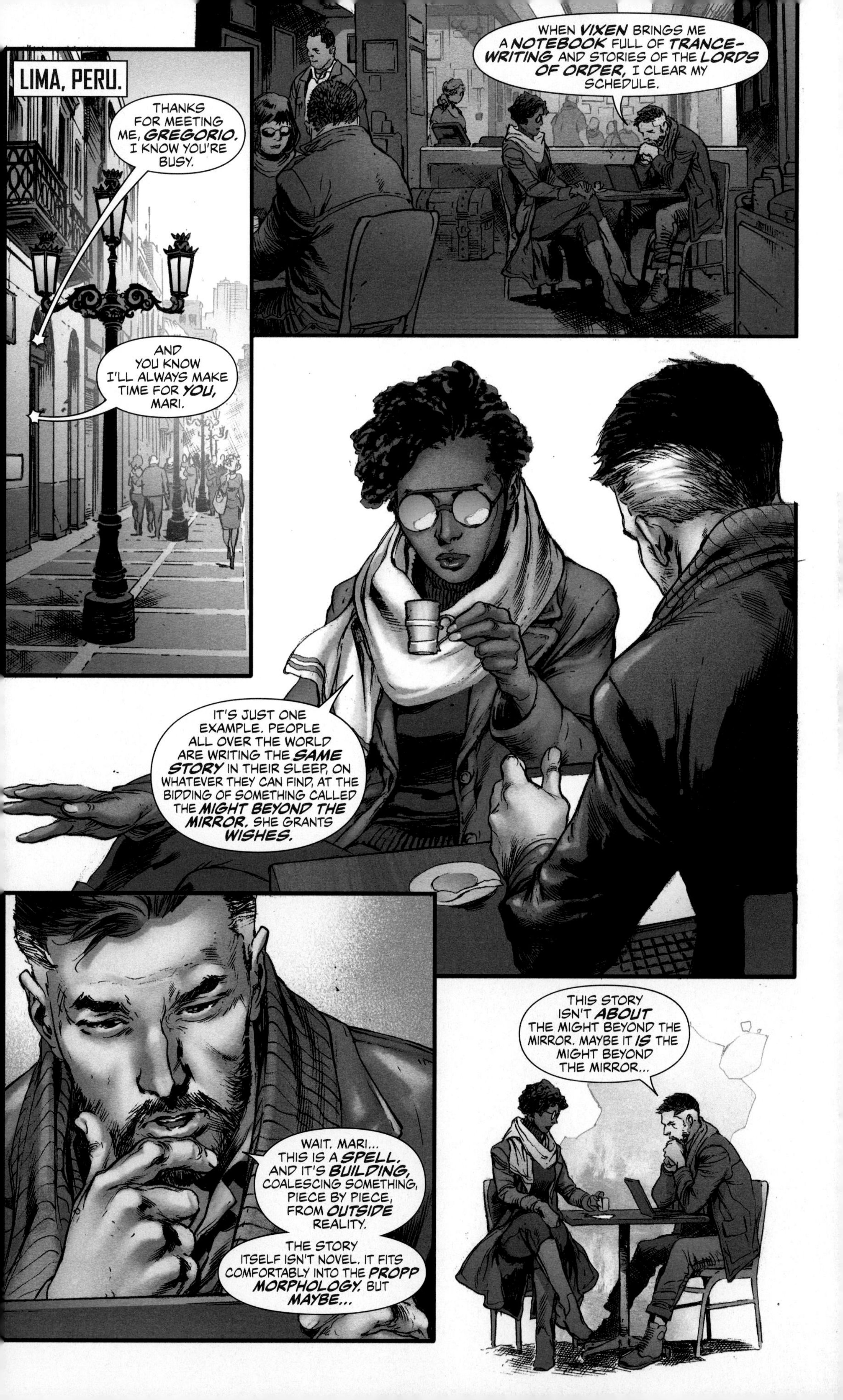

LIMA, PERU.
THANKS FOR MEETING ME, GREGORIO. I KNOW YOU'RE BUSY.
AND YOU KNOW I'LL ALWAYS MAKE TIME FOR YOU, MARI.
WHEN VIXEN BRINGS ME A NOTEBOOK FULL OF TRANCE-WRITING AND STORIES OF THE LORDS OF ORDER, I CLEAR MY SCHEDULE.
IT'S JUST ONE EXAMPLE. PEOPLE ALL OVER THE WORLD ARE WRITING THE SAME STORY IN THEIR SLEEP, ON WHATEVER THEY CAN FIND, AT THE BIDDING OF SOMETHING CALLED THE MIGHT BEYOND THE MIRROR. SHE GRANTS WISHES.
WAIT. MARI... THIS IS A SPELL, AND IT'S BUILDING, COALESCING SOMETHING, PIECE BY PIECE, FROM OUTSIDE REALITY.
THE STORY ITSELF ISN'T NOVEL. IT FITS COMFORTABLY INTO THE PROPP MORPHOLOGY. BUT MAYBE...
THIS STORY ISN'T ABOUT THE MIGHT BEYOND THE MIRROR. MAYBE IT IS THE MIGHT BEYOND THE MIRROR...

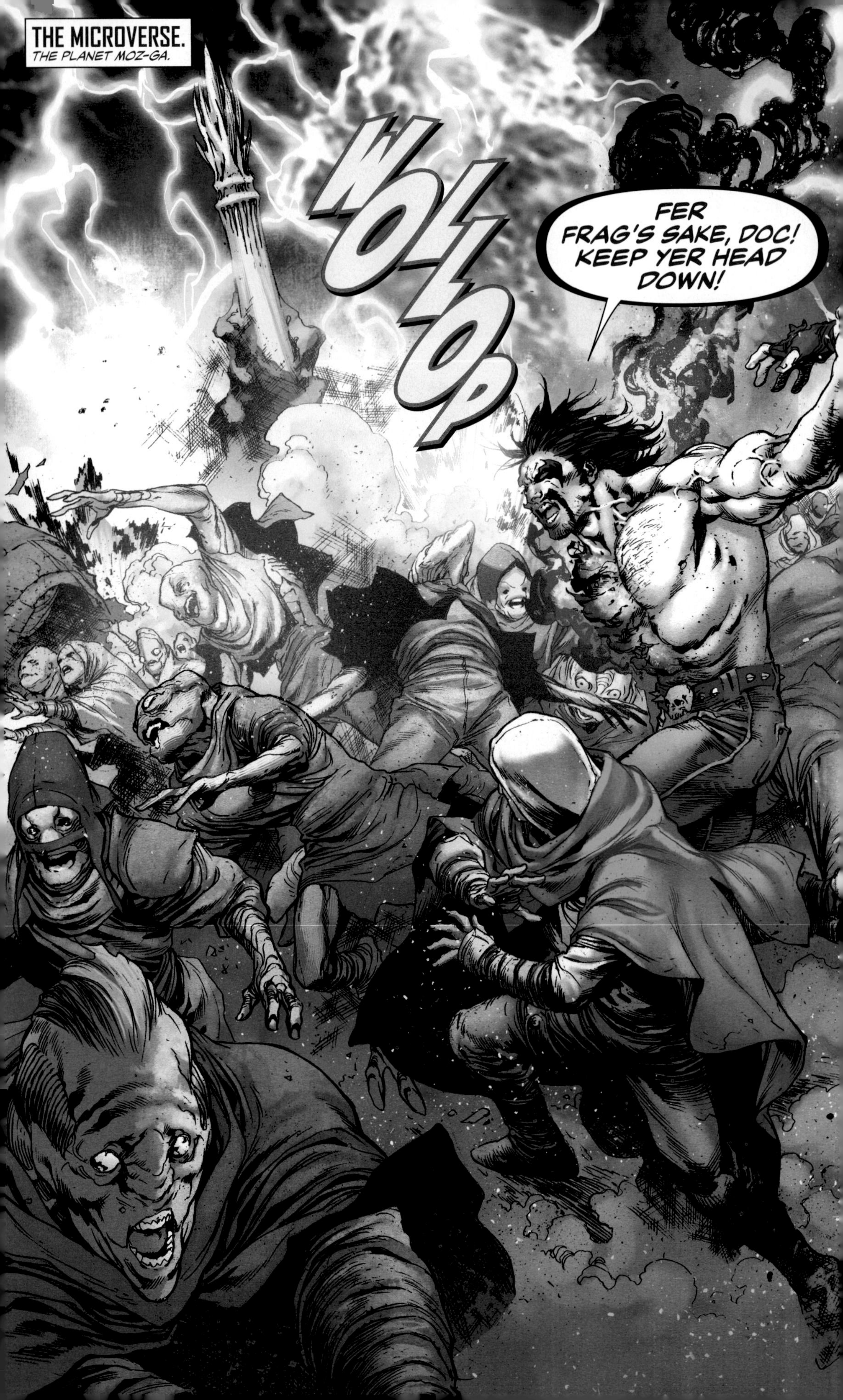
THE MICROVERSE.
THE PLANET MOZ-GA.
WOLLOP
FER FRAG'S SAKE, DOC! KEEP YER HEAD DOWN!

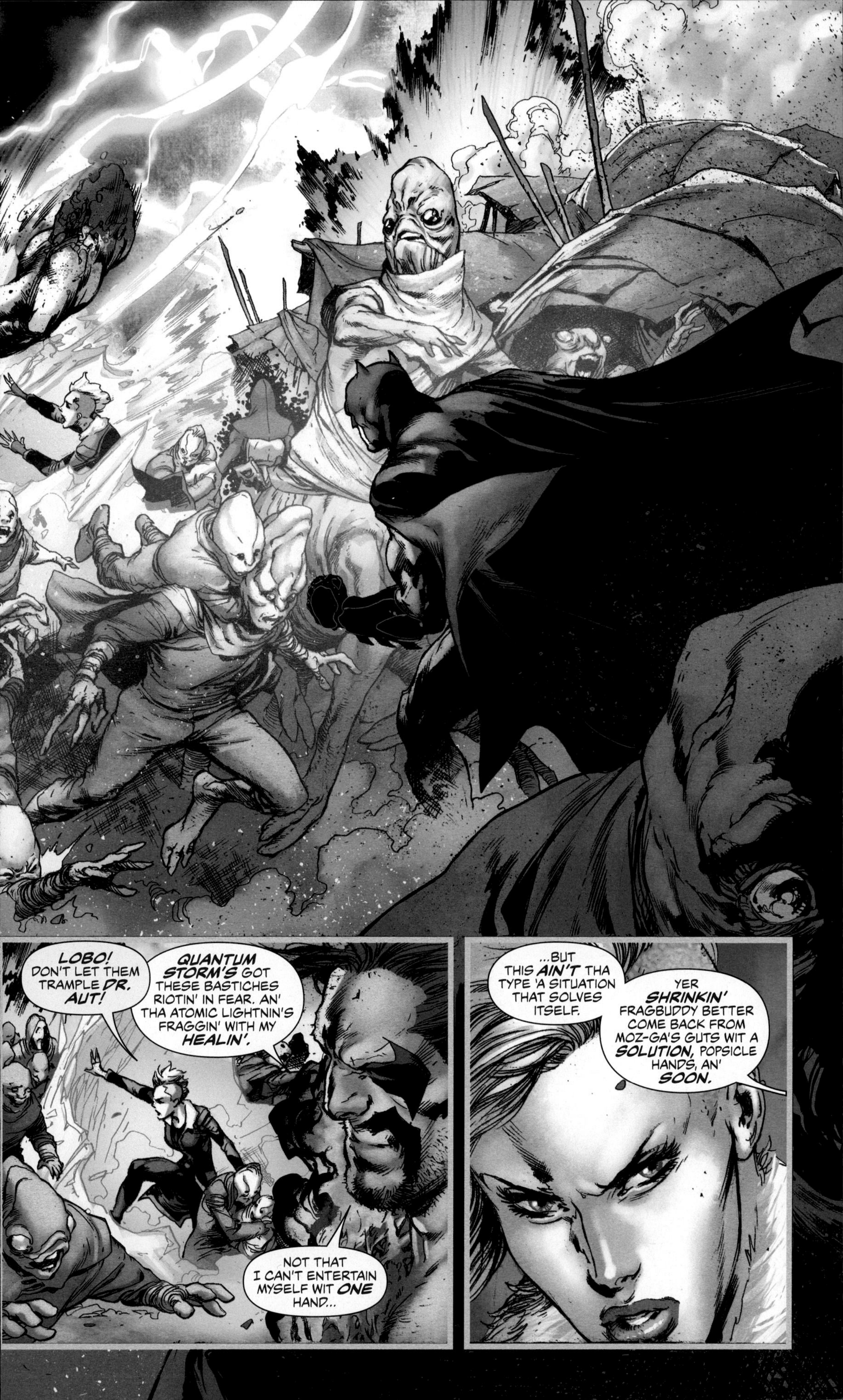

LOBO! DON'T LET THEM TRAMPLE DR. AUT!
QUANTUM STORM'S GOT THESE BASTICHES RIOTIN' IN FEAR. AN' THA ATOMIC LIGHTNIN'S FRAGGIN' WITH MY HEALIN'.
NOT THAT I CAN'T ENTERTAIN MYSELF WIT ONE HAND...
...BUT THIS AIN'T THA TYPE 'A SITUATION THAT SOLVES ITSELF.
YER SHRINKIN' FRAGBUDDY BETTER COME BACK FROM MOZ-GA'S GUTS WIT A SOLUTION, POPSICLE HANDS, AN' SOON.

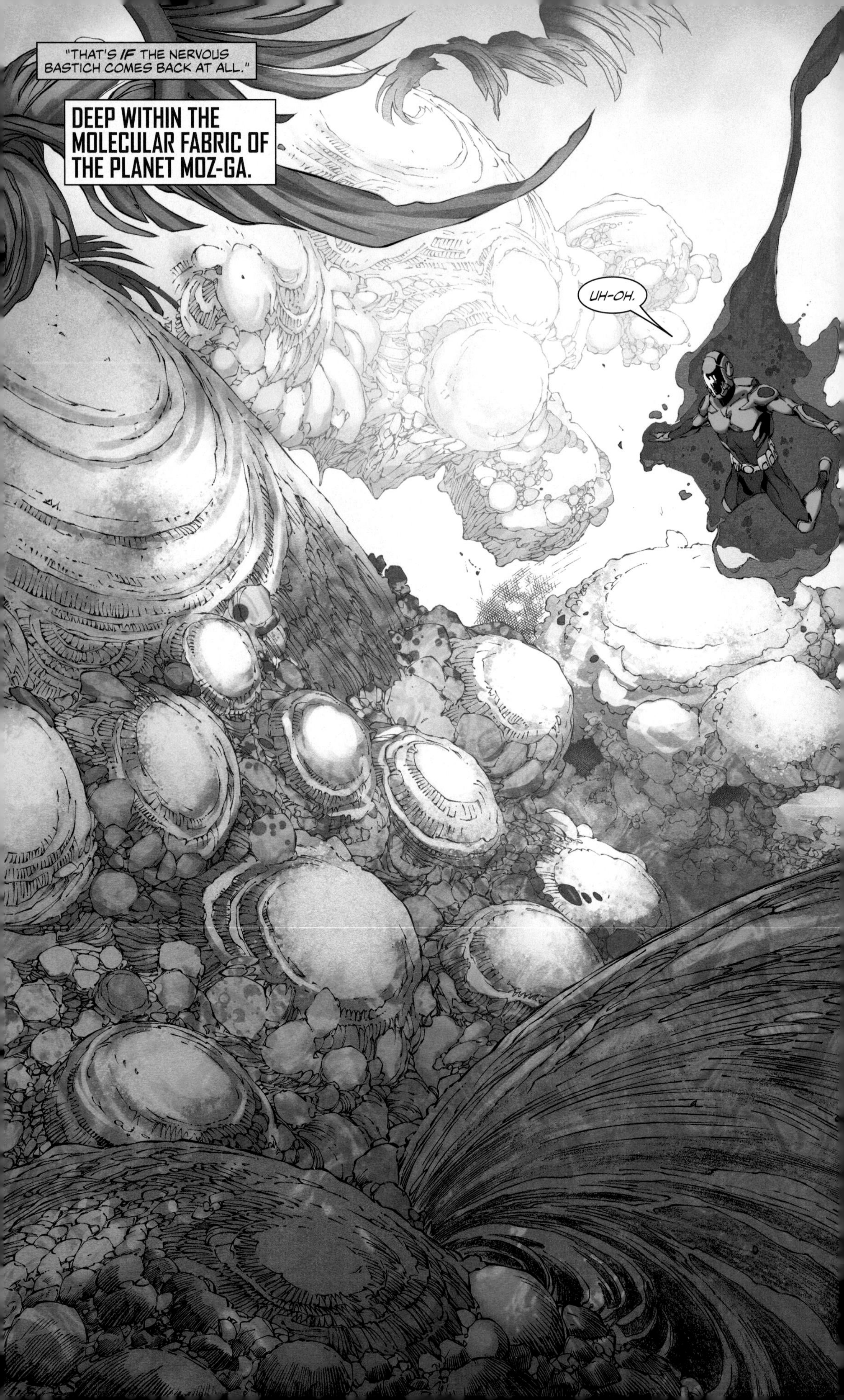
"THAT'S *IF* THE NERVOUS BASTICH COMES BACK AT ALL."
DEEP WITHIN THE MOLECULAR FABRIC OF THE PLANET MOZ-GA.
UH-OH.

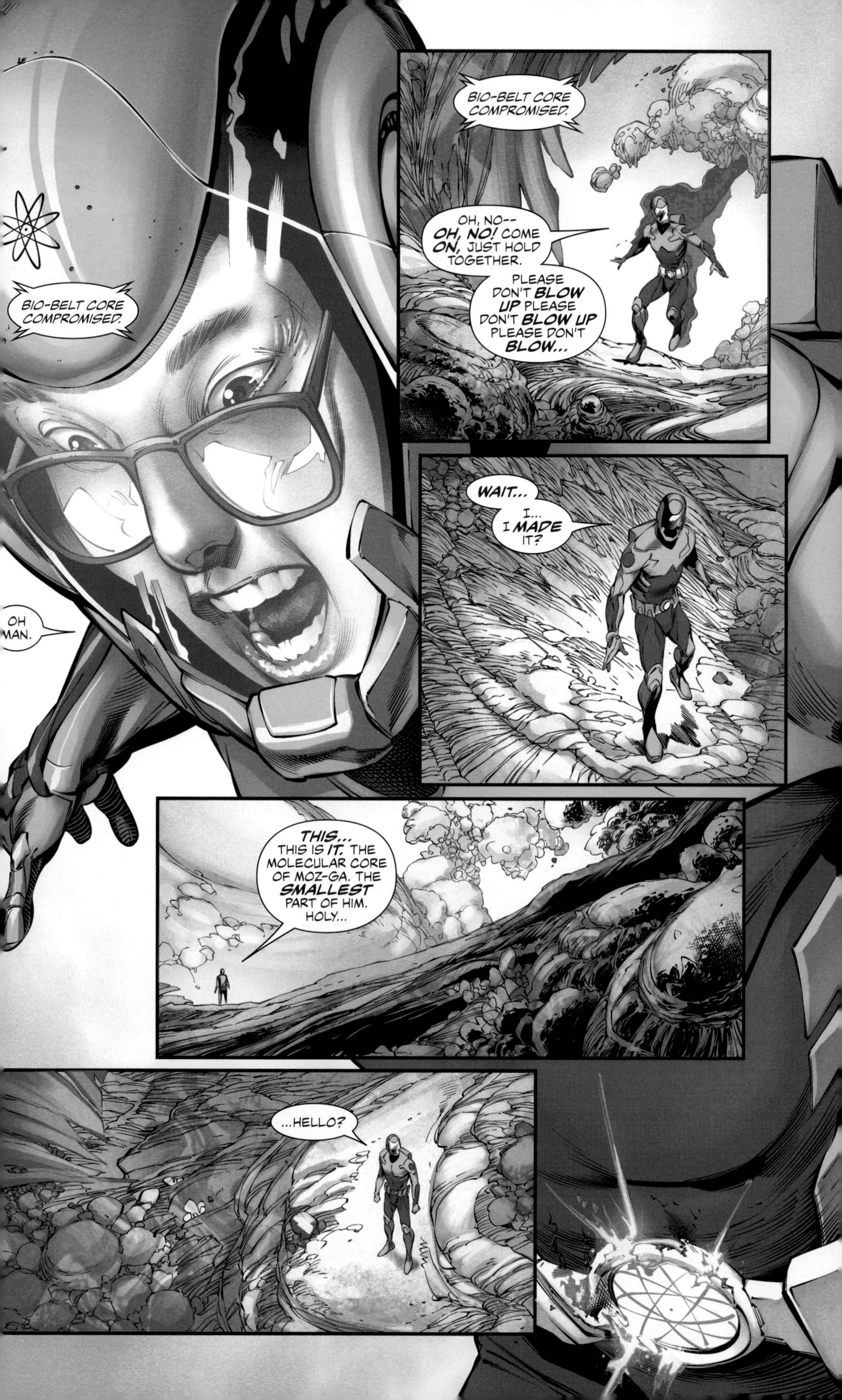
BIO-BELT CORE COMPROMISED.
BIO-BELT CORE COMPROMISED.
OH, NO-- OH, NO! COME ON, JUST HOLD TOGETHER.
PLEASE DON'T BLOW UP PLEASE DON'T BLOW UP PLEASE DON'T BLOW...
OH MAN.
WAIT...
I... I MADE IT?
THIS... THIS IS IT. THE MOLECULAR CORE OF MOZ-GA. THE SMALLEST PART OF HIM. HOLY...
...HELLO?

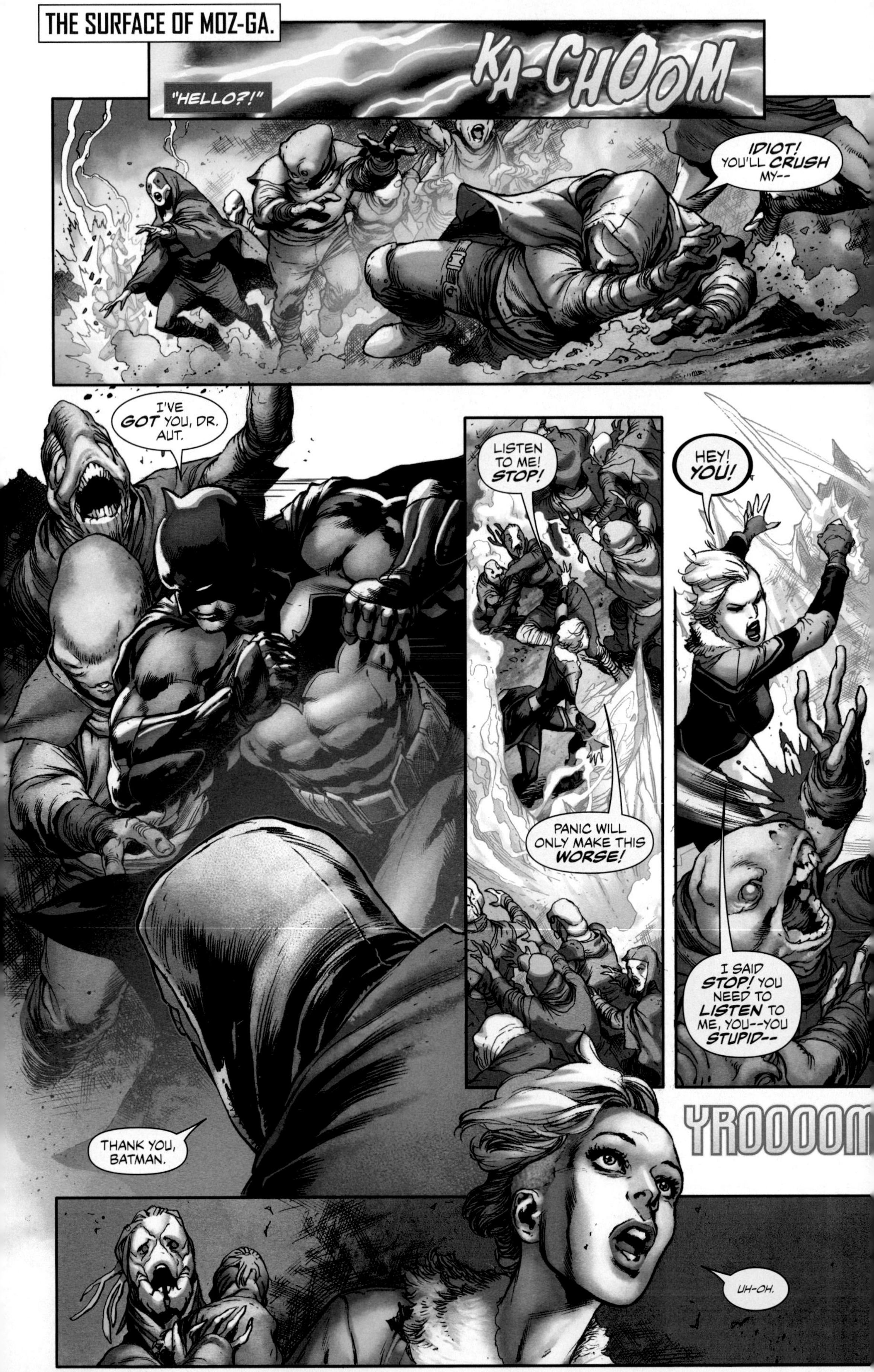
THE SURFACE OF MOZ-GA.
"HELLO?!"
KA-CHOOM
IDIOT! YOU'LL CRUSH MY--
I'VE GOT YOU, DR. AUT.
THANK YOU, BATMAN.
LISTEN TO ME! STOP!
PANIC WILL ONLY MAKE THIS WORSE!
HEY! YOU!
I SAID STOP! YOU NEED TO LISTEN TO ME, YOU--YOU STUPID--
YROOOOM
UH-OH.

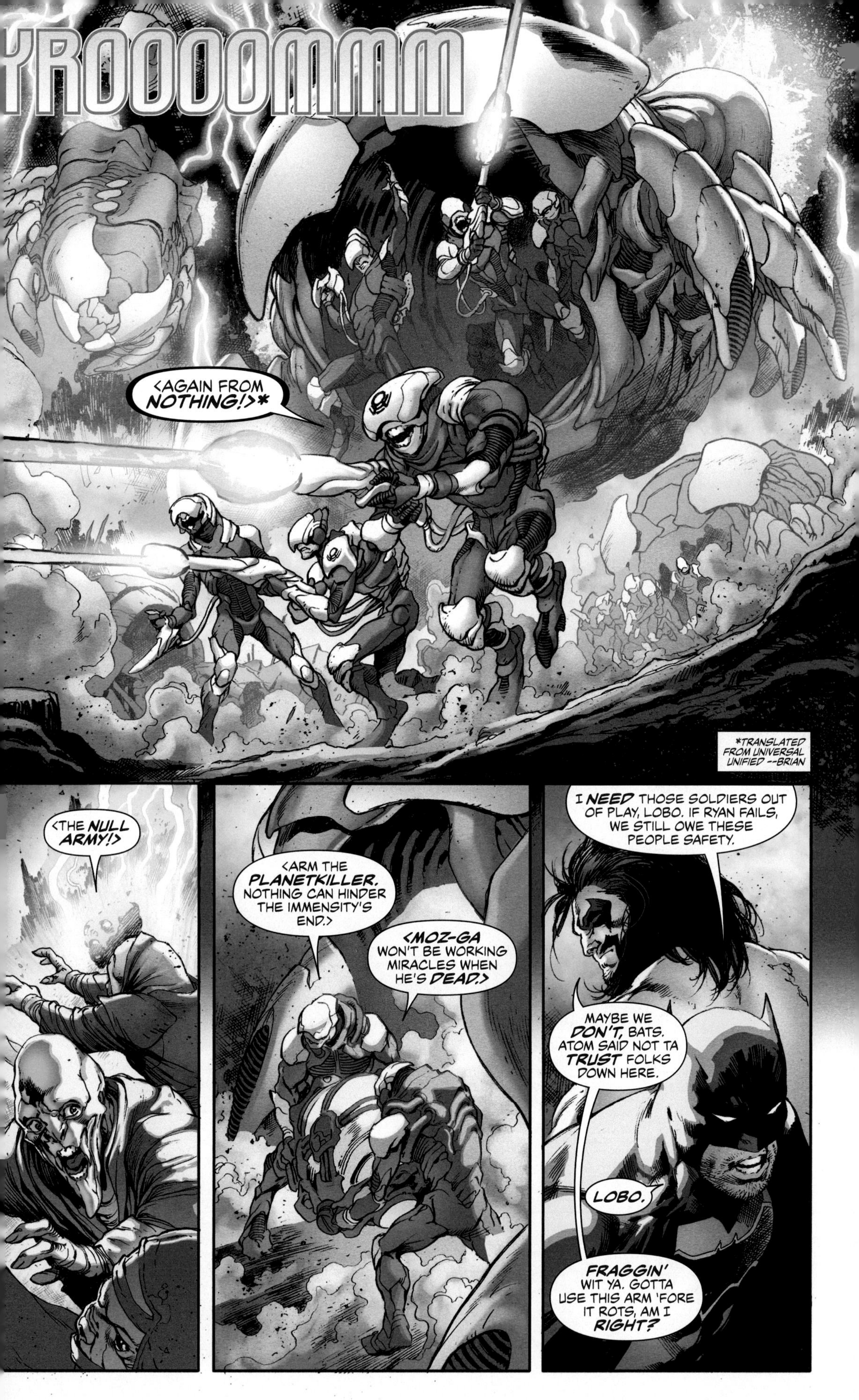

YROOOOMMMM
<AGAIN FROM NOTHING!>*
*TRANSLATED FROM UNIVERSAL UNIFIED --BRIAN
<THE NULL ARMY!>
<ARM THE PLANETKILLER. NOTHING CAN HINDER THE IMMENSITY'S END.>
<MOZ-GA WON'T BE WORKING MIRACLES WHEN HE'S DEAD.>
I NEED THOSE SOLDIERS OUT OF PLAY, LOBO. IF RYAN FAILS, WE STILL OWE THESE PEOPLE SAFETY.
MAYBE WE DON'T, BATS. ATOM SAID NOT TA TRUST FOLKS DOWN HERE.
LOBO.
FRAGGIN' WIT YA. GOTTA USE THIS ARM 'FORE IT ROTS, AM I RIGHT?

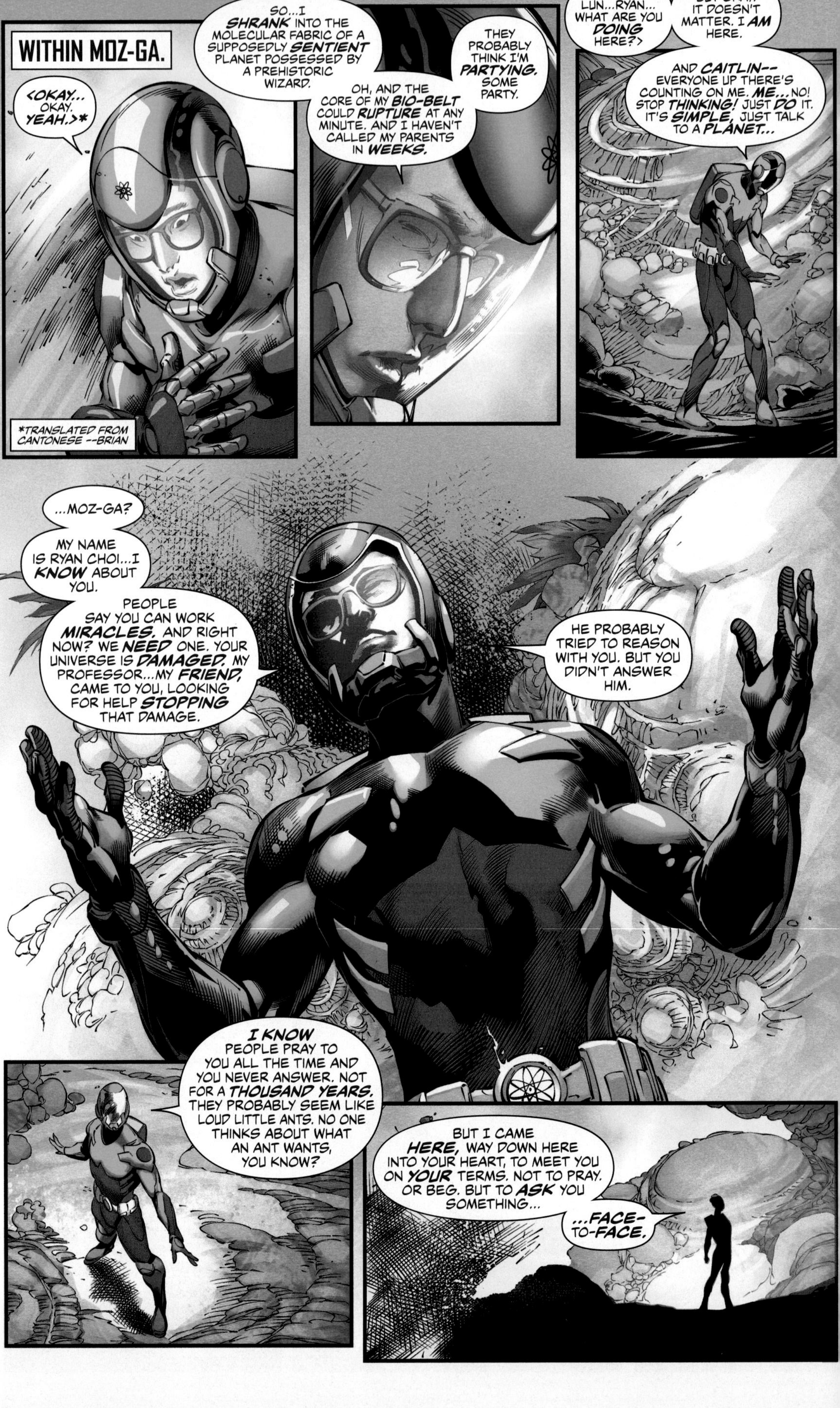
WITHIN MOZ-GA.
<OKAY... OKAY. YEAH.>*
*TRANSLATED FROM CANTONESE --BRIAN
SO...I SHRANK INTO THE MOLECULAR FABRIC OF A SUPPOSEDLY SENTIENT PLANET POSSESSED BY A PREHISTORIC WIZARD.
OH, AND THE CORE OF MY BIO-BELT COULD RUPTURE AT ANY MINUTE. AND I HAVEN'T CALLED MY PARENTS IN WEEKS.
THEY PROBABLY THINK I'M PARTYING. SOME PARTY.
<CHOI LUN...RYAN... WHAT ARE YOU DOING HERE?>
BUT OKAY. IT DOESN'T MATTER. I AM HERE.
AND CAITLIN-- EVERYONE UP THERE'S COUNTING ON ME. ME... NO! STOP THINKING! JUST DO IT. IT'S SIMPLE, JUST TALK TO A PLANET...
...MOZ-GA?
MY NAME IS RYAN CHOI...I KNOW ABOUT YOU.
PEOPLE SAY YOU CAN WORK MIRACLES. AND RIGHT NOW? WE NEED ONE. YOUR UNIVERSE IS DAMAGED. MY PROFESSOR...MY FRIEND, CAME TO YOU, LOOKING FOR HELP STOPPING THAT DAMAGE.
HE PROBABLY TRIED TO REASON WITH YOU. BUT YOU DIDN'T ANSWER HIM.
I KNOW PEOPLE PRAY TO YOU ALL THE TIME AND YOU NEVER ANSWER. NOT FOR A THOUSAND YEARS. THEY PROBABLY SEEM LIKE LOUD LITTLE ANTS. NO ONE THINKS ABOUT WHAT AN ANT WANTS, YOU KNOW?
BUT I CAME HERE, WAY DOWN HERE INTO YOUR HEART, TO MEET YOU ON YOUR TERMS. NOT TO PRAY. OR BEG. BUT TO ASK YOU SOMETHING...
...FACE-TO-FACE.

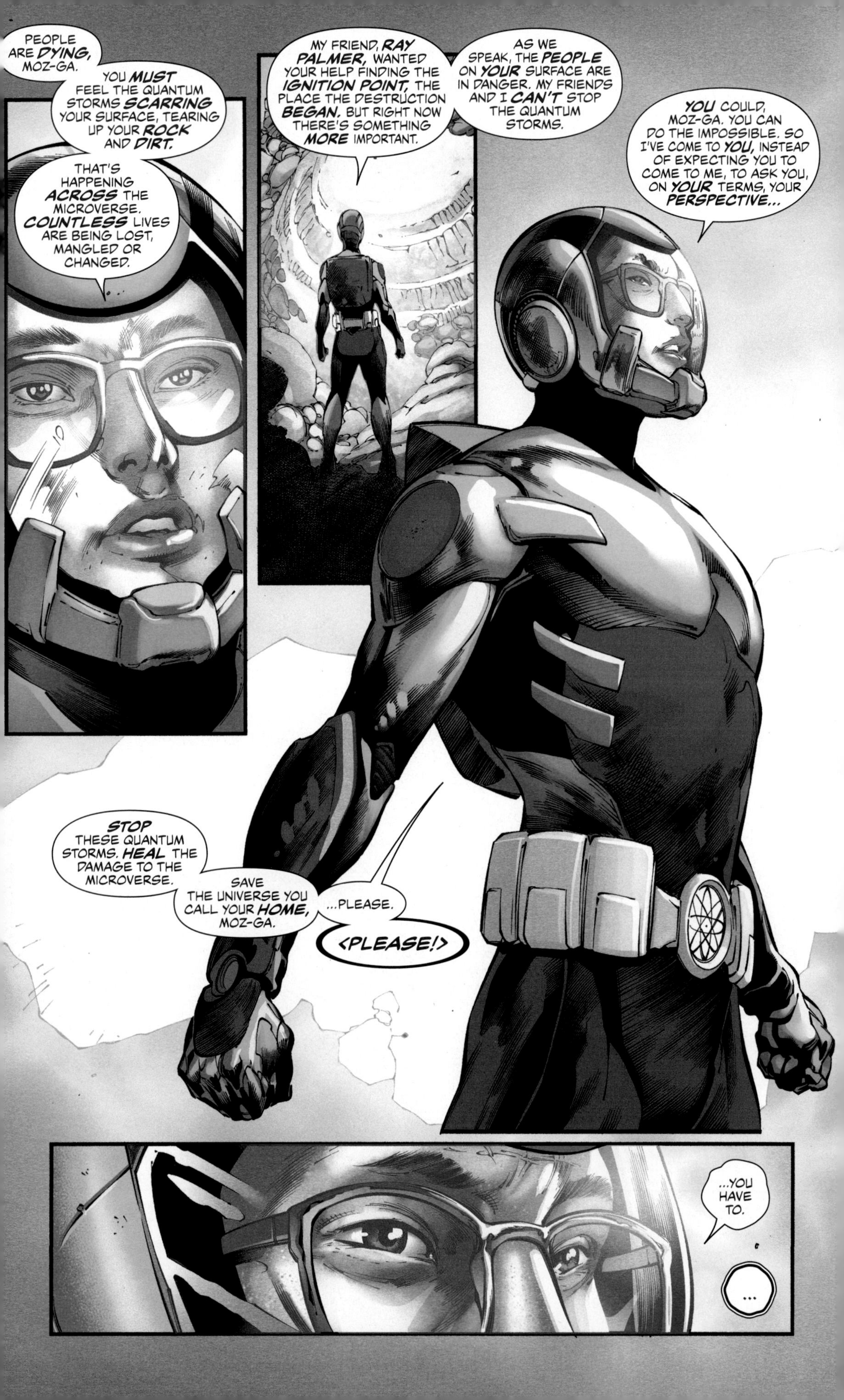
PEOPLE ARE DYING, MOZ-GA.
YOU MUST FEEL THE QUANTUM STORMS SCARRING YOUR SURFACE, TEARING UP YOUR ROCK AND DIRT.
THAT'S HAPPENING ACROSS THE MICROVERSE. COUNTLESS LIVES ARE BEING LOST, MANGLED OR CHANGED.
MY FRIEND, RAY PALMER, WANTED YOUR HELP FINDING THE IGNITION POINT, THE PLACE THE DESTRUCTION BEGAN. BUT RIGHT NOW THERE'S SOMETHING MORE IMPORTANT.
AS WE SPEAK, THE PEOPLE ON YOUR SURFACE ARE IN DANGER. MY FRIENDS AND I CAN'T STOP THE QUANTUM STORMS.
YOU COULD, MOZ-GA. YOU CAN DO THE IMPOSSIBLE. SO I'VE COME TO YOU, INSTEAD OF EXPECTING YOU TO COME TO ME, TO ASK YOU, ON YOUR TERMS, YOUR PERSPECTIVE...
STOP THESE QUANTUM STORMS. HEAL THE DAMAGE TO THE MICROVERSE.
SAVE THE UNIVERSE YOU CALL YOUR HOME, MOZ-GA.
...PLEASE.
<PLEASE!>
...YOU HAVE TO.
...

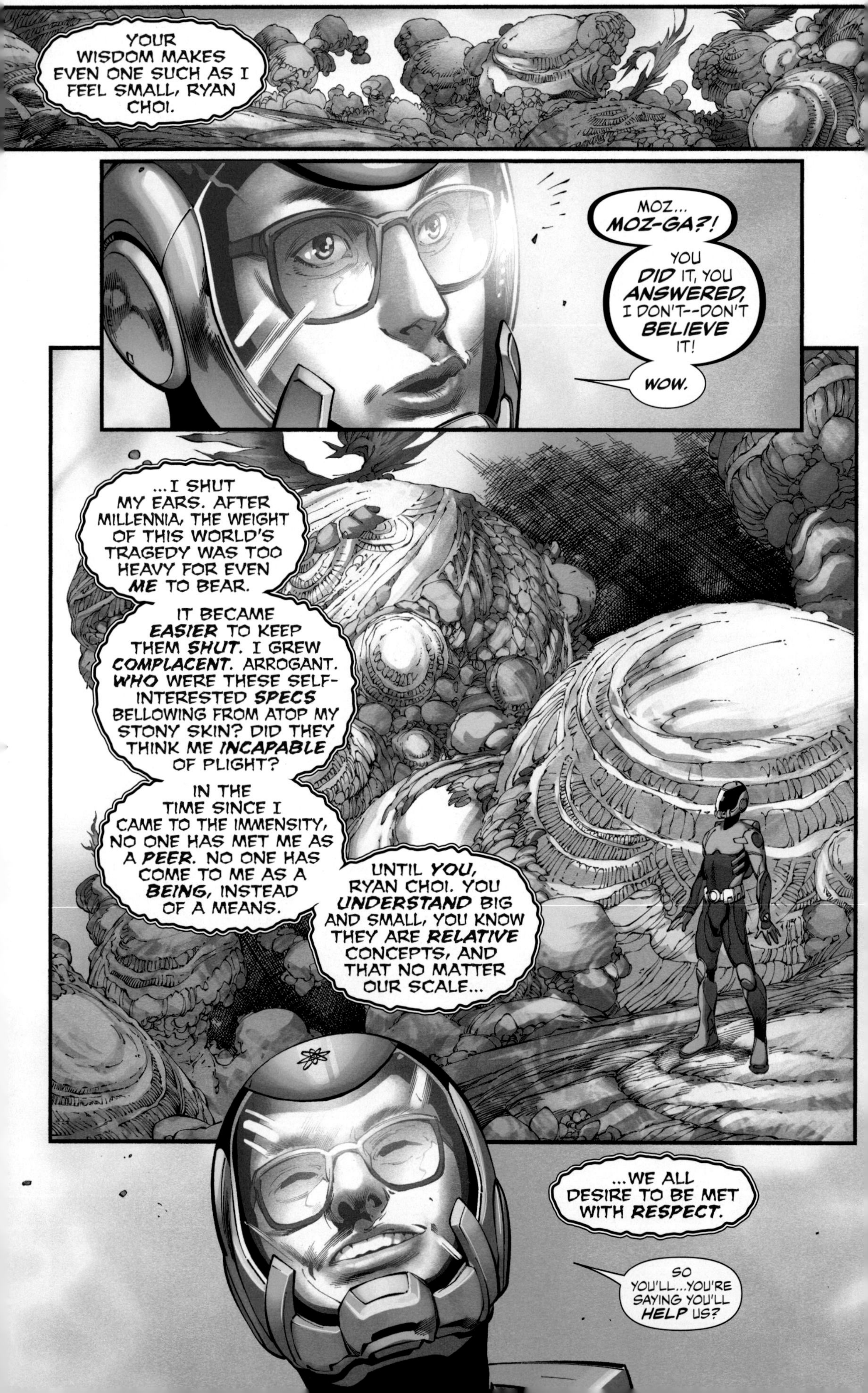
YOUR WISDOM MAKES EVEN ONE SUCH AS I FEEL SMALL, RYAN CHOI.
MOZ... MOZ-GA?!
YOU DID IT, YOU ANSWERED, I DON'T--DON'T BELIEVE IT!
WOW.
...I SHUT MY EARS. AFTER MILLENNIA, THE WEIGHT OF THIS WORLD'S TRAGEDY WAS TOO HEAVY FOR EVEN ME TO BEAR.
IT BECAME EASIER TO KEEP THEM SHUT. I GREW COMPLACENT. ARROGANT. WHO WERE THESE SELF-INTERESTED SPECS BELLOWING FROM ATOP MY STONY SKIN? DID THEY THINK ME INCAPABLE OF PLIGHT?
IN THE TIME SINCE I CAME TO THE IMMENSITY, NO ONE HAS MET ME AS A PEER. NO ONE HAS COME TO ME AS A BEING, INSTEAD OF A MEANS.
UNTIL YOU, RYAN CHOI. YOU UNDERSTAND BIG AND SMALL, YOU KNOW THEY ARE RELATIVE CONCEPTS, AND THAT NO MATTER OUR SCALE...
...WE ALL DESIRE TO BE MET WITH RESPECT.
SO YOU'LL...YOU'RE SAYING YOU'LL HELP US?

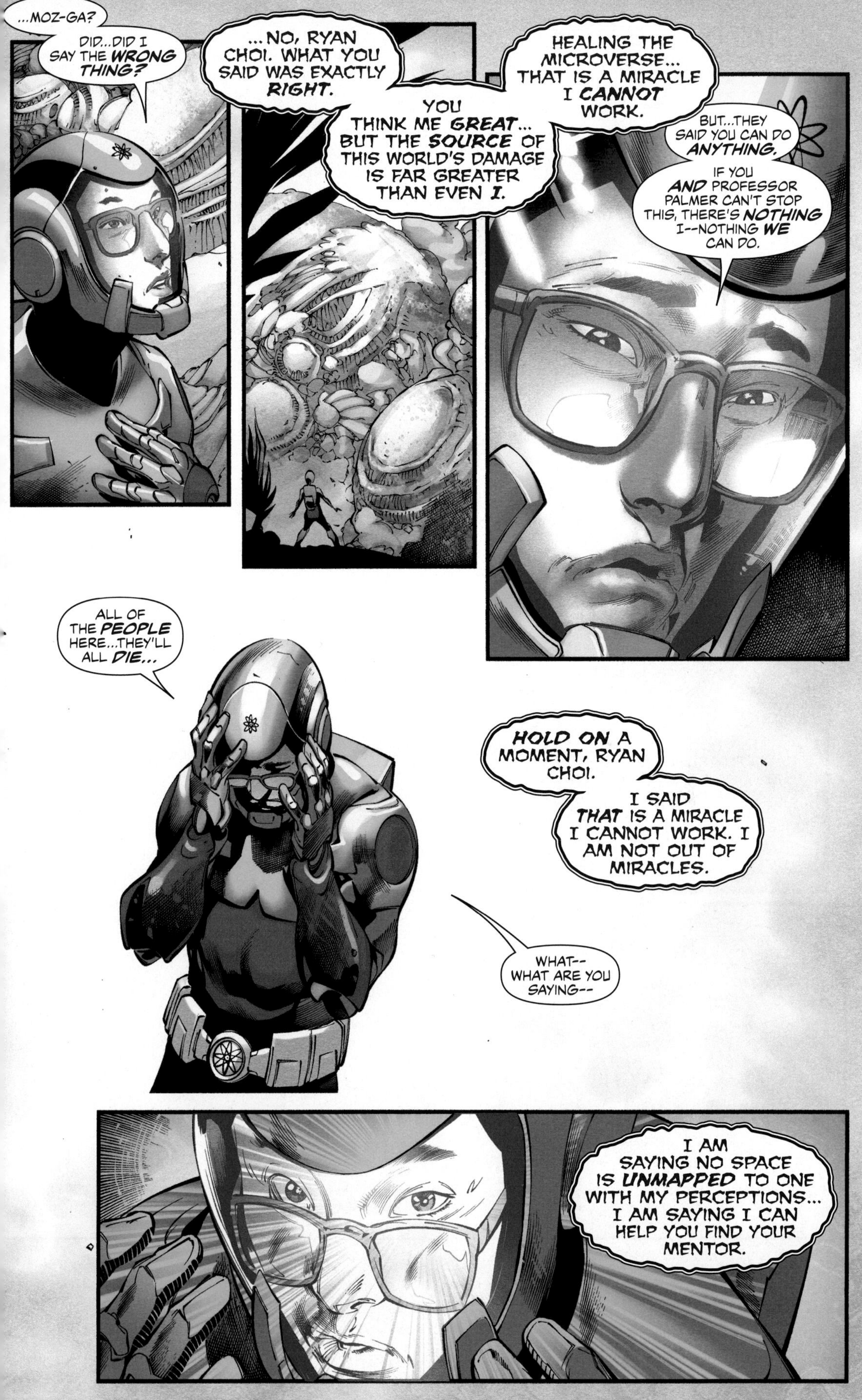
...MOZ-GA?
DID...DID I SAY THE WRONG THING?
...NO, RYAN CHOI. WHAT YOU SAID WAS EXACTLY RIGHT.
YOU THINK ME GREAT... BUT THE SOURCE OF THIS WORLD'S DAMAGE IS FAR GREATER THAN EVEN I.
HEALING THE MICROVERSE... THAT IS A MIRACLE I CANNOT WORK.
BUT...THEY SAID YOU CAN DO ANYTHING.
IF YOU AND PROFESSOR PALMER CAN'T STOP THIS, THERE'S NOTHING I--NOTHING WE CAN DO.
ALL OF THE PEOPLE HERE...THEY'LL ALL DIE...
HOLD ON A MOMENT, RYAN CHOI.
I SAID THAT IS A MIRACLE I CANNOT WORK. I AM NOT OUT OF MIRACLES.
WHAT--WHAT ARE YOU SAYING--
I AM SAYING NO SPACE IS UNMAPPED TO ONE WITH MY PERCEPTIONS... I AM SAYING I CAN HELP YOU FIND YOUR MENTOR.

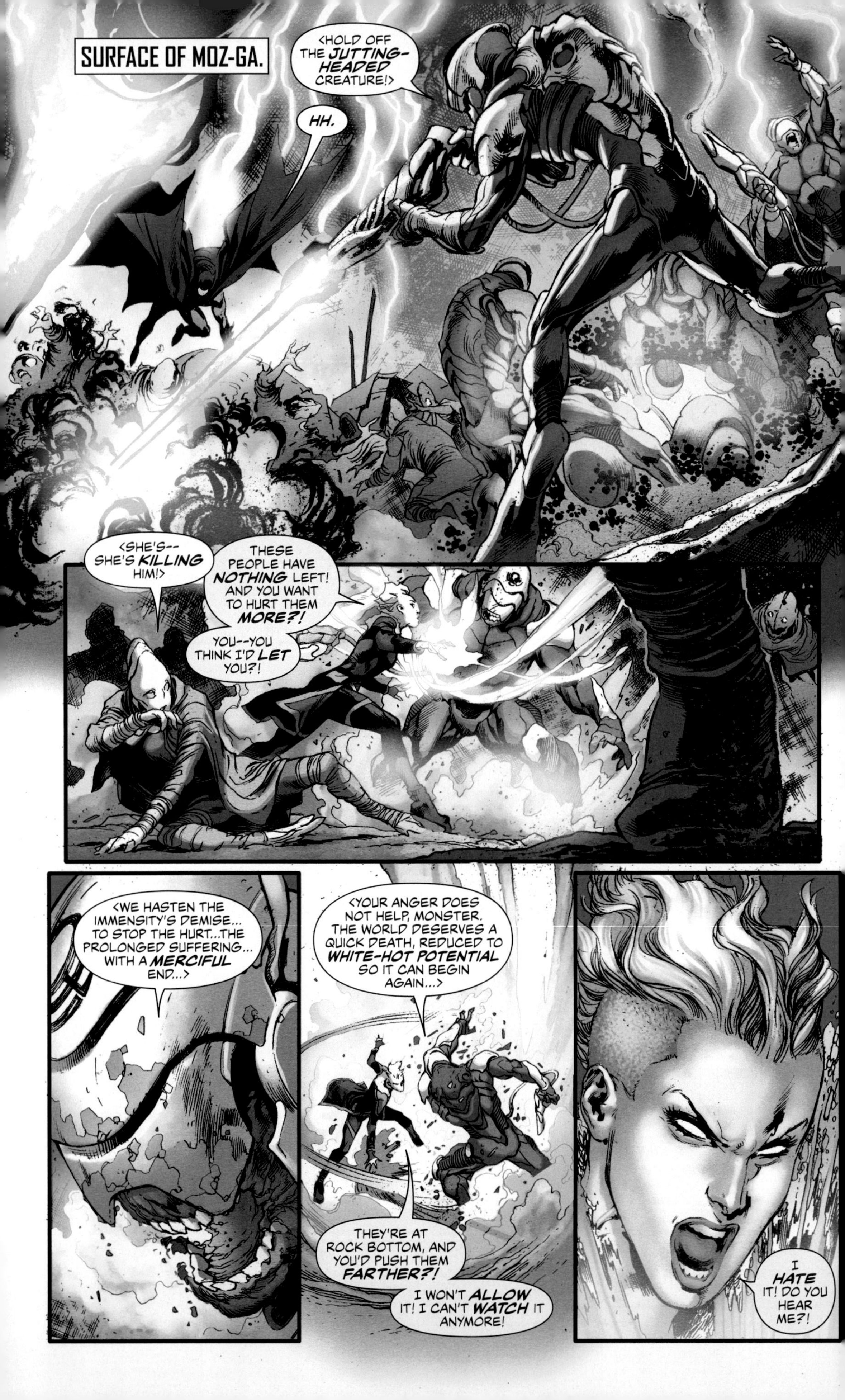
SURFACE OF MOZ-GA.
<HOLD OFF THE JUTTING-HEADED CREATURE!>
HH.
<SHE'S-- SHE'S KILLING HIM!>
THESE PEOPLE HAVE NOTHING LEFT! AND YOU WANT TO HURT THEM MORE?!
YOU--YOU THINK I'D LET YOU?!
<WE HASTEN THE IMMENSITY'S DEMISE... TO STOP THE HURT...THE PROLONGED SUFFERING... WITH A MERCIFUL END...>
<YOUR ANGER DOES NOT HELP, MONSTER. THE WORLD DESERVES A QUICK DEATH, REDUCED TO WHITE-HOT POTENTIAL SO IT CAN BEGIN AGAIN...>
THEY'RE AT ROCK BOTTOM, AND YOU'D PUSH THEM FARTHER?!
I WON'T ALLOW IT! I CAN'T WATCH IT ANYMORE!
I HATE IT! DO YOU HEAR ME?!

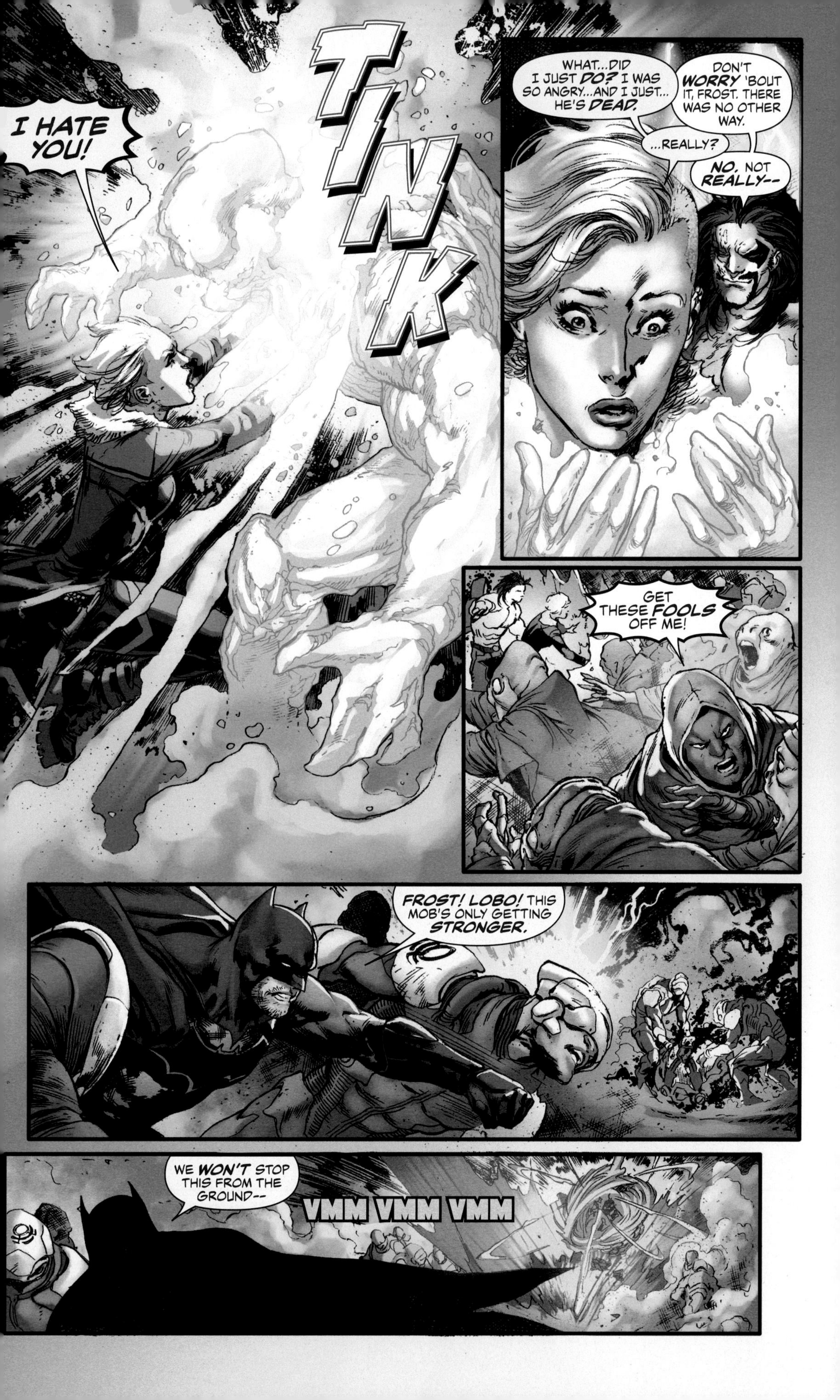
TINK
I HATE YOU!
WHAT...DID I JUST DO? I WAS SO ANGRY...AND I JUST... HE'S DEAD.
DON'T WORRY 'BOUT IT, FROST. THERE WAS NO OTHER WAY.
...REALLY?
NO, NOT REALLY--
GET THESE FOOLS OFF ME!
FROST! LOBO! THIS MOB'S ONLY GETTING STRONGER.
WE WON'T STOP THIS FROM THE GROUND--
VMM VMM VMM

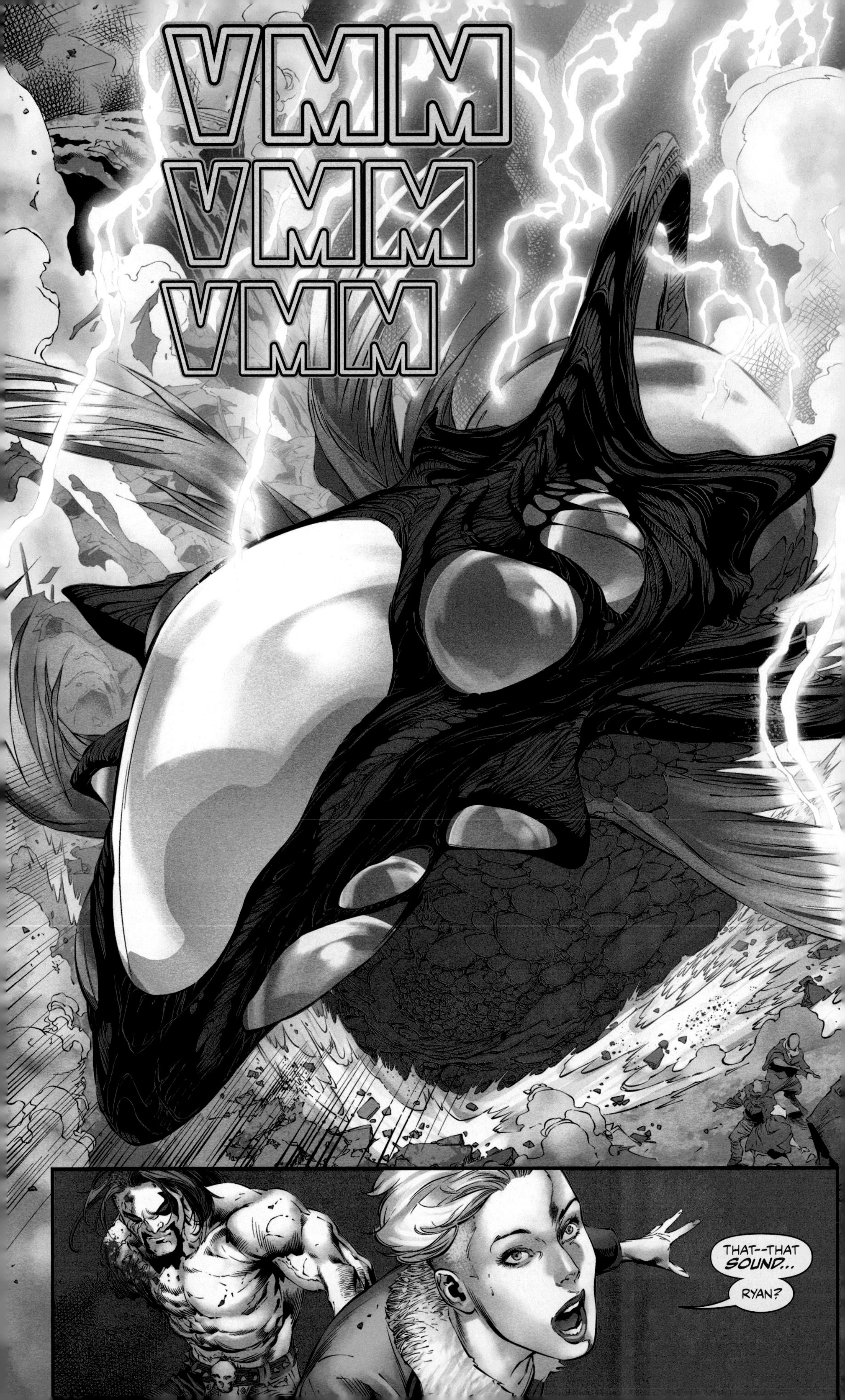
VMM VMM VMM
THAT--THAT SOUND...
RYAN?

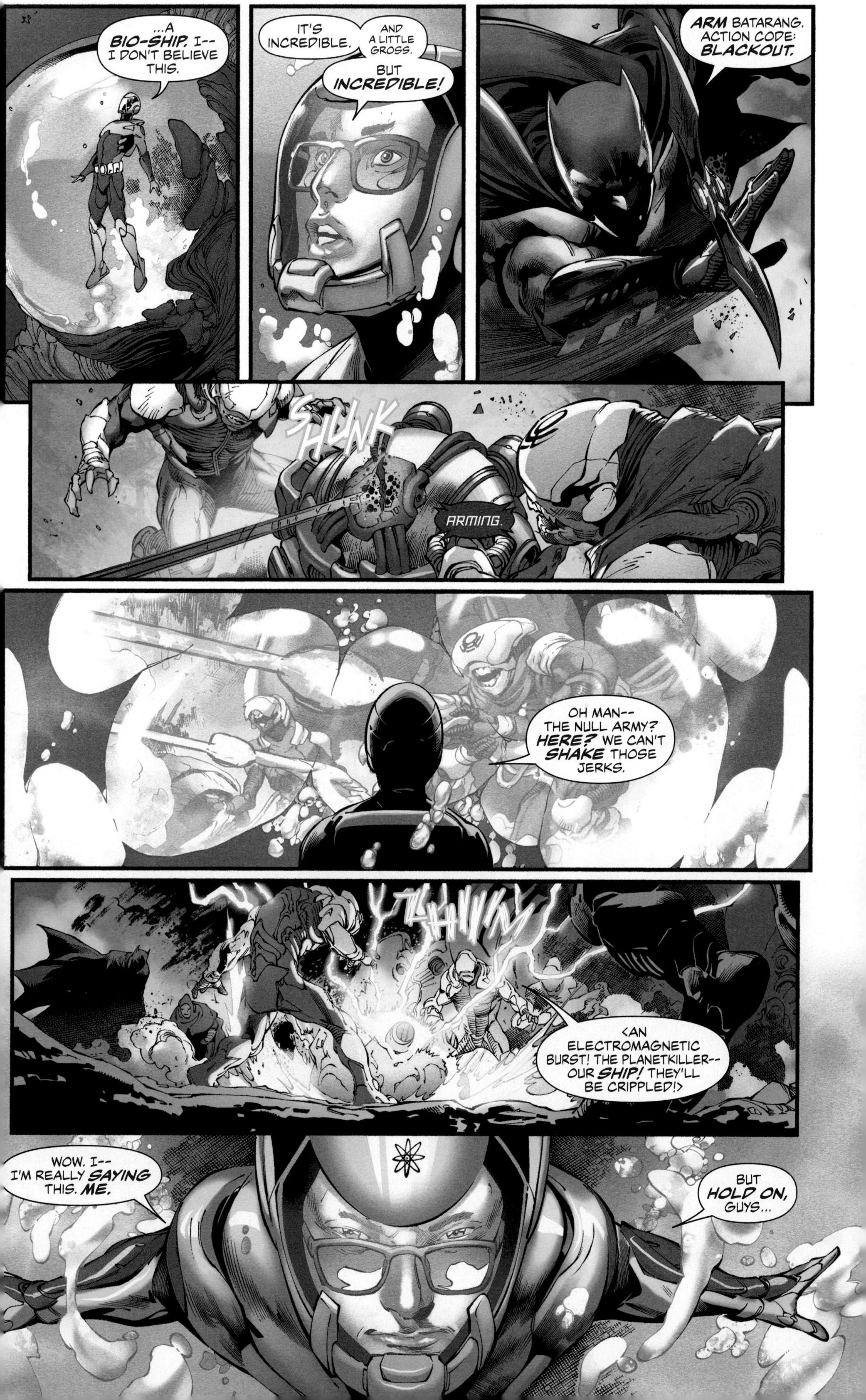
...A BIO-SHIP. I-- I DON'T BELIEVE THIS.
IT'S INCREDIBLE.
AND A LITTLE GROSS.
BUT INCREDIBLE!
ARM BATARANG. ACTION CODE: BLACKOUT.
SHUNK
ARMING.
OH MAN-- THE NULL ARMY? HERE? WE CAN'T SHAKE THOSE JERKS.
<AN ELECTROMAGNETIC BURST! THE PLANETKILLER-- OUR SHIP! THEY'LL BE CRIPPLED!>
WOW. I-- I'M REALLY SAYING THIS. ME.
BUT HOLD ON, GUYS...

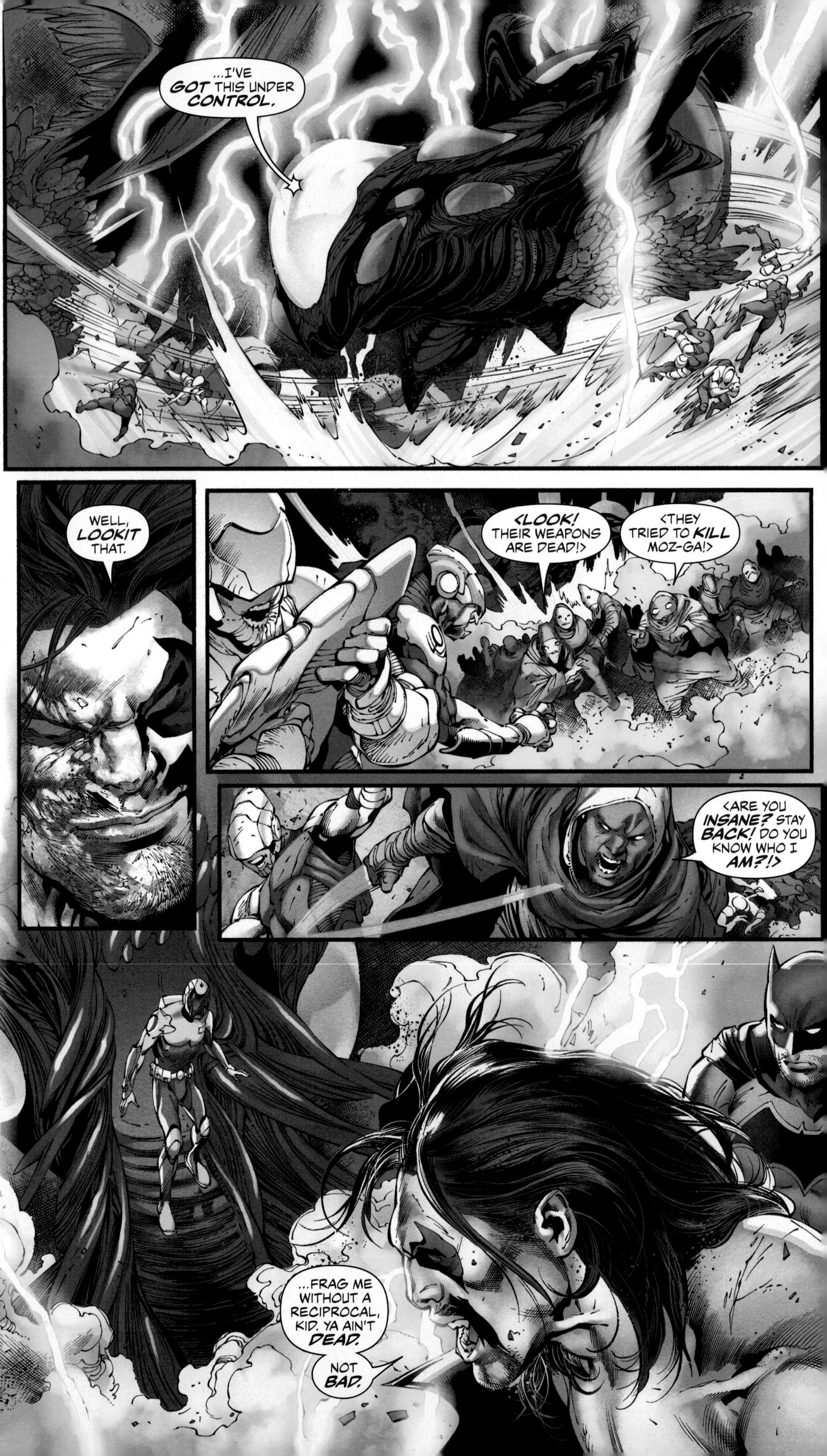
...I'VE GOT THIS UNDER CONTROL.
WELL, LOOKIT THAT.
<LOOK! THEIR WEAPONS ARE DEAD!>
<THEY TRIED TO KILL MOZ-GA!>
<ARE YOU INSANE? STAY BACK! DO YOU KNOW WHO I AM?!>
...FRAG ME WITHOUT A RECIPROCAL, KID. YA AIN'T DEAD.
NOT BAD.

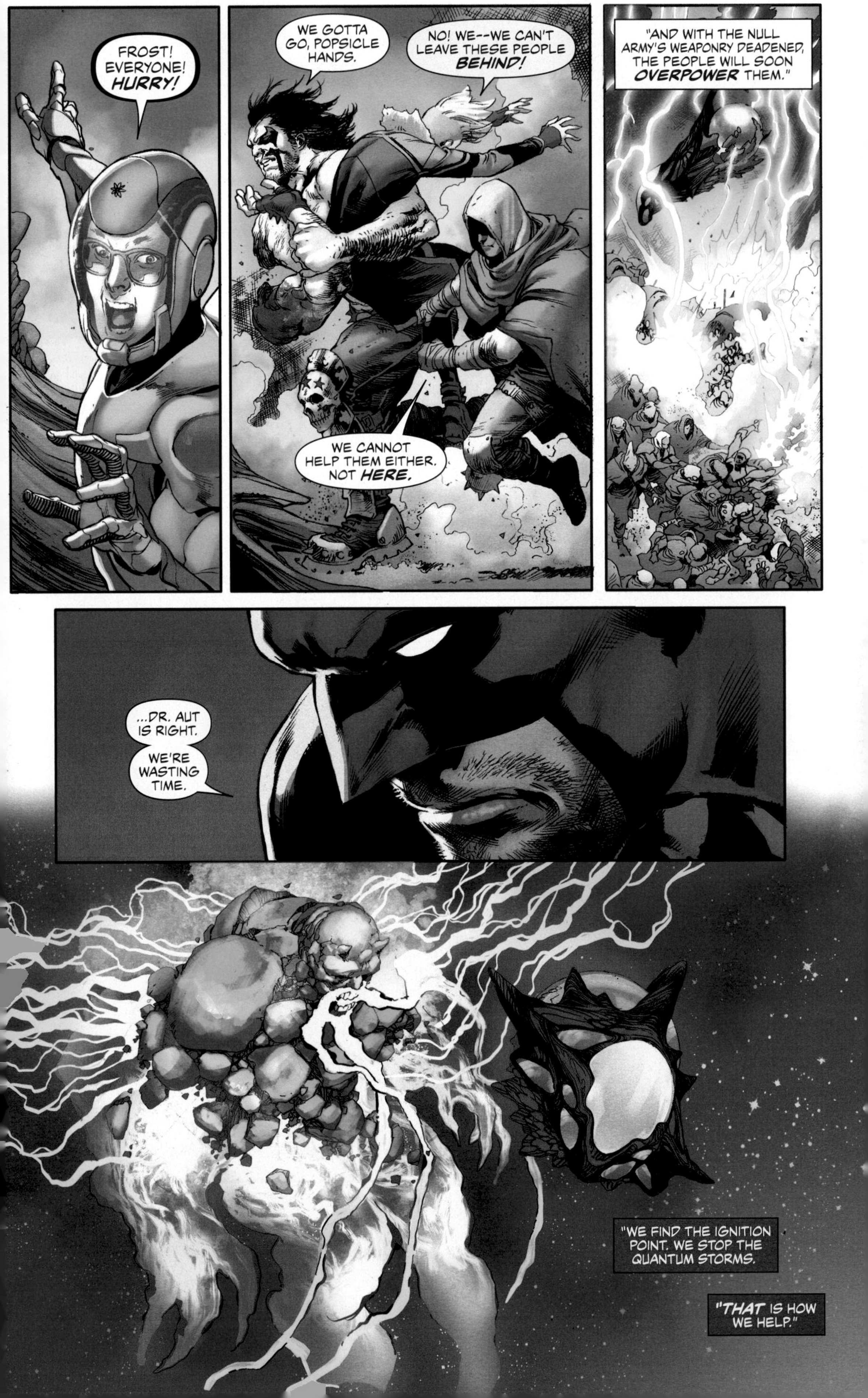
FROST! EVERYONE! HURRY!
WE GOTTA GO, POPSICLE HANDS.
NO! WE--WE CAN'T LEAVE THESE PEOPLE BEHIND!
WE CANNOT HELP THEM EITHER. NOT HERE.
"AND WITH THE NULL ARMY'S WEAPONRY DEADENED, THE PEOPLE WILL SOON OVERPOWER THEM."
...DR. AUT IS RIGHT.
WE'RE WASTING TIME.
"WE FIND THE IGNITION POINT. WE STOP THE QUANTUM STORMS.
"THAT IS HOW WE HELP."

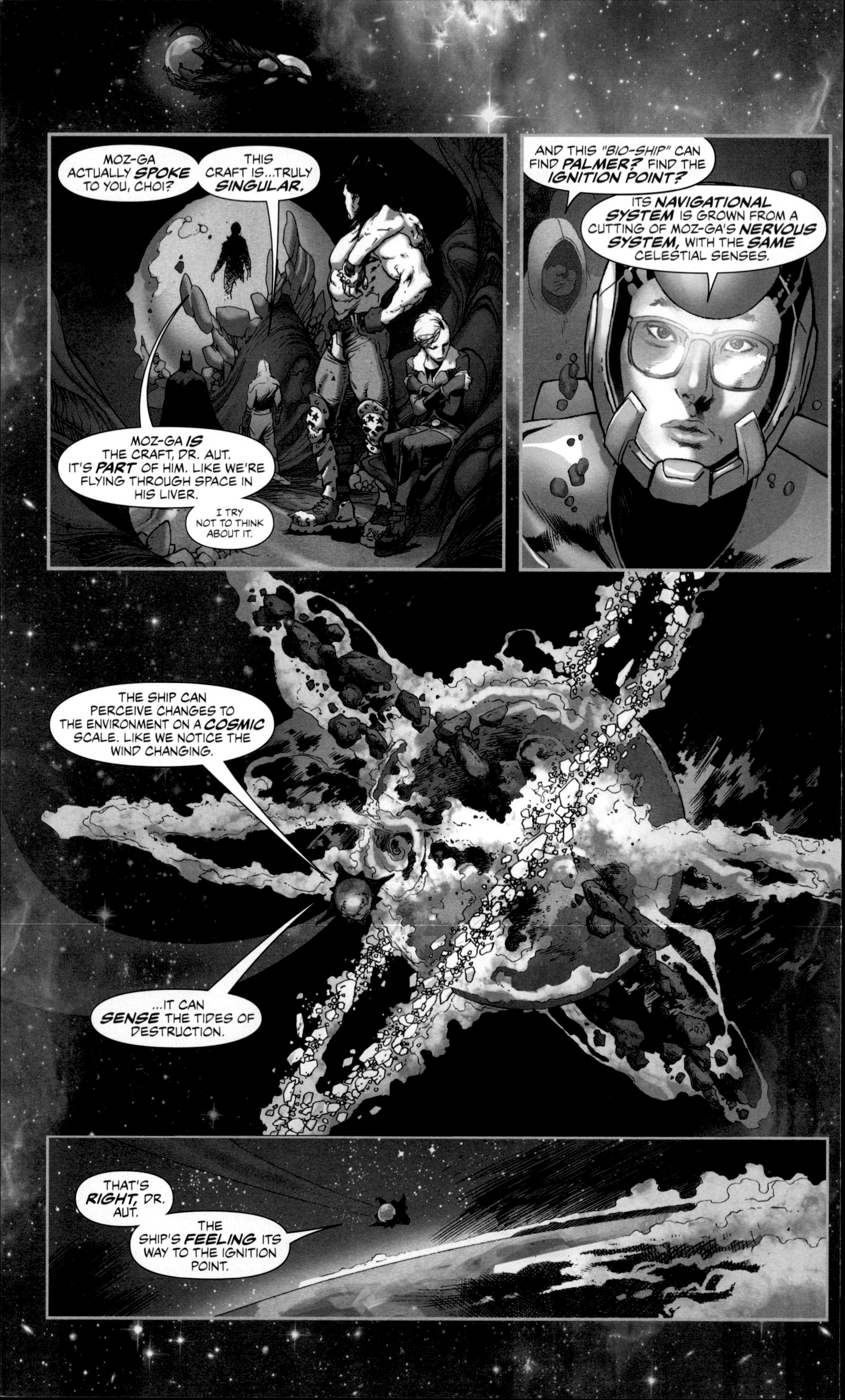
MOZ-GA ACTUALLY SPOKE TO YOU, CHOI?
THIS CRAFT IS...TRULY SINGULAR.
MOZ-GA IS THE CRAFT, DR. AUT. IT'S PART OF HIM. LIKE WE'RE FLYING THROUGH SPACE IN HIS LIVER.
I TRY NOT TO THINK ABOUT IT.
AND THIS "BIO-SHIP" CAN FIND PALMER? FIND THE IGNITION POINT?
ITS NAVIGATIONAL SYSTEM IS GROWN FROM A CUTTING OF MOZ-GA'S NERVOUS SYSTEM, WITH THE SAME CELESTIAL SENSES.
THE SHIP CAN PERCEIVE CHANGES TO THE ENVIRONMENT ON A COSMIC SCALE. LIKE WE NOTICE THE WIND CHANGING.
...IT CAN SENSE THE TIDES OF DESTRUCTION.
THAT'S RIGHT, DR. AUT.
THE SHIP'S FEELING ITS WAY TO THE IGNITION POINT.

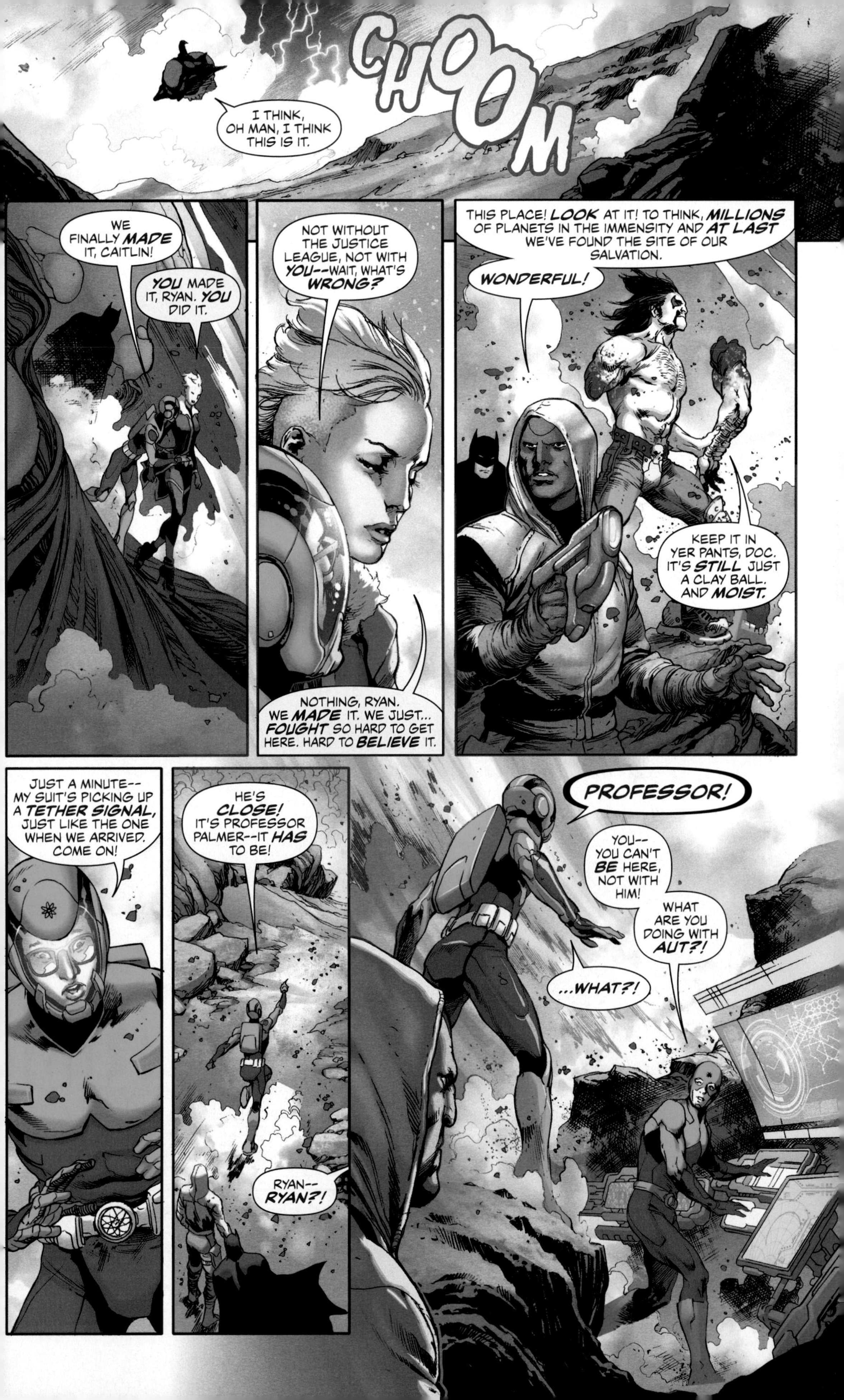

CHOOOM
I THINK, OH MAN, I THINK THIS IS IT.
WE FINALLY MADE IT, CAITLIN!
YOU MADE IT, RYAN. YOU DID IT.
NOT WITHOUT THE JUSTICE LEAGUE, NOT WITH YOU--WAIT, WHAT'S WRONG?
NOTHING, RYAN. WE MADE IT. WE JUST... FOUGHT SO HARD TO GET HERE. HARD TO BELIEVE IT.
THIS PLACE! LOOK AT IT! TO THINK, MILLIONS OF PLANETS IN THE IMMENSITY AND AT LAST WE'VE FOUND THE SITE OF OUR SALVATION.
WONDERFUL!
KEEP IT IN YER PANTS, DOC. IT'S STILL JUST A CLAY BALL. AND MOIST.
JUST A MINUTE-- MY SUIT'S PICKING UP A TETHER SIGNAL, JUST LIKE THE ONE WHEN WE ARRIVED. COME ON!
HE'S CLOSE! IT'S PROFESSOR PALMER--IT HAS TO BE!
RYAN-- RYAN?!
PROFESSOR!
YOU-- YOU CAN'T BE HERE, NOT WITH HIM!
WHAT ARE YOU DOING WITH AUT?!
...WHAT?!

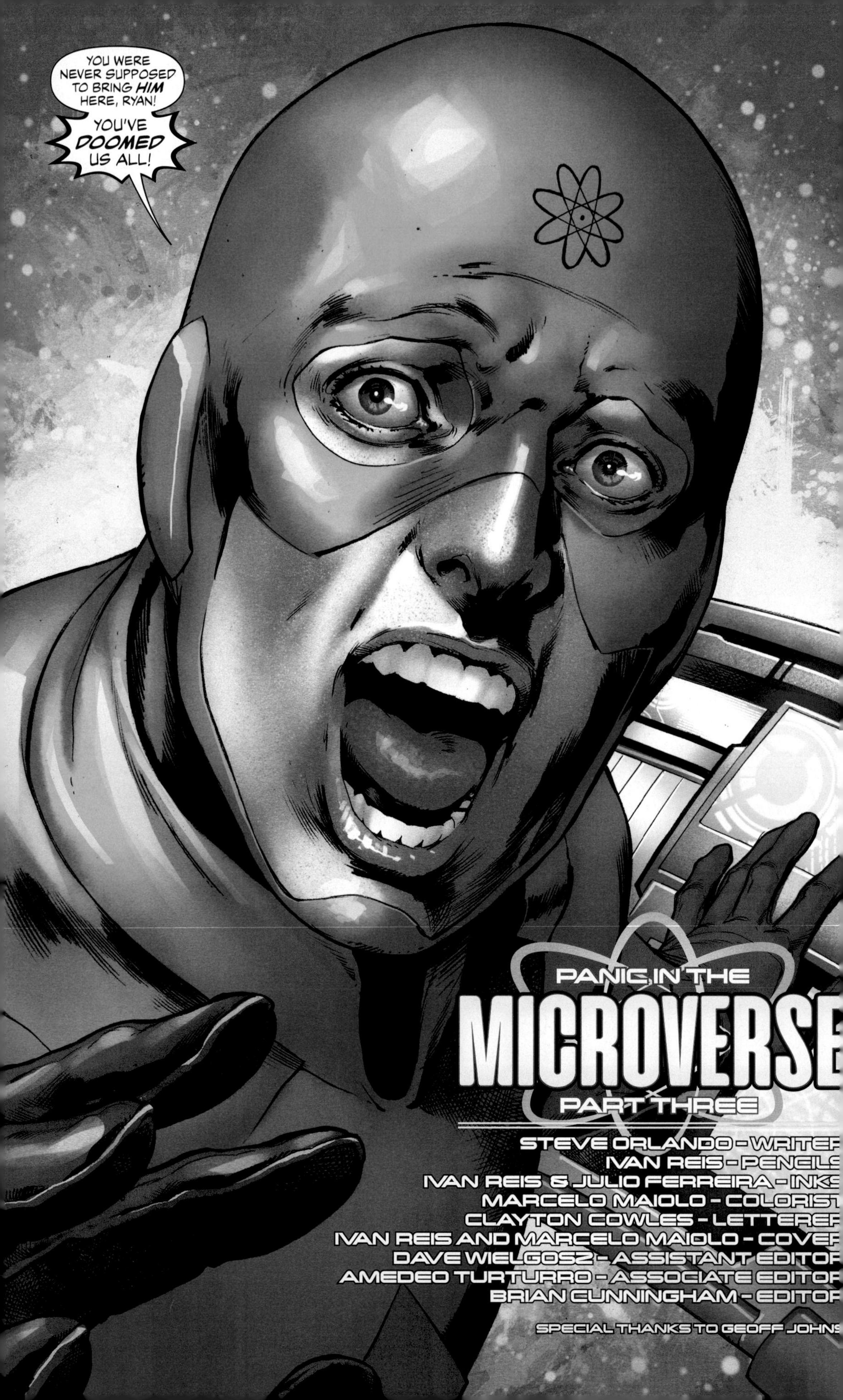
YOU WERE NEVER SUPPOSED TO BRING HIM HERE, RYAN!
YOU'VE DOOMED US ALL!
PANIC IN THE MICROVERSE PART THREE
STEVE ORLANDO - WRITER
IVAN REIS - PENCILS
IVAN REIS & JULIO FERREIRA - INKS
MARCELO MAIOLO - COLORIST
CLAYTON COWLES - LETTERER
IVAN REIS AND MARCELO MAIOLO - COVER
DAVE WIELGOSZ - ASSISTANT EDITOR
AMEDEO TURTURRO - ASSOCIATE EDITOR
BRIAN CUNNINGHAM - EDITOR
SPECIAL THANKS TO GEOFF JOHNS

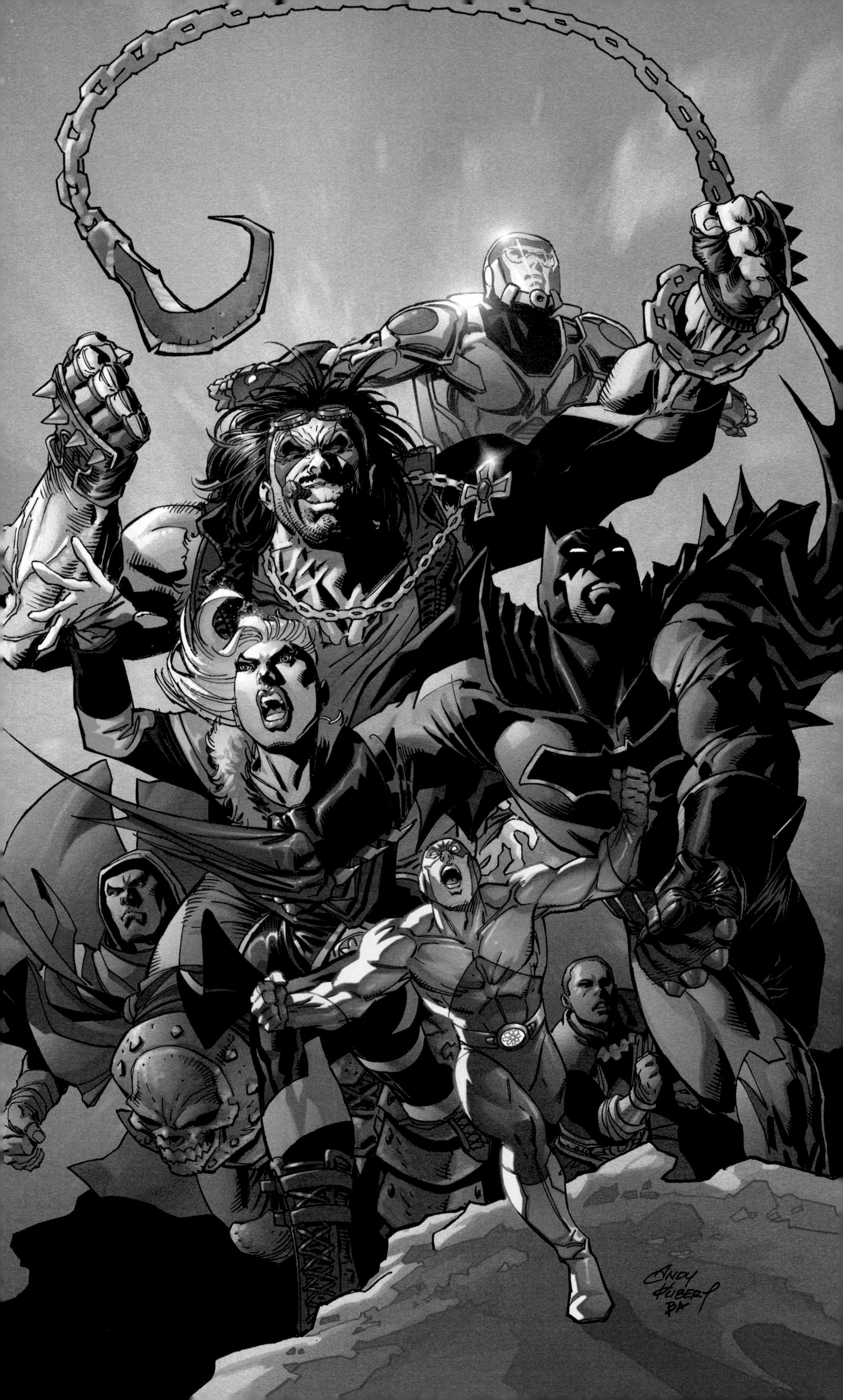
ANDY KUBERT
BA

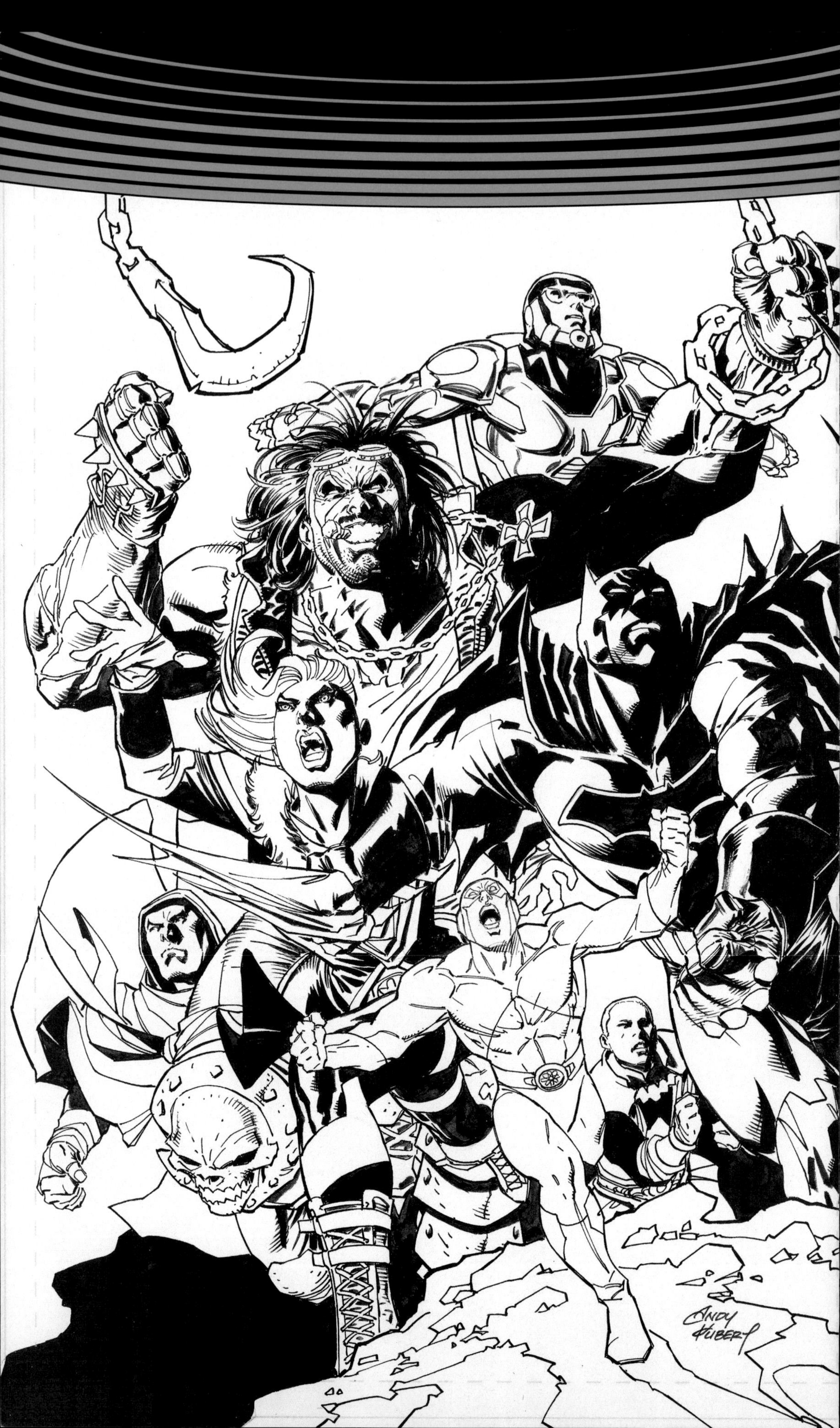
ANDY KUBERT

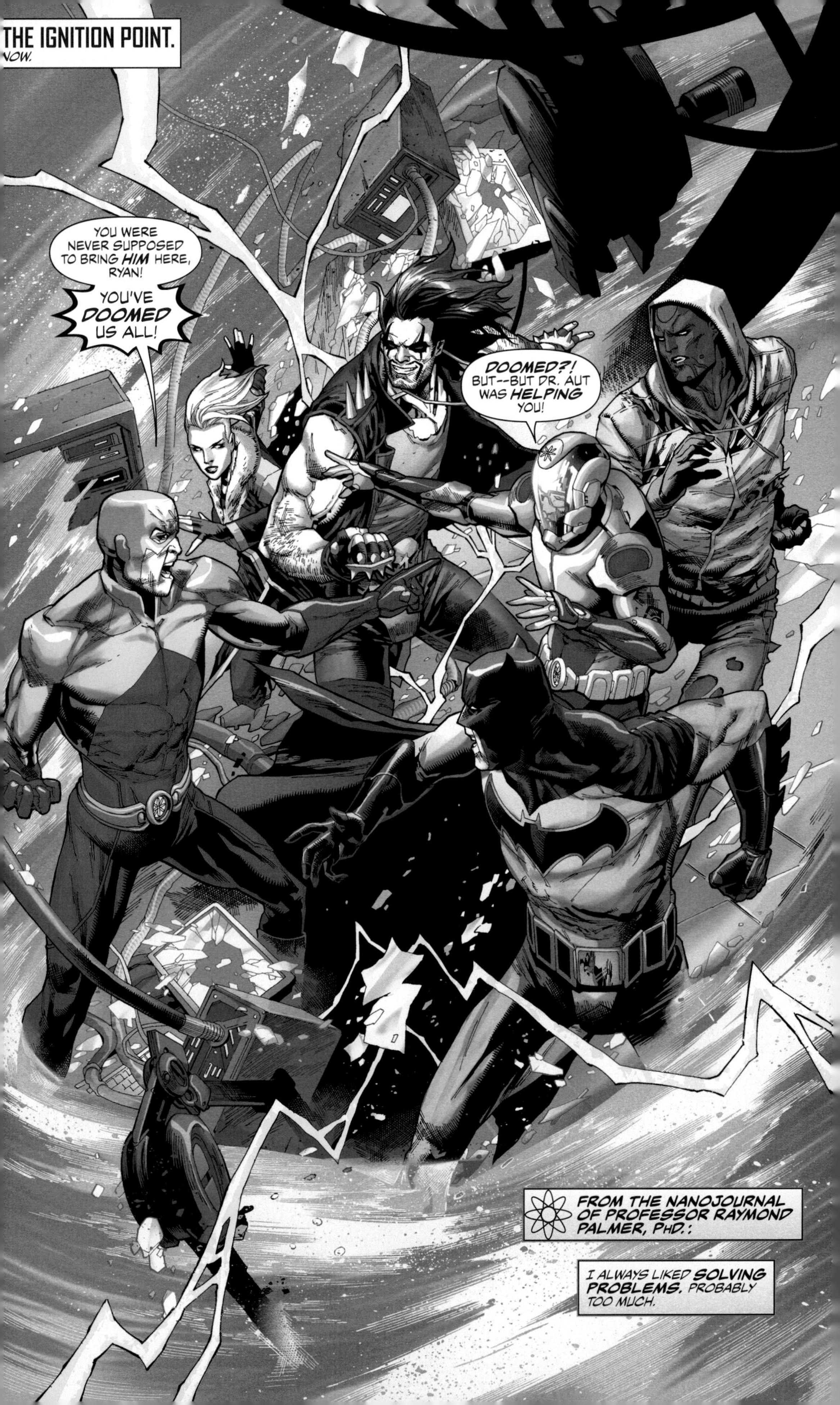
THE IGNITION POINT.
NOW.
YOU WERE NEVER SUPPOSED TO BRING HIM HERE, RYAN!
YOU'VE DOOMED US ALL!
DOOMED?! BUT--BUT DR. AUT WAS HELPING YOU!
FROM THE NANOJOURNAL OF PROFESSOR RAYMOND PALMER, PhD.:
I ALWAYS LIKED SOLVING PROBLEMS. PROBABLY TOO MUCH.

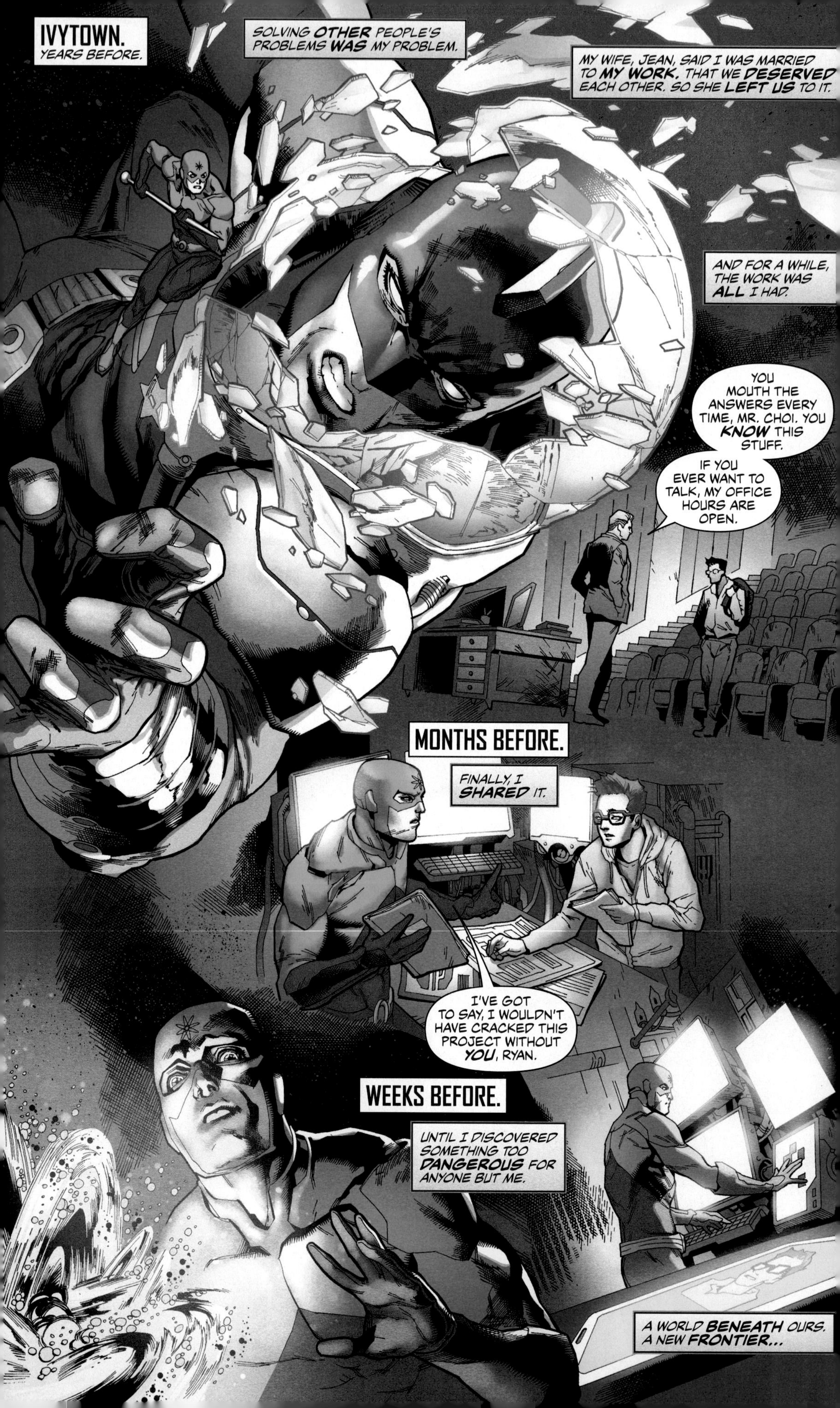

IVYTOWN. YEARS BEFORE.
SOLVING OTHER PEOPLE'S PROBLEMS WAS MY PROBLEM.
MY WIFE, JEAN, SAID I WAS MARRIED TO MY WORK. THAT WE DESERVED EACH OTHER. SO SHE LEFT US TO IT.
AND FOR A WHILE, THE WORK WAS ALL I HAD.
YOU MOUTH THE ANSWERS EVERY TIME, MR. CHOI. YOU KNOW THIS STUFF.
IF YOU EVER WANT TO TALK, MY OFFICE HOURS ARE OPEN.
MONTHS BEFORE.
FINALLY, I SHARED IT.
I'VE GOT TO SAY, I WOULDN'T HAVE CRACKED THIS PROJECT WITHOUT YOU, RYAN.
WEEKS BEFORE.
UNTIL I DISCOVERED SOMETHING TOO DANGEROUS FOR ANYONE BUT ME.
A WORLD BENEATH OURS. A NEW FRONTIER...

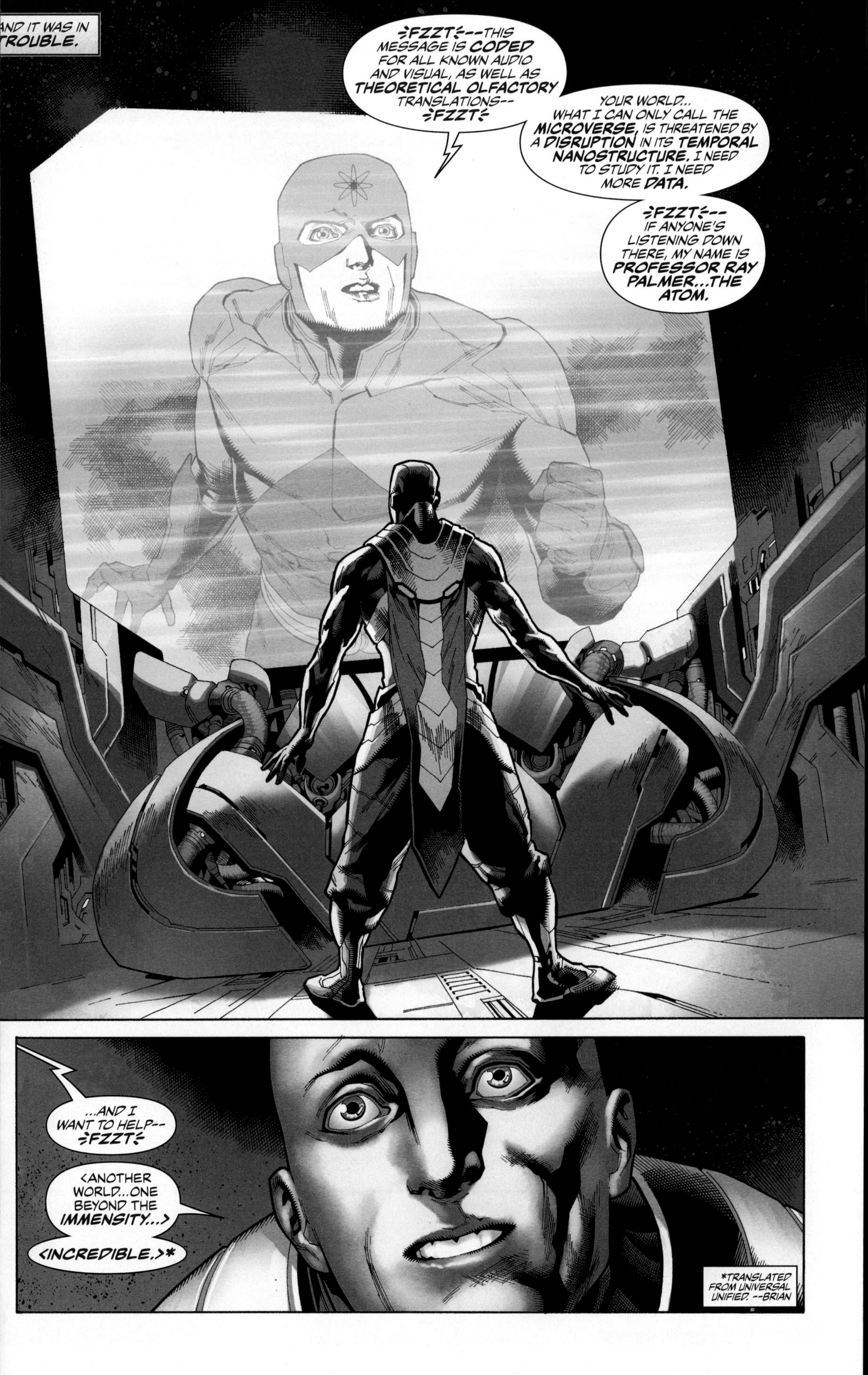
AND IT WAS IN TROUBLE.
FZZT--THIS MESSAGE IS CODED FOR ALL KNOWN AUDIO AND VISUAL, AS WELL AS THEORETICAL OLFACTORY TRANSLATIONS-- FZZT
YOUR WORLD... WHAT I CAN ONLY CALL THE MICROVERSE, IS THREATENED BY A DISRUPTION IN ITS TEMPORAL NANOSTRUCTURE. I NEED TO STUDY IT. I NEED MORE DATA.
FZZT-- IF ANYONE'S LISTENING DOWN THERE, MY NAME IS PROFESSOR RAY PALMER...THE ATOM.
...AND I WANT TO HELP-- FZZT
<ANOTHER WORLD...ONE BEYOND THE IMMENSITY...>
<INCREDIBLE.>*
*TRANSLATED FROM UNIVERSAL UNIFIED. --BRIAN

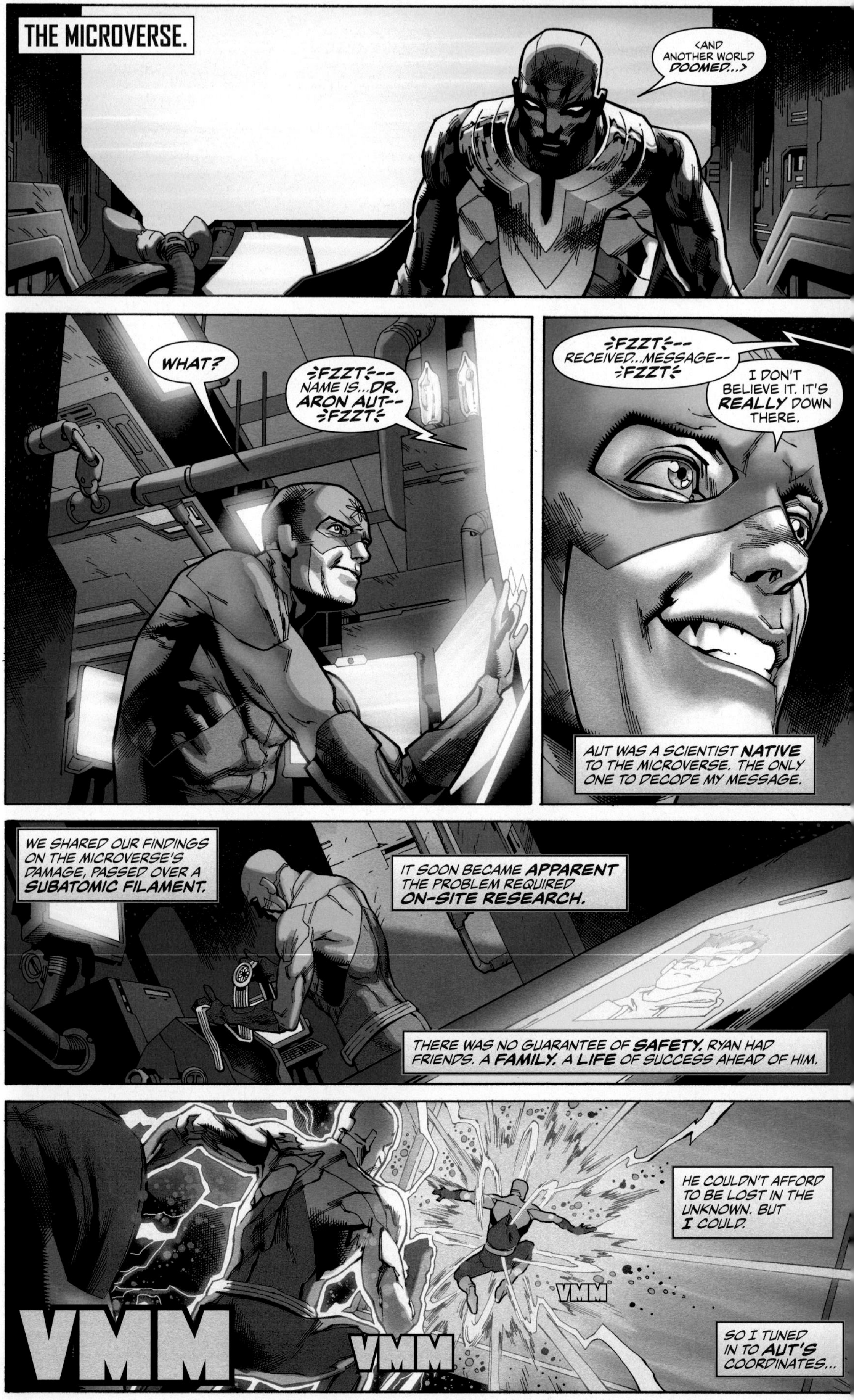
THE MICROVERSE.
<AND ANOTHER WORLD DOOMED...>
WHAT?
FZZT-- NAME IS...DR. ARON AUT-- FZZT
FZZT-- RECEIVED...MESSAGE-- FZZT
I DON'T BELIEVE IT. IT'S REALLY DOWN THERE.
AUT WAS A SCIENTIST NATIVE TO THE MICROVERSE. THE ONLY ONE TO DECODE MY MESSAGE.
WE SHARED OUR FINDINGS ON THE MICROVERSE'S DAMAGE, PASSED OVER A SUBATOMIC FILAMENT.
IT SOON BECAME APPARENT THE PROBLEM REQUIRED ON-SITE RESEARCH.
THERE WAS NO GUARANTEE OF SAFETY. RYAN HAD FRIENDS. A FAMILY. A LIFE OF SUCCESS AHEAD OF HIM.
HE COULDN'T AFFORD TO BE LOST IN THE UNKNOWN. BUT I COULD.
VMM
VMM
VMM
SO I TUNED IN TO AUT'S COORDINATES...

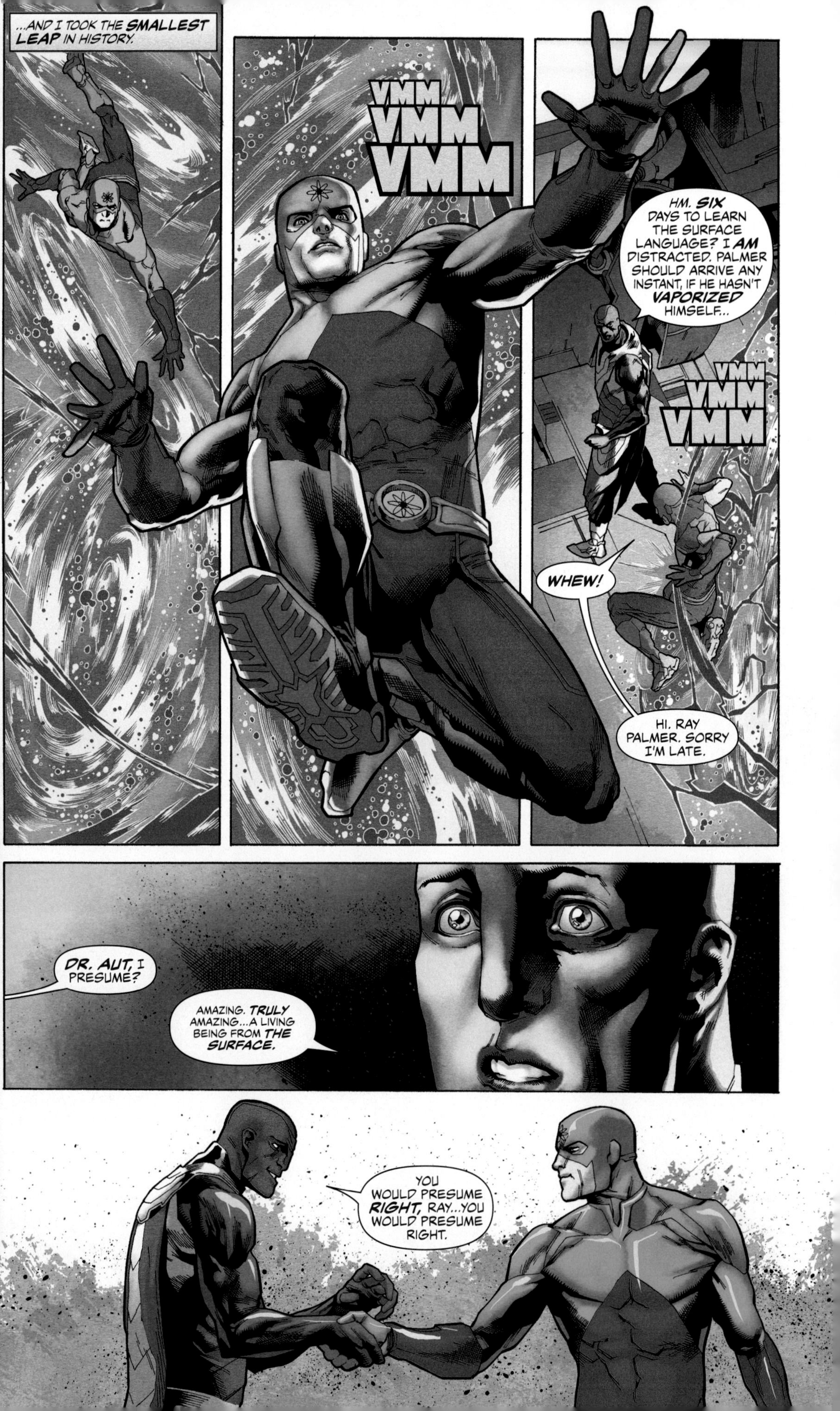

...AND I TOOK THE SMALLEST LEAP IN HISTORY.
VMM VMM VMM
HM. SIX DAYS TO LEARN THE SURFACE LANGUAGE? I AM DISTRACTED. PALMER SHOULD ARRIVE ANY INSTANT, IF HE HASN'T VAPORIZED HIMSELF...
VMM VMM VMM
WHEW!
HI. RAY PALMER. SORRY I'M LATE.
DR. AUT, I PRESUME?
AMAZING. TRULY AMAZING...A LIVING BEING FROM THE SURFACE.
YOU WOULD PRESUME RIGHT, RAY...YOU WOULD PRESUME RIGHT.

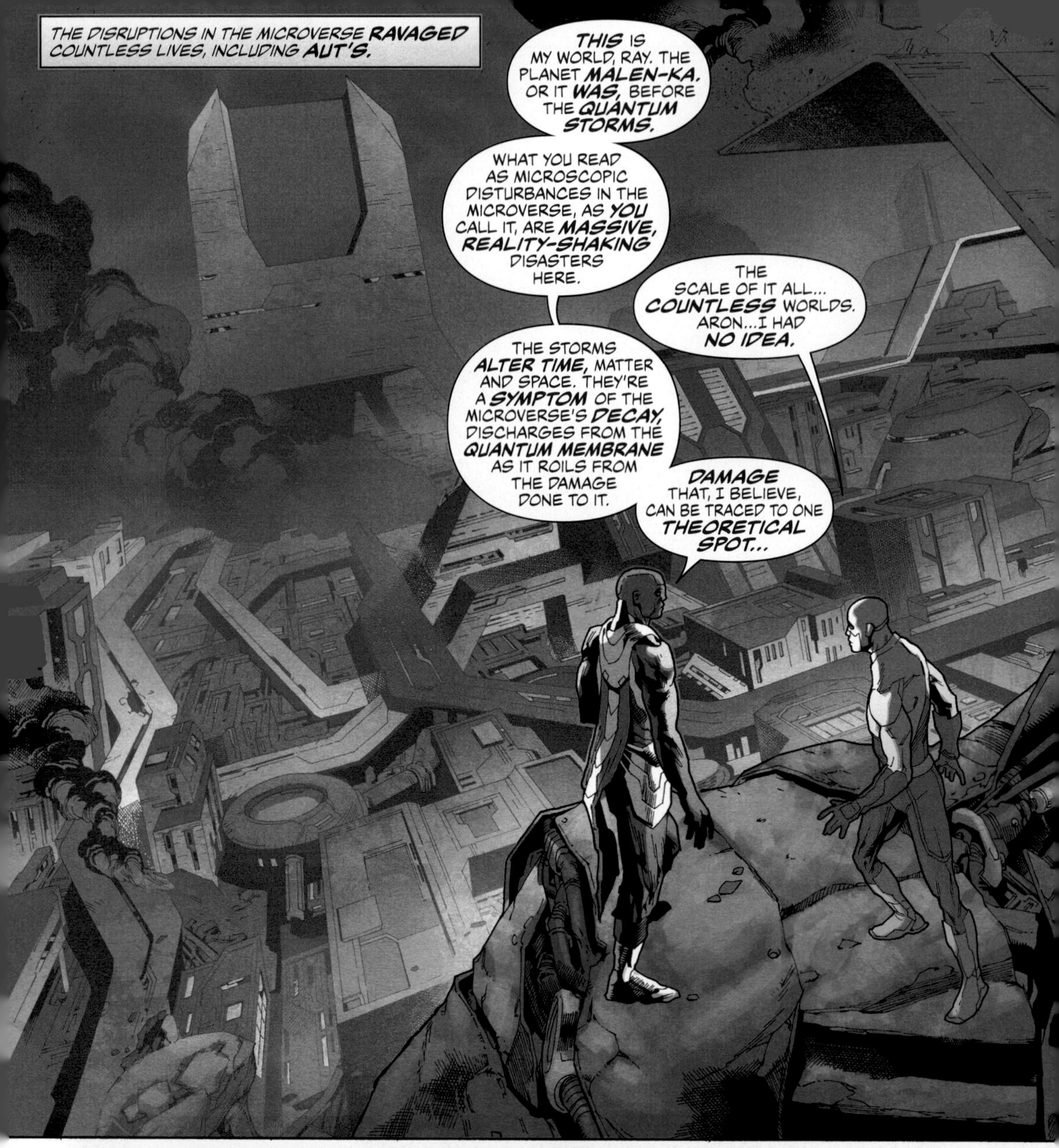
THE DISRUPTIONS IN THE MICROVERSE RAVAGED COUNTLESS LIVES, INCLUDING AUT'S.
THIS IS MY WORLD, RAY. THE PLANET MALEN-KA. OR IT WAS, BEFORE THE QUANTUM STORMS.
WHAT YOU READ AS MICROSCOPIC DISTURBANCES IN THE MICROVERSE, AS YOU CALL IT, ARE MASSIVE, REALITY-SHAKING DISASTERS HERE.
THE SCALE OF IT ALL... COUNTLESS WORLDS. ARON...I HAD NO IDEA.
THE STORMS ALTER TIME, MATTER AND SPACE. THEY'RE A SYMPTOM OF THE MICROVERSE'S DECAY, DISCHARGES FROM THE QUANTUM MEMBRANE AS IT ROILS FROM THE DAMAGE DONE TO IT.
DAMAGE THAT, I BELIEVE, CAN BE TRACED TO ONE THEORETICAL SPOT...

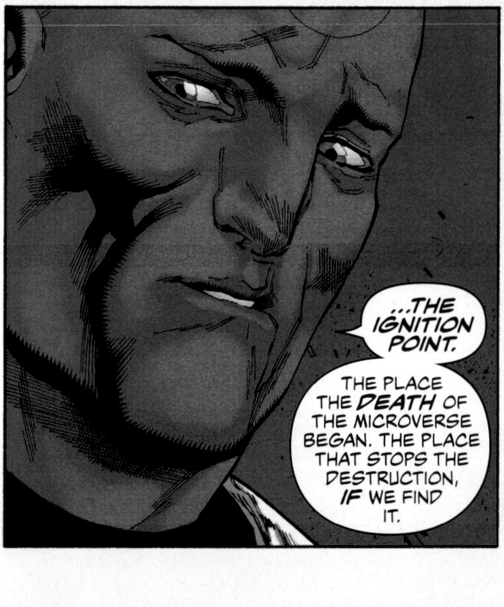
...THE IGNITION POINT.
THE PLACE THE DEATH OF THE MICROVERSE BEGAN. THE PLACE THAT STOPS THE DESTRUCTION, IF WE FIND IT.

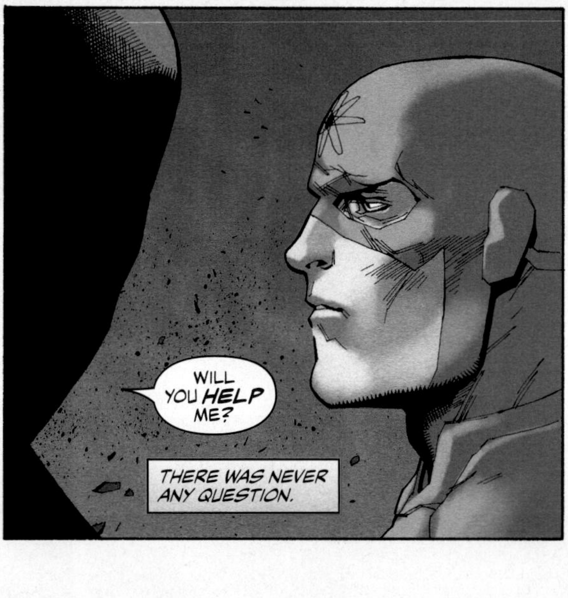
WILL YOU HELP ME?
THERE WAS NEVER ANY QUESTION.

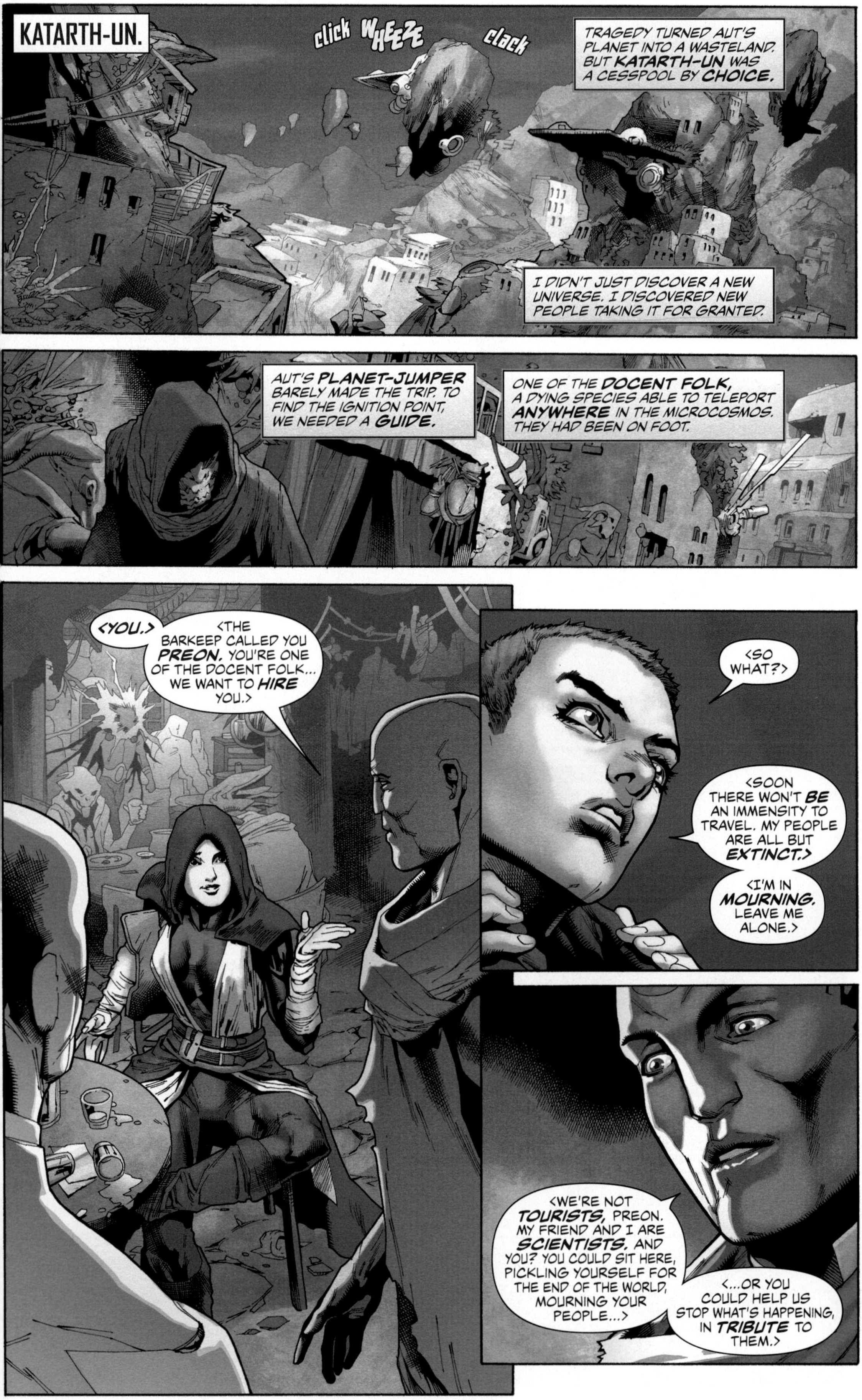
KATARTH-UN.
click WHEEZE clack
TRAGEDY TURNED AUT'S PLANET INTO A WASTELAND. BUT KATARTH-UN WAS A CESSPOOL BY CHOICE.
I DIDN'T JUST DISCOVER A NEW UNIVERSE. I DISCOVERED NEW PEOPLE TAKING IT FOR GRANTED.
AUT'S PLANET-JUMPER BARELY MADE THE TRIP. TO FIND THE IGNITION POINT, WE NEEDED A GUIDE.
ONE OF THE DOCENT FOLK, A DYING SPECIES ABLE TO TELEPORT ANYWHERE IN THE MICROCOSMOS. THEY HAD BEEN ON FOOT.
<YOU.>
<THE BARKEEP CALLED YOU PREON. YOU'RE ONE OF THE DOCENT FOLK... WE WANT TO HIRE YOU.>
<SO WHAT?>
<SOON THERE WON'T BE AN IMMENSITY TO TRAVEL. MY PEOPLE ARE ALL BUT EXTINCT.>
<I'M IN MOURNING. LEAVE ME ALONE.>
<WE'RE NOT TOURISTS, PREON. MY FRIEND AND I ARE SCIENTISTS. AND YOU? YOU COULD SIT HERE, PICKLING YOURSELF FOR THE END OF THE WORLD, MOURNING YOUR PEOPLE...>
<...OR YOU COULD HELP US STOP WHAT'S HAPPENING, IN TRIBUTE TO THEM.>

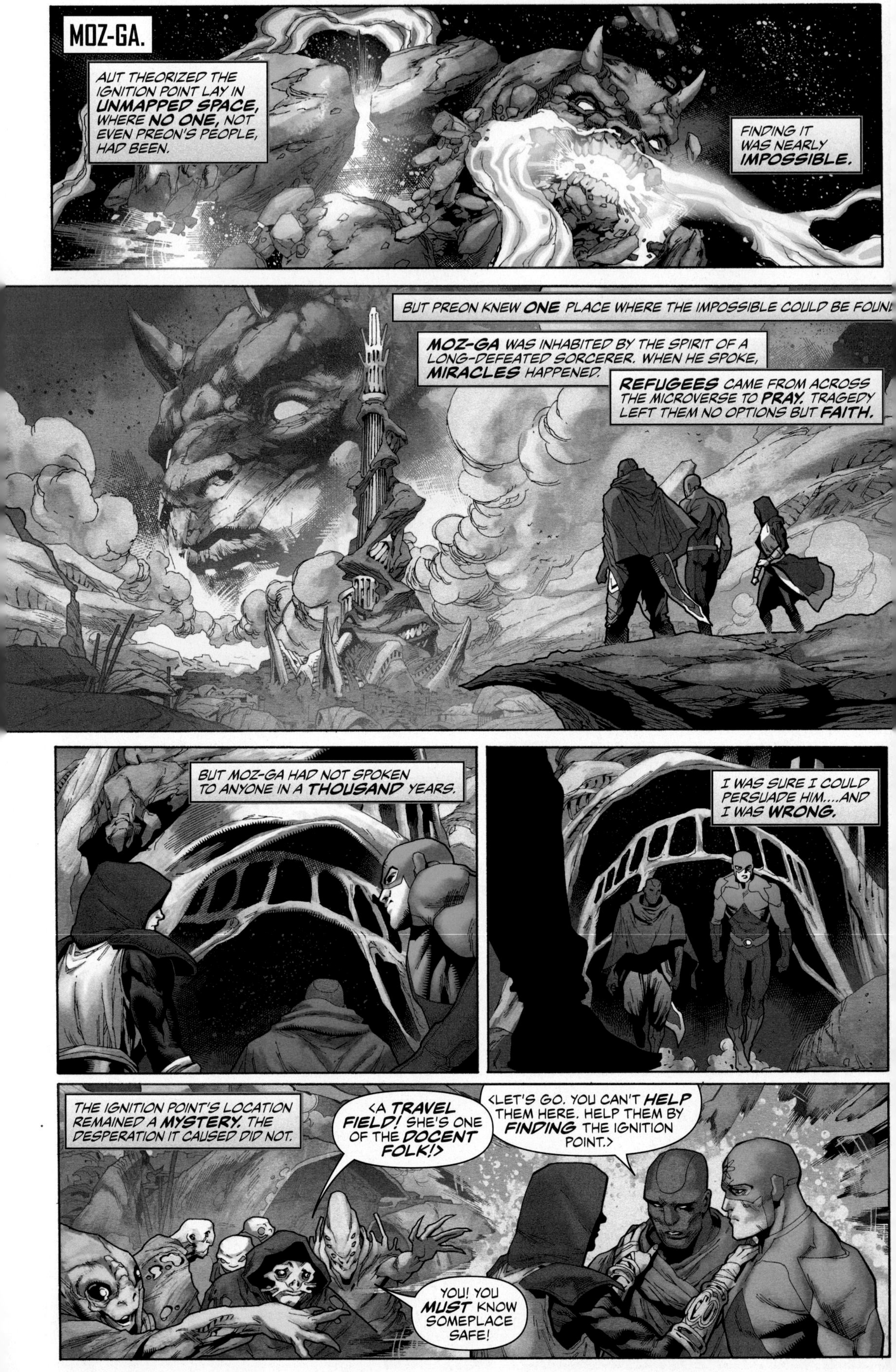
MOZ-GA.
AUT THEORIZED THE IGNITION POINT LAY IN UNMAPPED SPACE, WHERE NO ONE, NOT EVEN PREON'S PEOPLE, HAD BEEN.
FINDING IT WAS NEARLY IMPOSSIBLE.
BUT PREON KNEW ONE PLACE WHERE THE IMPOSSIBLE COULD BE FOUN
MOZ-GA WAS INHABITED BY THE SPIRIT OF A LONG-DEFEATED SORCERER. WHEN HE SPOKE, MIRACLES HAPPENED.
REFUGEES CAME FROM ACROSS THE MICROVERSE TO PRAY. TRAGEDY LEFT THEM NO OPTIONS BUT FAITH.
BUT MOZ-GA HAD NOT SPOKEN TO ANYONE IN A THOUSAND YEARS.
I WAS SURE I COULD PERSUADE HIM....AND I WAS WRONG.
THE IGNITION POINT'S LOCATION REMAINED A MYSTERY. THE DESPERATION IT CAUSED DID NOT.
<A TRAVEL FIELD! SHE'S ONE OF THE DOCENT FOLK!>
YOU! YOU MUST KNOW SOMEPLACE SAFE!
<LET'S GO. YOU CAN'T HELP THEM HERE. HELP THEM BY FINDING THE IGNITION POINT.>

PREON COULDN'T TELEPORT INTO **UNMAPPED SPACE** BLIND. WE COULD MATERIALIZE IN A **SUN.**

click WHEEZE *clack*

OUR SEARCH BECAME PART **ARCHAEOLOGY** AND PART **CARTOGRAPHY.** IT WAS A NEEDLE IN A HAYSTACK OF ASTROPHYSICS.

WE WERE FORCED TO EXPLORE **NONTRADITIONAL** METHODS.

AUT WAS SO **FOCUSED.** THE LOSS OF HIS PLANET, **HIS PEOPLE,** HAD CLEARLY AFFECTED HIM. BUT HE SHUT IT OUT. PUT IT AWAY FOR LATER, ONCE THE MICROVERSE WAS **SAFE.**

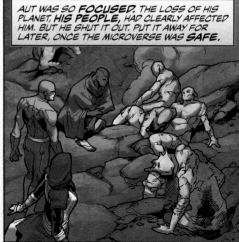

PREON COULDN'T HIDE THE **PAIN** OF HER LOSS. BUT THE CHANCE TO EXPLORE THE UNMAPPED MICROVERSE, TO REPRESENT A RACE OF TRAVELERS WHERE HER PEOPLE HAD NEVER SET FOOT, **INVIGORATED** HER.

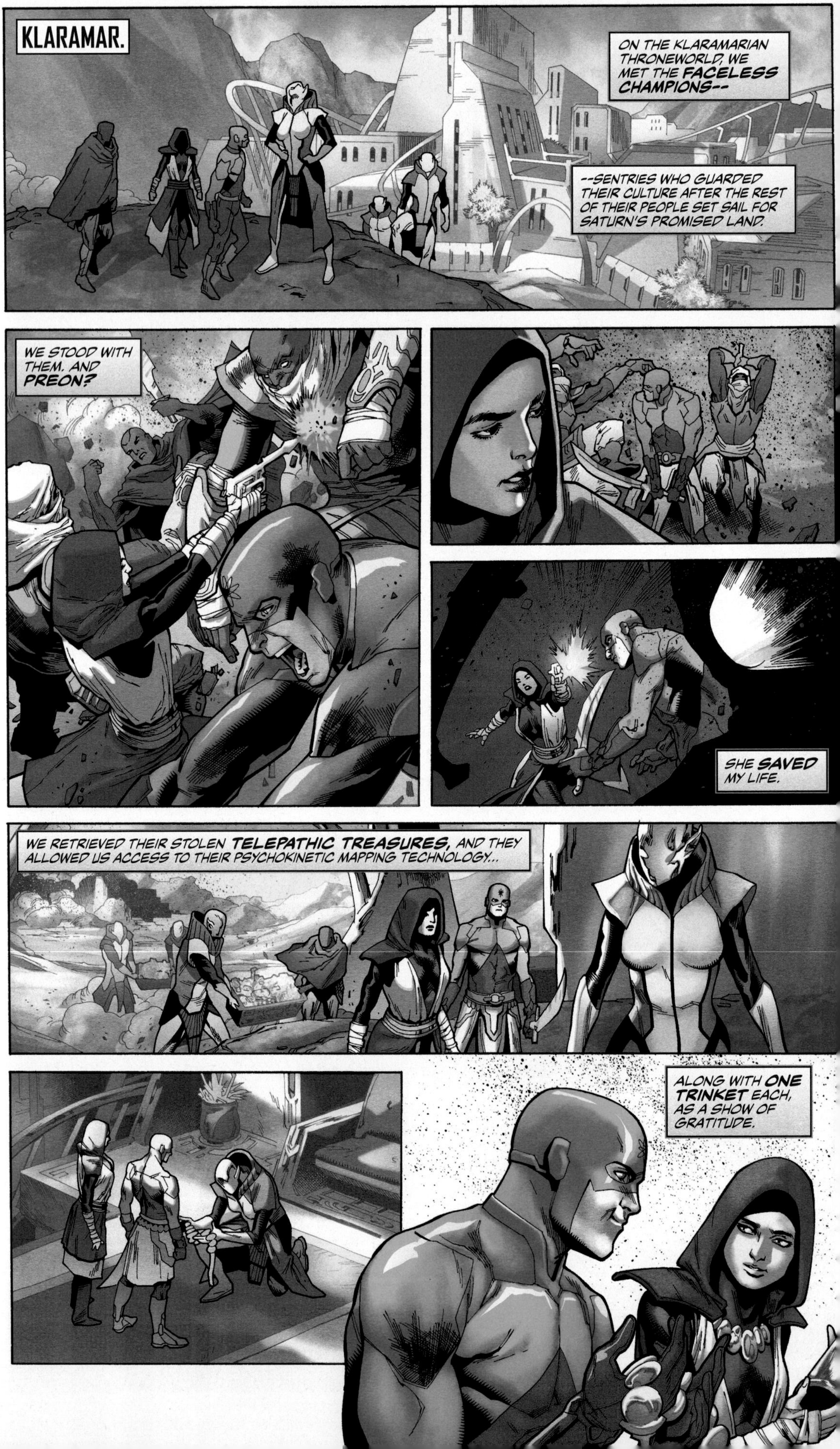
KLARAMAR.
ON THE KLARAMARIAN THRONEWORLD, WE MET THE FACELESS CHAMPIONS--
--SENTRIES WHO GUARDED THEIR CULTURE AFTER THE REST OF THEIR PEOPLE SET SAIL FOR SATURN'S PROMISED LAND.
WE STOOD WITH THEM. AND PREON?
SHE SAVED MY LIFE.
WE RETRIEVED THEIR STOLEN TELEPATHIC TREASURES, AND THEY ALLOWED US ACCESS TO THEIR PSYCHOKINETIC MAPPING TECHNOLOGY...
ALONG WITH ONE TRINKET EACH, AS A SHOW OF GRATITUDE.

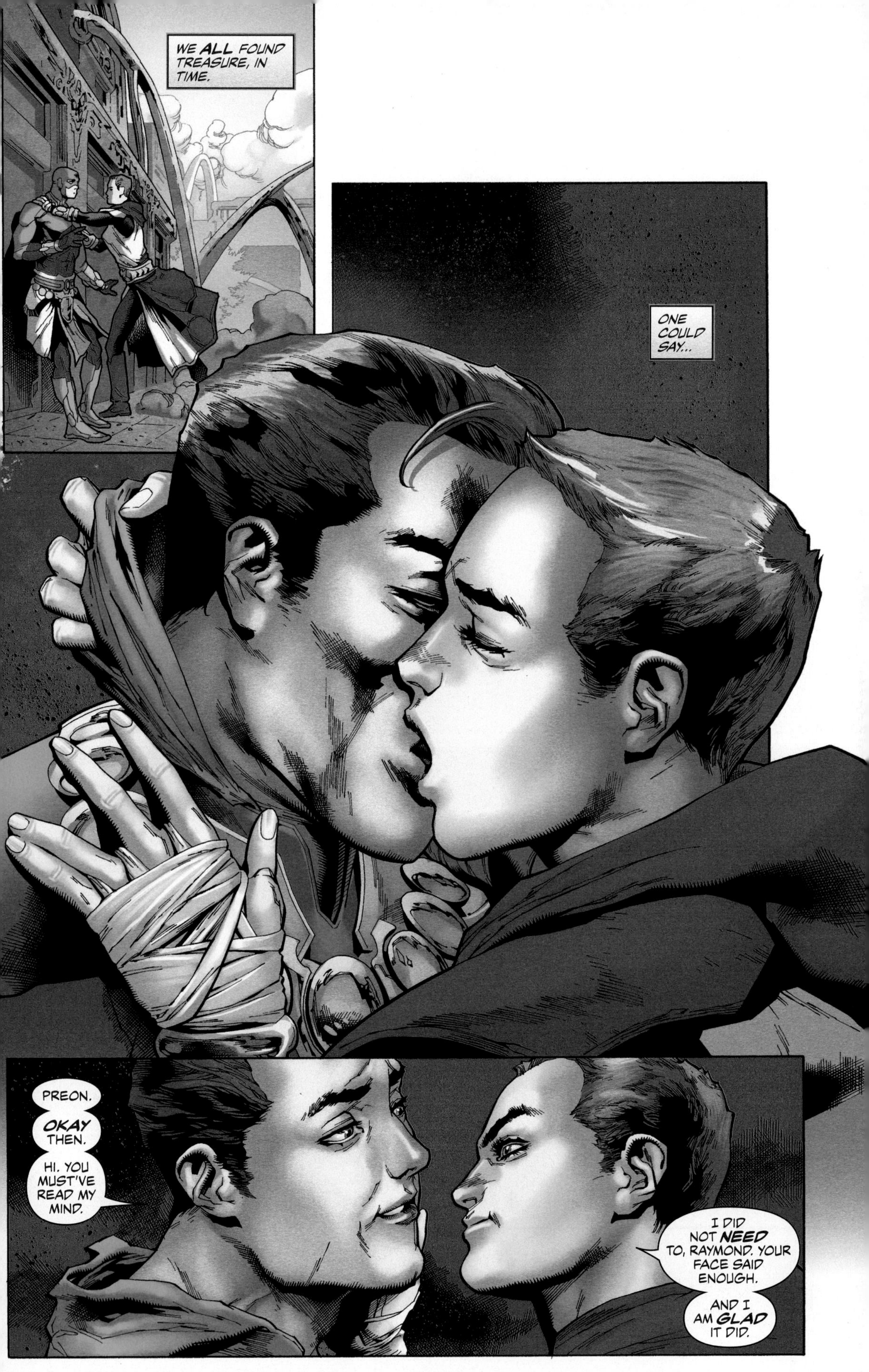
WE ALL FOUND TREASURE, IN TIME.
ONE COULD SAY...
PREON.
OKAY THEN.
HI. YOU MUST'VE READ MY MIND.
I DID NOT NEED TO, RAYMOND. YOUR FACE SAID ENOUGH.
AND I AM GLAD IT DID.

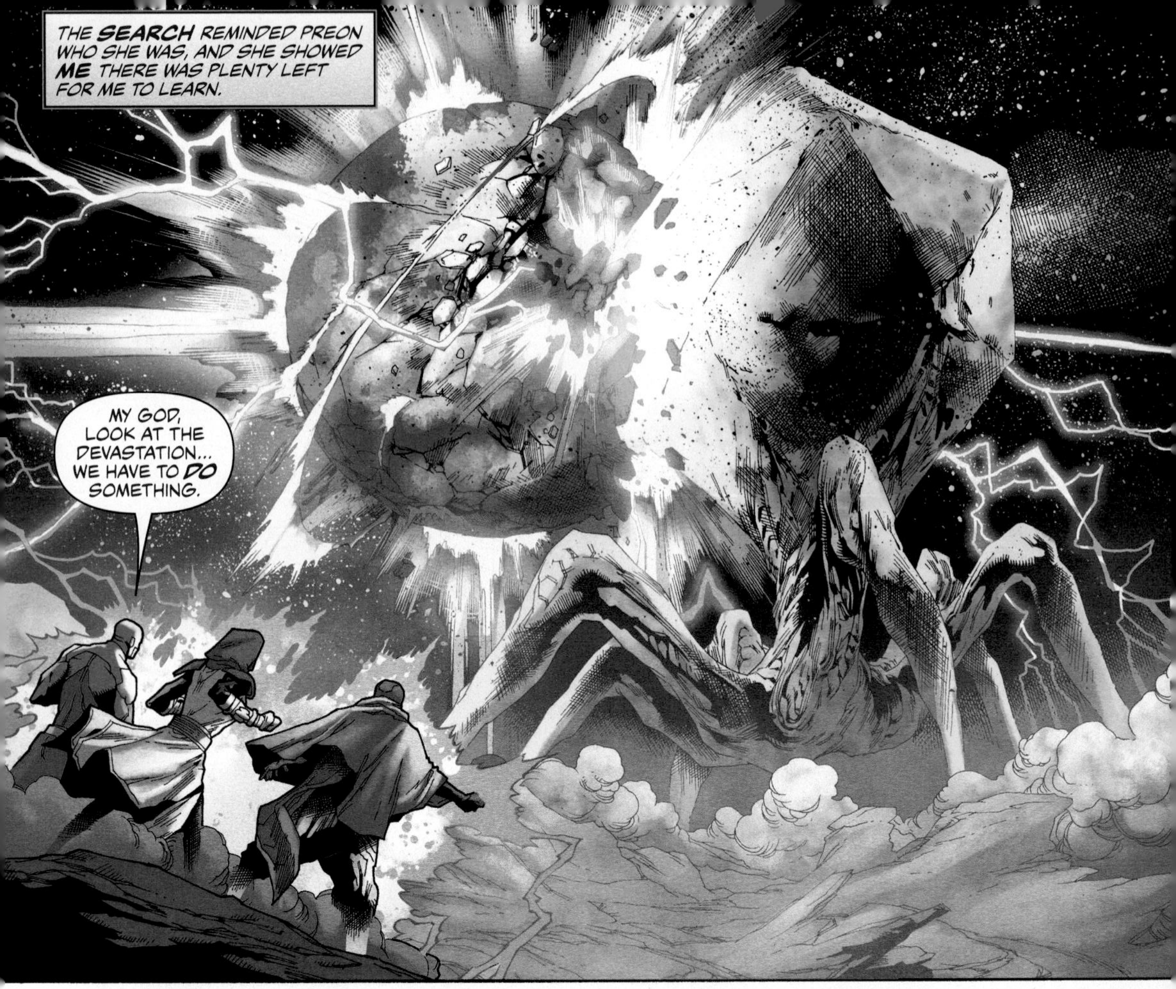
THE SEARCH REMINDED PREON WHO SHE WAS, AND SHE SHOWED ME THERE WAS PLENTY LEFT FOR ME TO LEARN.
MY GOD, LOOK AT THE DEVASTATION... WE HAVE TO DO SOMETHING.

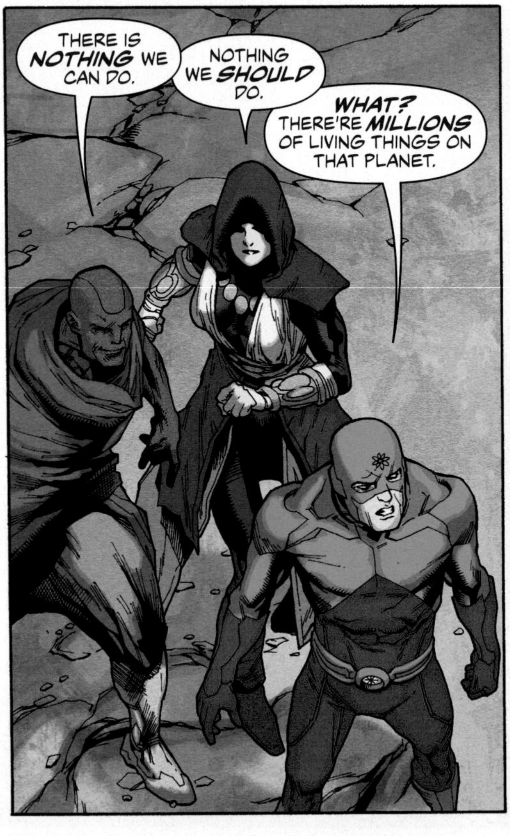
THERE IS NOTHING WE CAN DO.
NOTHING WE SHOULD DO.
WHAT? THERE'RE MILLIONS OF LIVING THINGS ON THAT PLANET.

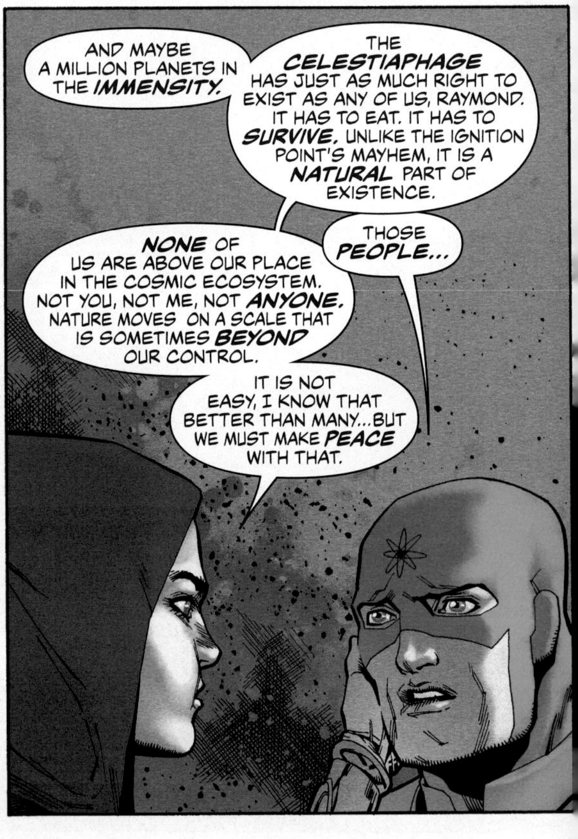
AND MAYBE A MILLION PLANETS IN THE IMMENSITY.
THE CELESTIAPHAGE HAS JUST AS MUCH RIGHT TO EXIST AS ANY OF US, RAYMOND. IT HAS TO EAT. IT HAS TO SURVIVE. UNLIKE THE IGNITION POINT'S MAYHEM, IT IS A NATURAL PART OF EXISTENCE.
THOSE PEOPLE...
NONE OF US ARE ABOVE OUR PLACE IN THE COSMIC ECOSYSTEM. NOT YOU, NOT ME, NOT ANYONE. NATURE MOVES ON A SCALE THAT IS SOMETIMES BEYOND OUR CONTROL.
IT IS NOT EASY, I KNOW THAT BETTER THAN MANY...BUT WE MUST MAKE PEACE WITH THAT.

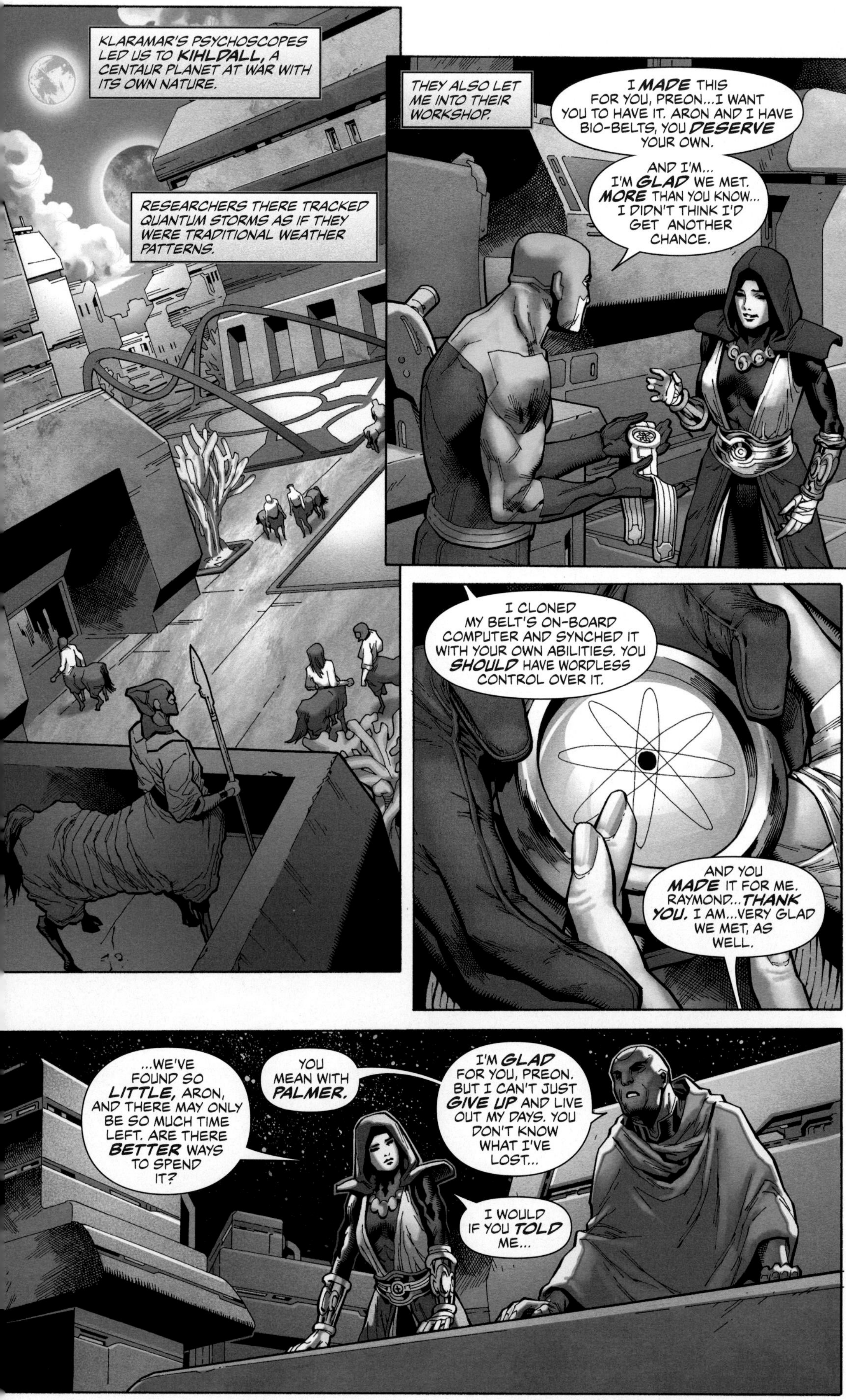
KLARAMAR'S PSYCHOSCOPES LED US TO KIHLDALL, A CENTAUR PLANET AT WAR WITH ITS OWN NATURE.
RESEARCHERS THERE TRACKED QUANTUM STORMS AS IF THEY WERE TRADITIONAL WEATHER PATTERNS.
THEY ALSO LET ME INTO THEIR WORKSHOP.
I MADE THIS FOR YOU, PREON...I WANT YOU TO HAVE IT. ARON AND I HAVE BIO-BELTS, YOU DESERVE YOUR OWN.
AND I'M... I'M GLAD WE MET. MORE THAN YOU KNOW... I DIDN'T THINK I'D GET ANOTHER CHANCE.
I CLONED MY BELT'S ON-BOARD COMPUTER AND SYNCHED IT WITH YOUR OWN ABILITIES. YOU SHOULD HAVE WORDLESS CONTROL OVER IT.
AND YOU MADE IT FOR ME. RAYMOND...THANK YOU. I AM...VERY GLAD WE MET, AS WELL.
...WE'VE FOUND SO LITTLE, ARON, AND THERE MAY ONLY BE SO MUCH TIME LEFT. ARE THERE BETTER WAYS TO SPEND IT?
YOU MEAN WITH PALMER.
I'M GLAD FOR YOU, PREON. BUT I CAN'T JUST GIVE UP AND LIVE OUT MY DAYS. YOU DON'T KNOW WHAT I'VE LOST...
I WOULD IF YOU TOLD ME...

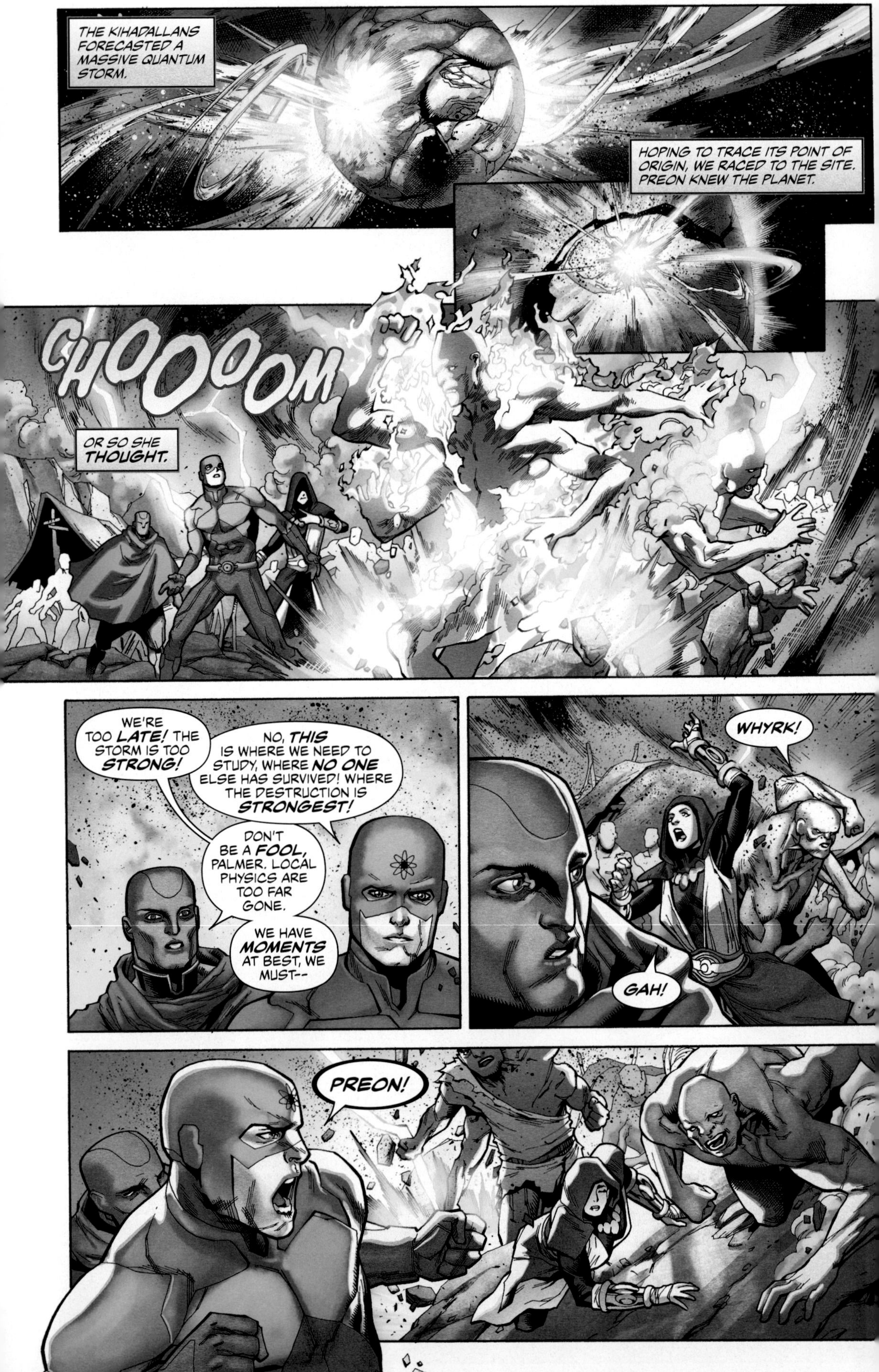
THE KIHADALLANS FORECASTED A MASSIVE QUANTUM STORM.
HOPING TO TRACE ITS POINT OF ORIGIN, WE RACED TO THE SITE. PREON KNEW THE PLANET.
CHOOOOOM
OR SO SHE THOUGHT.
WE'RE TOO LATE! THE STORM IS TOO STRONG!
NO, THIS IS WHERE WE NEED TO STUDY, WHERE NO ONE ELSE HAS SURVIVED! WHERE THE DESTRUCTION IS STRONGEST!
DON'T BE A FOOL, PALMER. LOCAL PHYSICS ARE TOO FAR GONE.
WE HAVE MOMENTS AT BEST, WE MUST--
WHYRK!
GAH!
PREON!

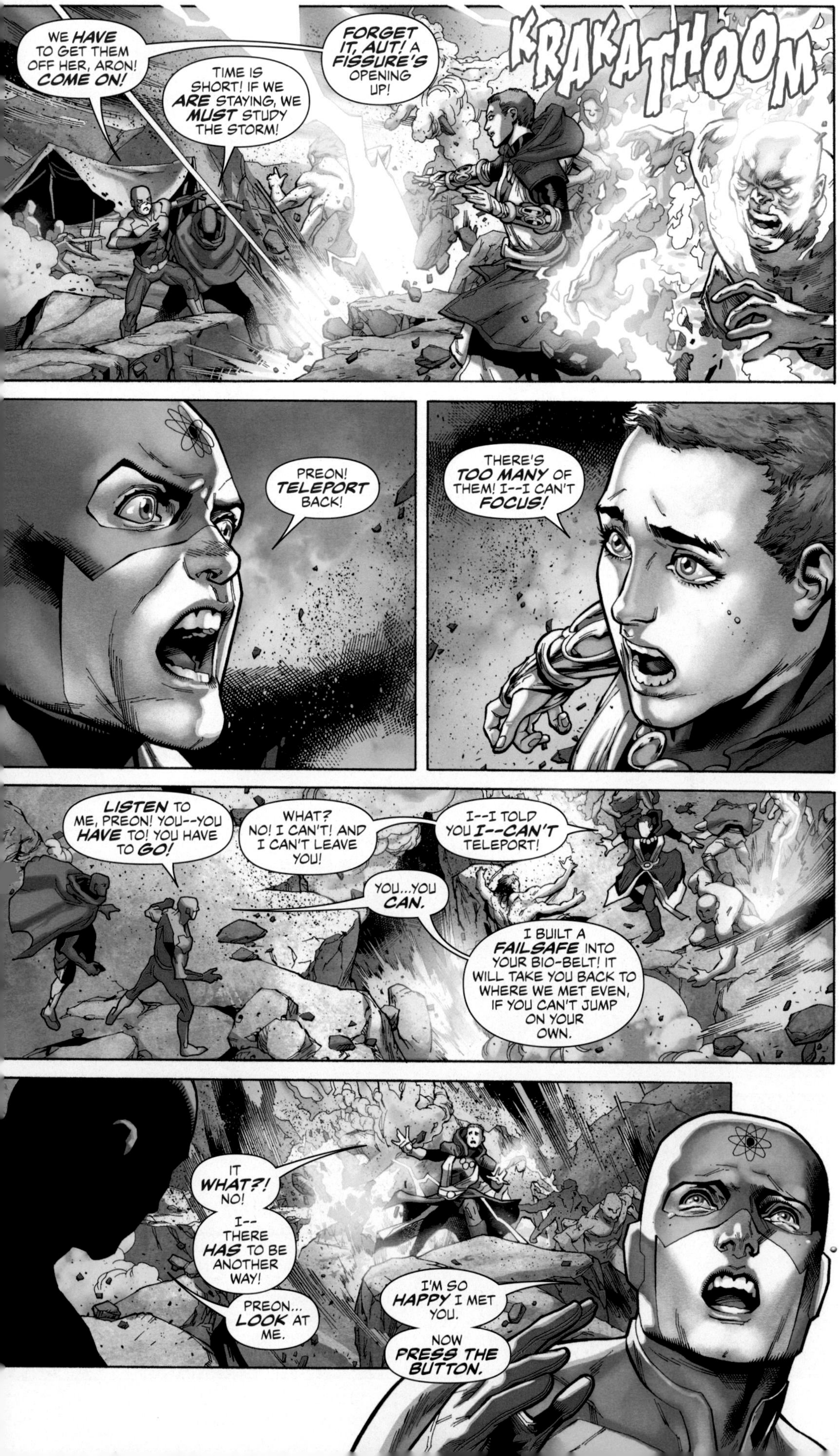
WE HAVE TO GET THEM OFF HER, ARON! COME ON!
TIME IS SHORT! IF WE ARE STAYING, WE MUST STUDY THE STORM!
FORGET IT, AUT! A FISSURE'S OPENING UP!
KRAKATHOOM
PREON! TELEPORT BACK!
THERE'S TOO MANY OF THEM! I--I CAN'T FOCUS!
LISTEN TO ME, PREON! YOU--YOU HAVE TO! YOU HAVE TO GO!
WHAT? NO! I CAN'T! AND I CAN'T LEAVE YOU!
I--I TOLD YOU I--CAN'T TELEPORT!
YOU...YOU CAN.
I BUILT A FAILSAFE INTO YOUR BIO-BELT! IT WILL TAKE YOU BACK TO WHERE WE MET EVEN, IF YOU CAN'T JUMP ON YOUR OWN.
IT WHAT?! NO!
I-- THERE HAS TO BE ANOTHER WAY!
PREON... LOOK AT ME.
I'M SO HAPPY I MET YOU.
NOW PRESS THE BUTTON.

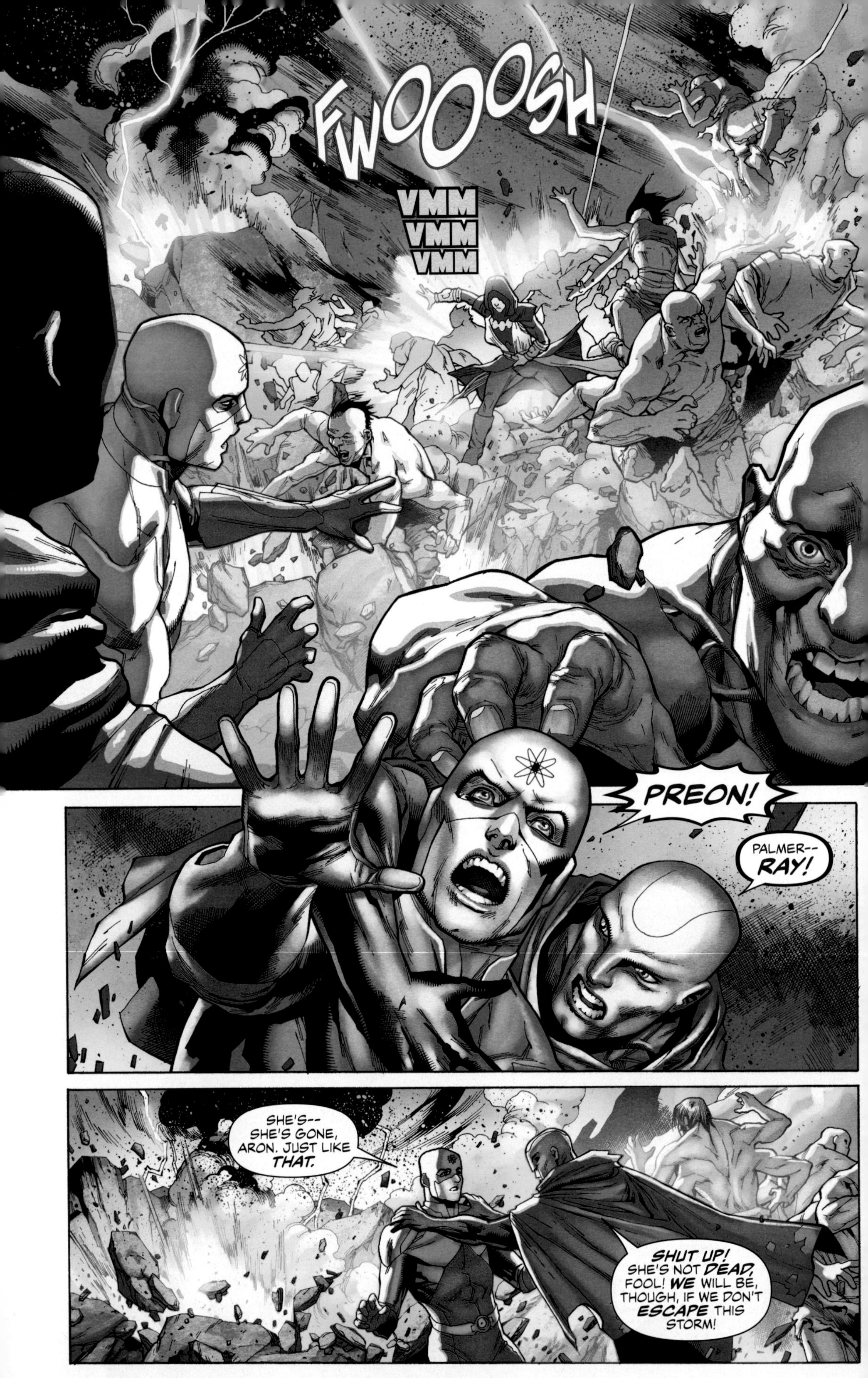
FWOOOSH
VMM VMM VMM
PREON!
PALMER-- RAY!
SHE'S-- SHE'S GONE, ARON. JUST LIKE THAT.
SHUT UP! SHE'S NOT DEAD, FOOL! WE WILL BE, THOUGH, IF WE DON'T ESCAPE THIS STORM!

RUMBLE-
CHOOM

WE NEED TO SAVE **OURSELVES**, PALMER! WE NEED TO **THINK**--AND **FAST**!

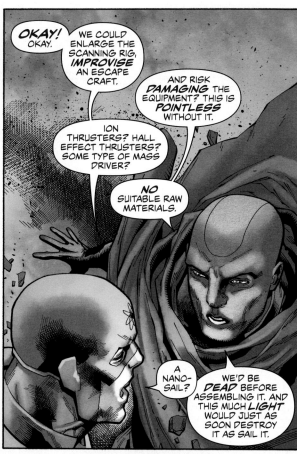

OKAY! OKAY.

WE COULD ENLARGE THE SCANNING RIG, **IMPROVISE** AN ESCAPE CRAFT.

AND RISK **DAMAGING** THE EQUIPMENT? THIS IS **POINTLESS** WITHOUT IT.

ION THRUSTERS? HALL EFFECT THRUSTERS? SOME TYPE OF MASS DRIVER?

NO SUITABLE RAW MATERIALS.

A NANO-SAIL?

WE'D BE **DEAD** BEFORE ASSEMBLING IT. AND THIS MUCH **LIGHT** WOULD JUST AS SOON DESTROY IT AS SAIL IT.

...THE **LIGHT**...

ARON? DO... DO YOU **TRUST** ME?

I TRUST YOUR **MIND**.

...THEN **HOLD ON.**

VMM
VMM
VMM

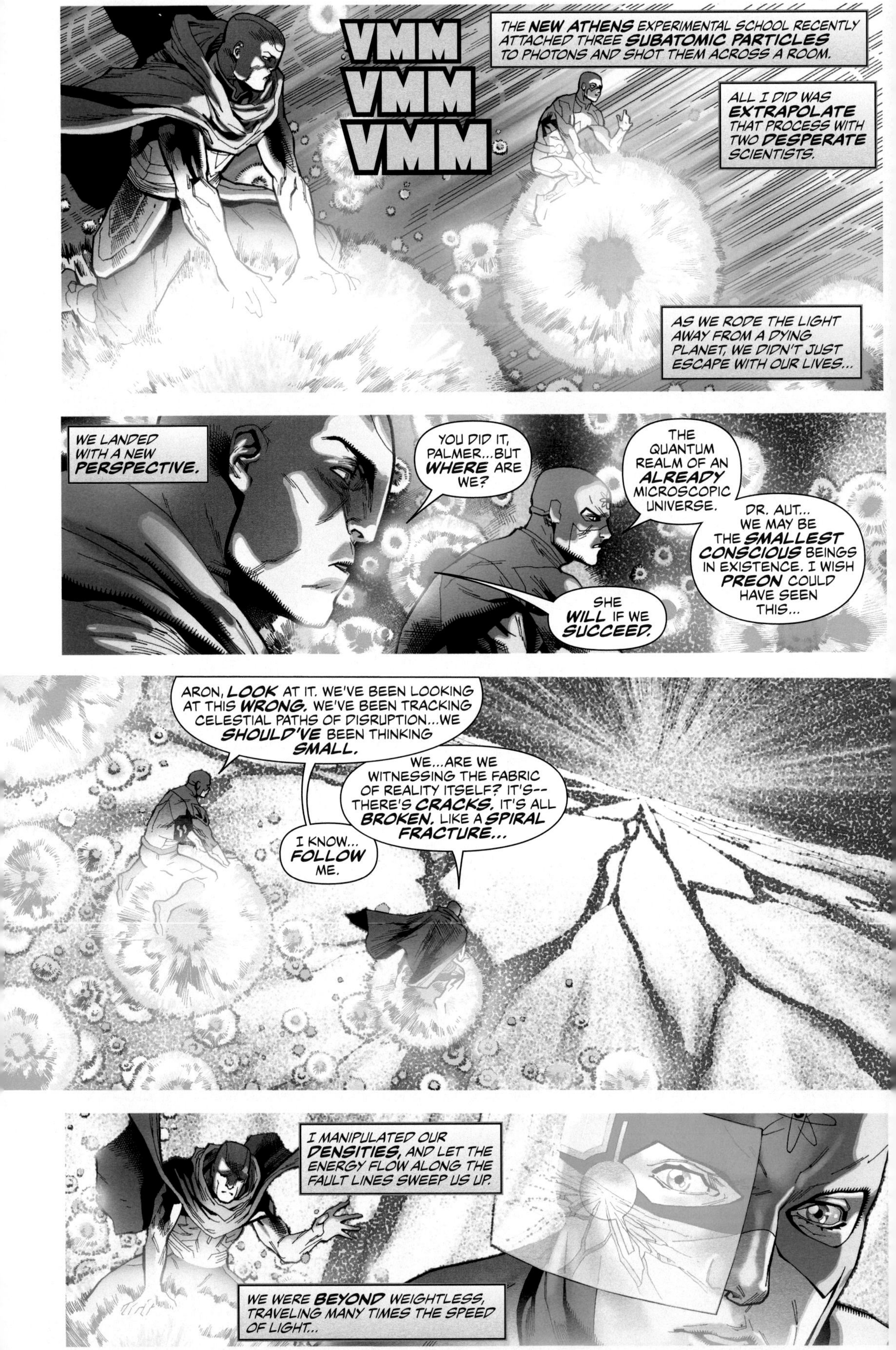
VMM VMM VMM
THE NEW ATHENS EXPERIMENTAL SCHOOL RECENTLY ATTACHED THREE SUBATOMIC PARTICLES TO PHOTONS AND SHOT THEM ACROSS A ROOM.
ALL I DID WAS EXTRAPOLATE THAT PROCESS WITH TWO DESPERATE SCIENTISTS.
AS WE RODE THE LIGHT AWAY FROM A DYING PLANET, WE DIDN'T JUST ESCAPE WITH OUR LIVES...
WE LANDED WITH A NEW PERSPECTIVE.
YOU DID IT, PALMER...BUT WHERE ARE WE?
THE QUANTUM REALM OF AN ALREADY MICROSCOPIC UNIVERSE.
DR. AUT... WE MAY BE THE SMALLEST CONSCIOUS BEINGS IN EXISTENCE. I WISH PREON COULD HAVE SEEN THIS...
SHE WILL IF WE SUCCEED.
ARON, LOOK AT IT. WE'VE BEEN LOOKING AT THIS WRONG. WE'VE BEEN TRACKING CELESTIAL PATHS OF DISRUPTION...WE SHOULD'VE BEEN THINKING SMALL.
WE...ARE WE WITNESSING THE FABRIC OF REALITY ITSELF? IT'S-- THERE'S CRACKS. IT'S ALL BROKEN. LIKE A SPIRAL FRACTURE...
I KNOW... FOLLOW ME.
I MANIPULATED OUR DENSITIES, AND LET THE ENERGY FLOW ALONG THE FAULT LINES SWEEP US UP.
WE WERE BEYOND WEIGHTLESS, TRAVELING MANY TIMES THE SPEED OF LIGHT...

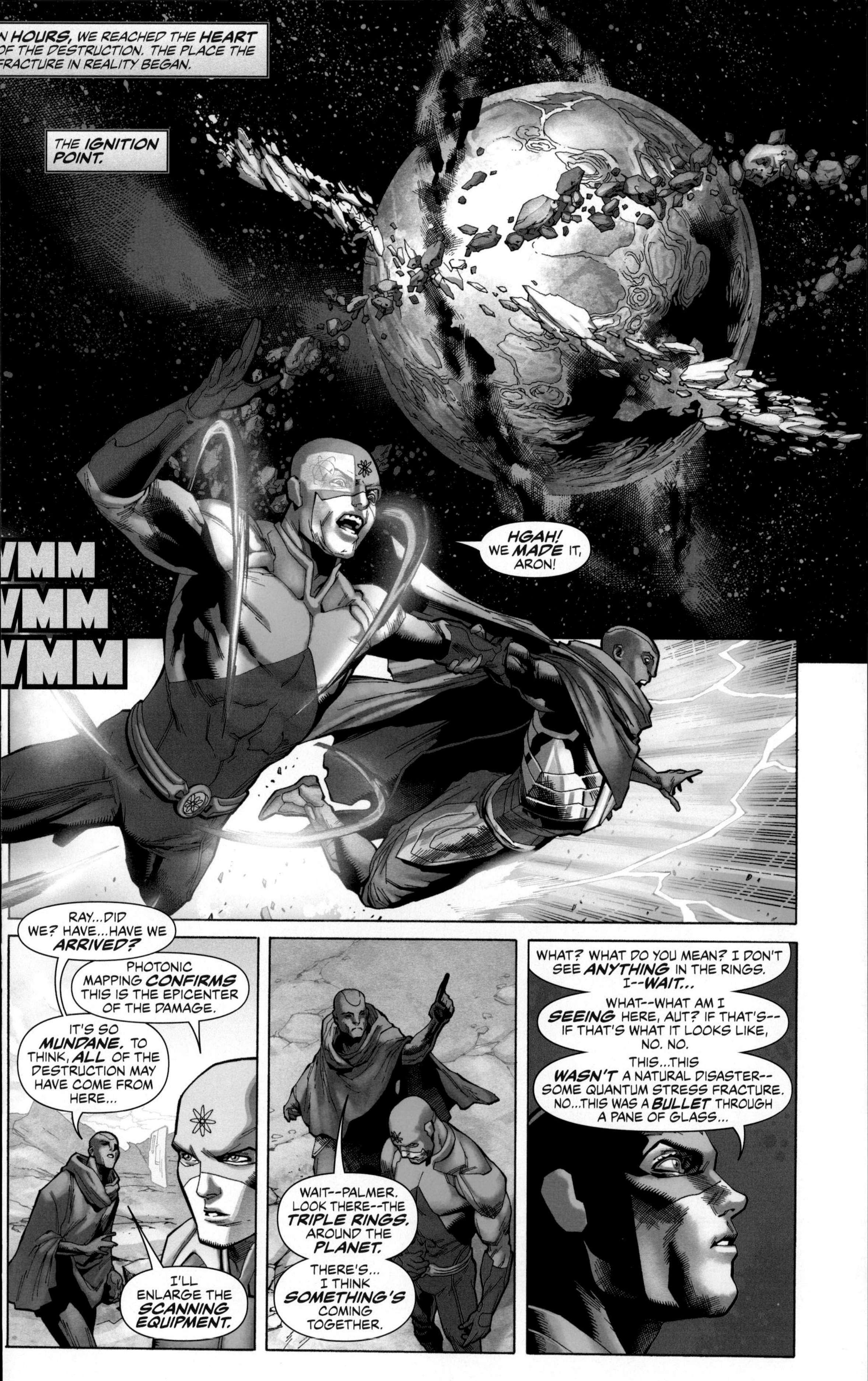

N HOURS, WE REACHED THE HEART OF THE DESTRUCTION. THE PLACE THE FRACTURE IN REALITY BEGAN.
THE IGNITION POINT.
HGAH! WE MADE IT, ARON!
VMM
VMM
VMM
RAY...DID WE? HAVE...HAVE WE ARRIVED?
PHOTONIC MAPPING CONFIRMS THIS IS THE EPICENTER OF THE DAMAGE.
IT'S SO MUNDANE. TO THINK, ALL OF THE DESTRUCTION MAY HAVE COME FROM HERE...
I'LL ENLARGE THE SCANNING EQUIPMENT.
WAIT--PALMER. LOOK THERE--THE TRIPLE RINGS. AROUND THE PLANET.
THERE'S... I THINK SOMETHING'S COMING TOGETHER.
WHAT? WHAT DO YOU MEAN? I DON'T SEE ANYTHING IN THE RINGS. I--WAIT...
WHAT--WHAT AM I SEEING HERE, AUT? IF THAT'S--IF THAT'S WHAT IT LOOKS LIKE, NO. NO.
THIS...THIS WASN'T A NATURAL DISASTER--SOME QUANTUM STRESS FRACTURE. NO...THIS WAS A BULLET THROUGH A PANE OF GLASS...

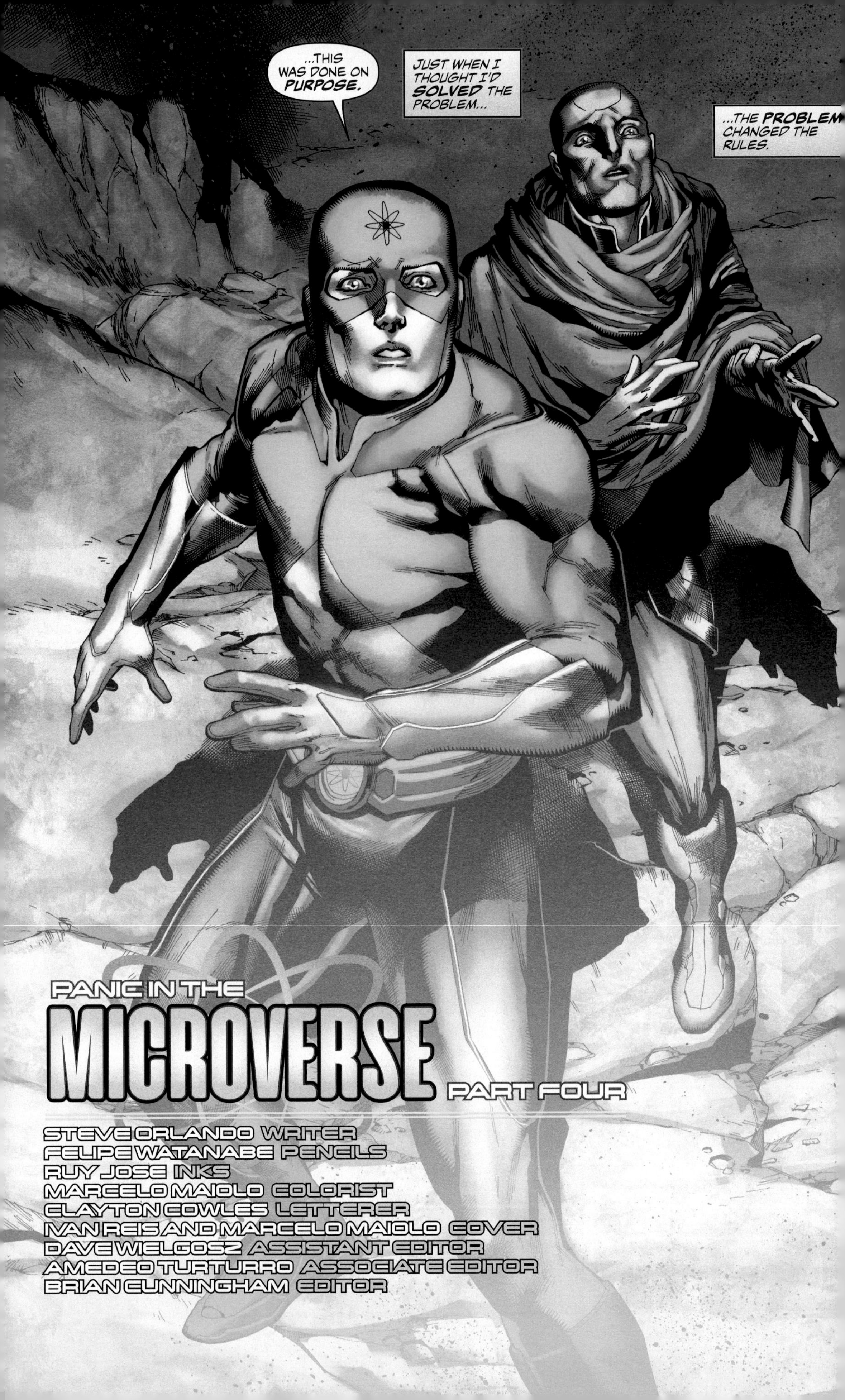
...THIS WAS DONE ON PURPOSE.
JUST WHEN I THOUGHT I'D SOLVED THE PROBLEM...
...THE PROBLEM CHANGED THE RULES.
PANIC IN THE MICROVERSE PART FOUR
STEVE ORLANDO WRITER
FELIPE WATANABE PENCILS
RUY JOSE INKS
MARCELO MAIOLO COLORIST
CLAYTON COWLES LETTERER
IVAN REIS AND MARCELO MAIOLO COVER
DAVE WIELGOSZ ASSISTANT EDITOR
AMEDEO TURTURRO ASSOCIATE EDITOR
BRIAN CUNNINGHAM EDITOR

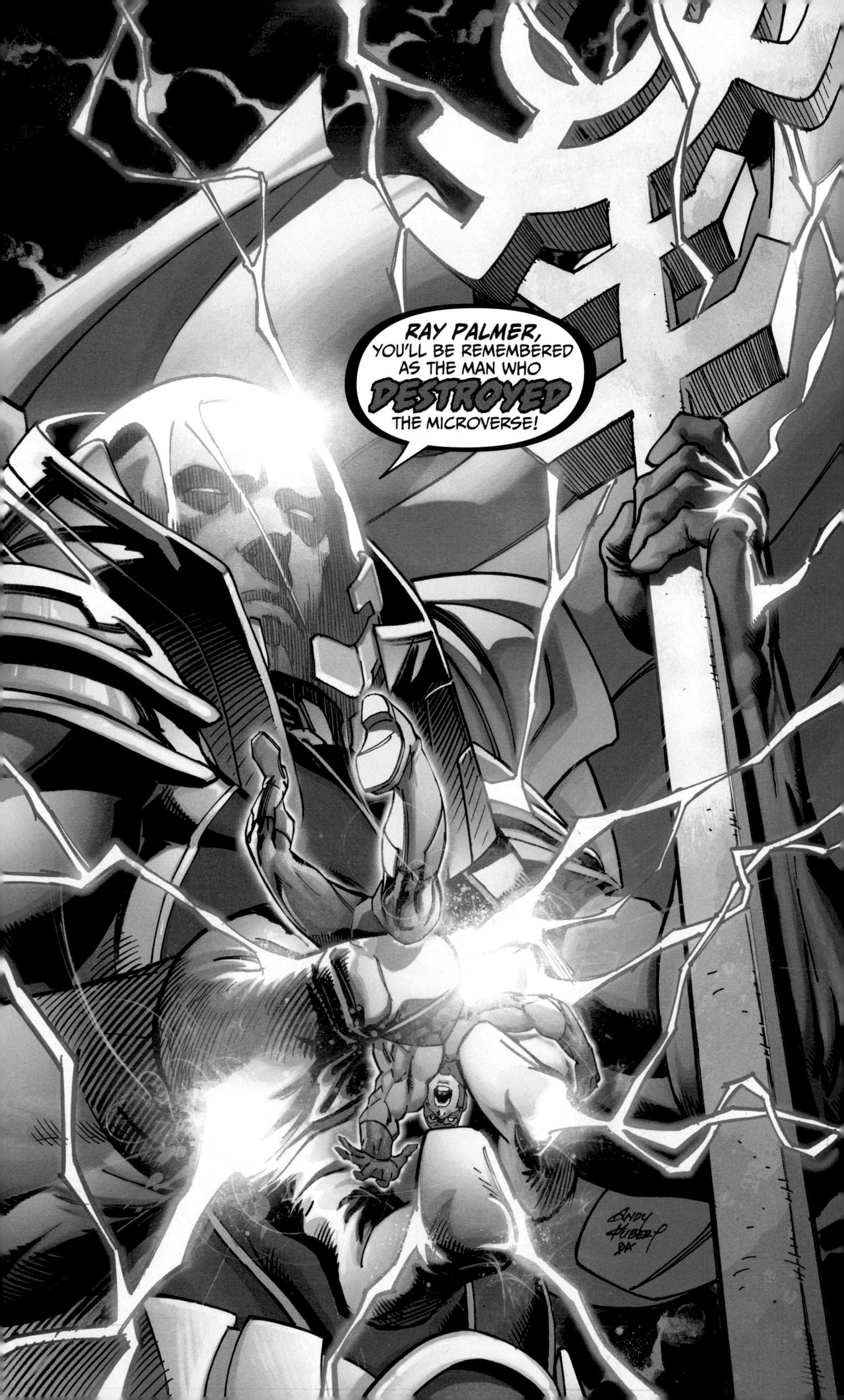
RAY PALMER, YOU'LL BE REMEMBERED AS THE MAN WHO DESTROYED THE MICROVERSE!
ANDY KUBERT

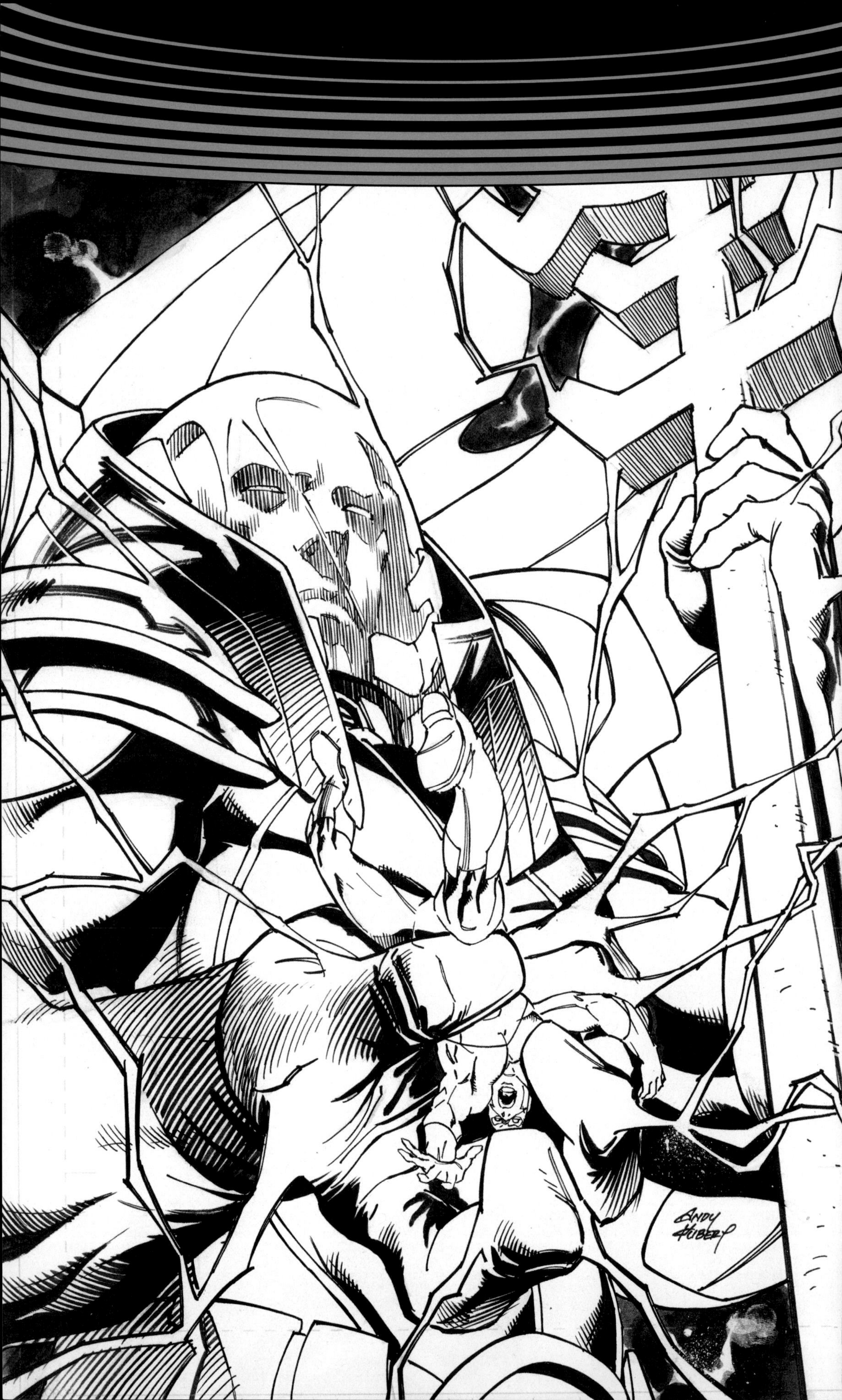
ANDY KUBERT

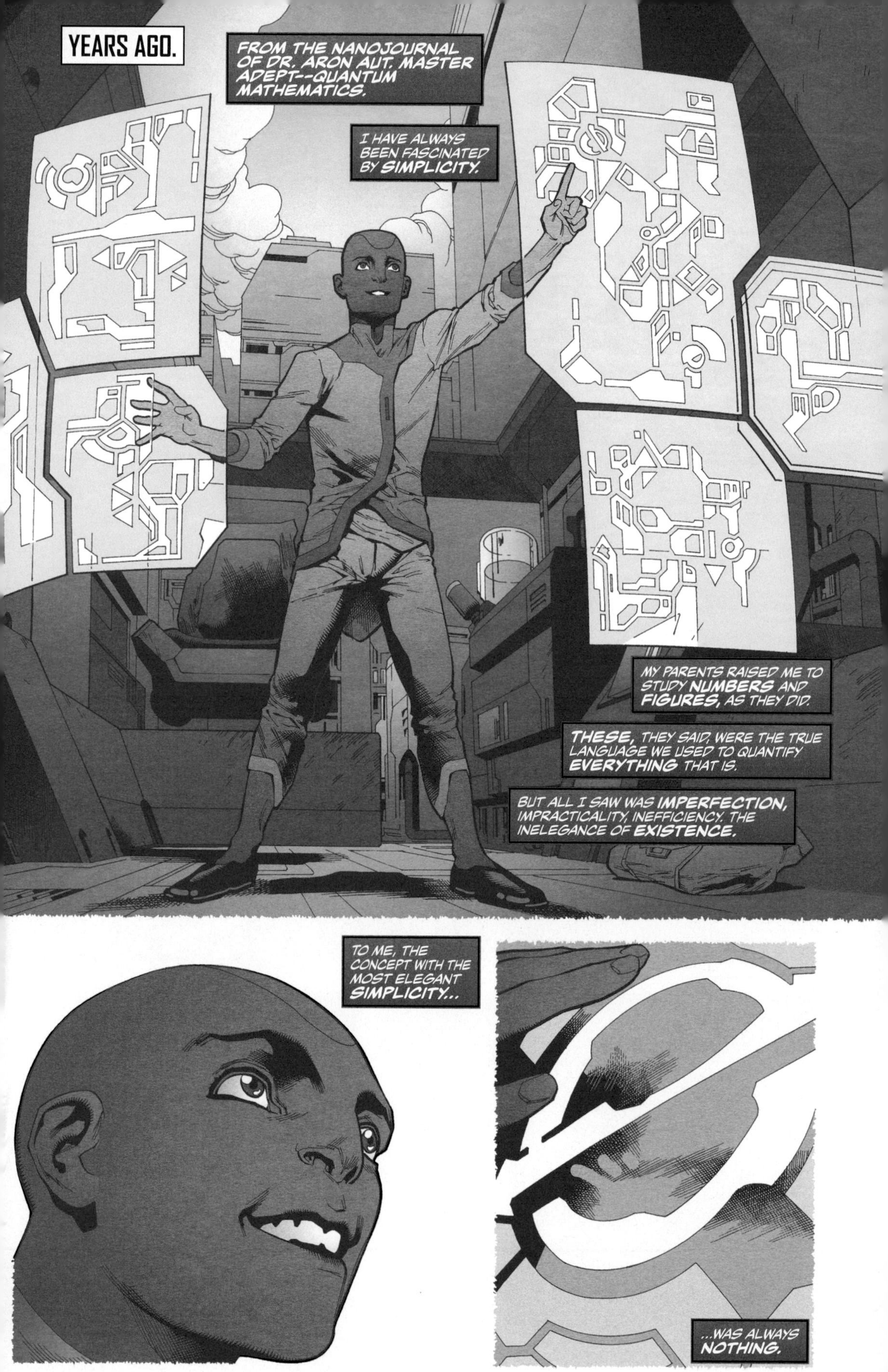
YEARS AGO.
FROM THE NANOJOURNAL OF DR. ARON AUT, MASTER ADEPT--QUANTUM MATHEMATICS.
I HAVE ALWAYS BEEN FASCINATED BY SIMPLICITY.
MY PARENTS RAISED ME TO STUDY NUMBERS AND FIGURES, AS THEY DID.
THESE, THEY SAID, WERE THE TRUE LANGUAGE WE USED TO QUANTIFY EVERYTHING THAT IS.
BUT ALL I SAW WAS IMPERFECTION, IMPRACTICALITY, INEFFICIENCY. THE INELEGANCE OF EXISTENCE.
TO ME, THE CONCEPT WITH THE MOST ELEGANT SIMPLICITY...
...WAS ALWAYS NOTHING.

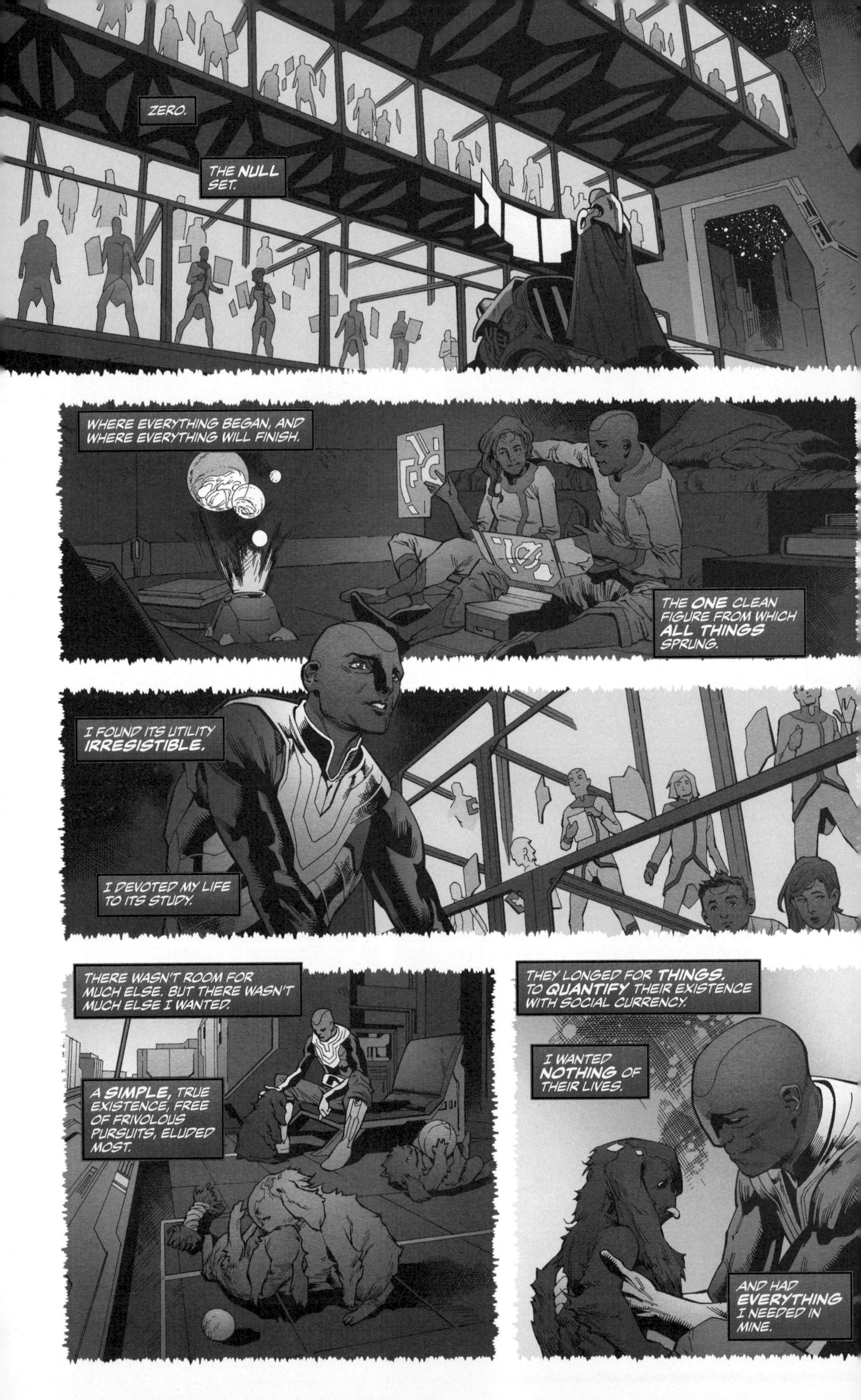
ZERO.
THE NULL SET.
WHERE EVERYTHING BEGAN, AND WHERE EVERYTHING WILL FINISH.
THE ONE CLEAN FIGURE FROM WHICH ALL THINGS SPRUNG.
I FOUND ITS UTILITY IRRESISTIBLE.
I DEVOTED MY LIFE TO ITS STUDY.
THERE WASN'T ROOM FOR MUCH ELSE. BUT THERE WASN'T MUCH ELSE I WANTED.
A SIMPLE, TRUE EXISTENCE, FREE OF FRIVOLOUS PURSUITS, ELUDED MOST.
THEY LONGED FOR THINGS. TO QUANTIFY THEIR EXISTENCE WITH SOCIAL CURRENCY.
I WANTED NOTHING OF THEIR LIVES.
AND HAD EVERYTHING I NEEDED IN MINE.

UNTIL THE **QUANTUM STORMS.**

THAT ABRUPT, INDELIBLE **SHOCK** CREEPING ACROSS CREATION.

SUDDENLY, A **SIMPLE** EXISTENCE WAS **IMPOSSIBLE.**

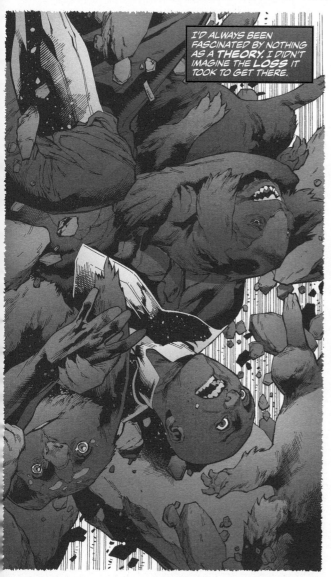

I'D ALWAYS BEEN FASCINATED BY NOTHING AS A **THEORY.** I DIDN'T IMAGINE THE **LOSS** IT TOOK TO GET THERE.

IT **HURT.** BUT IT SHOWED ME WHAT IT WOULD TAKE FOR IT, FOR **EVERYTHING,** TO END AND START **ANEW.**

SIMPLE. AGAIN FROM **NOTHING.**

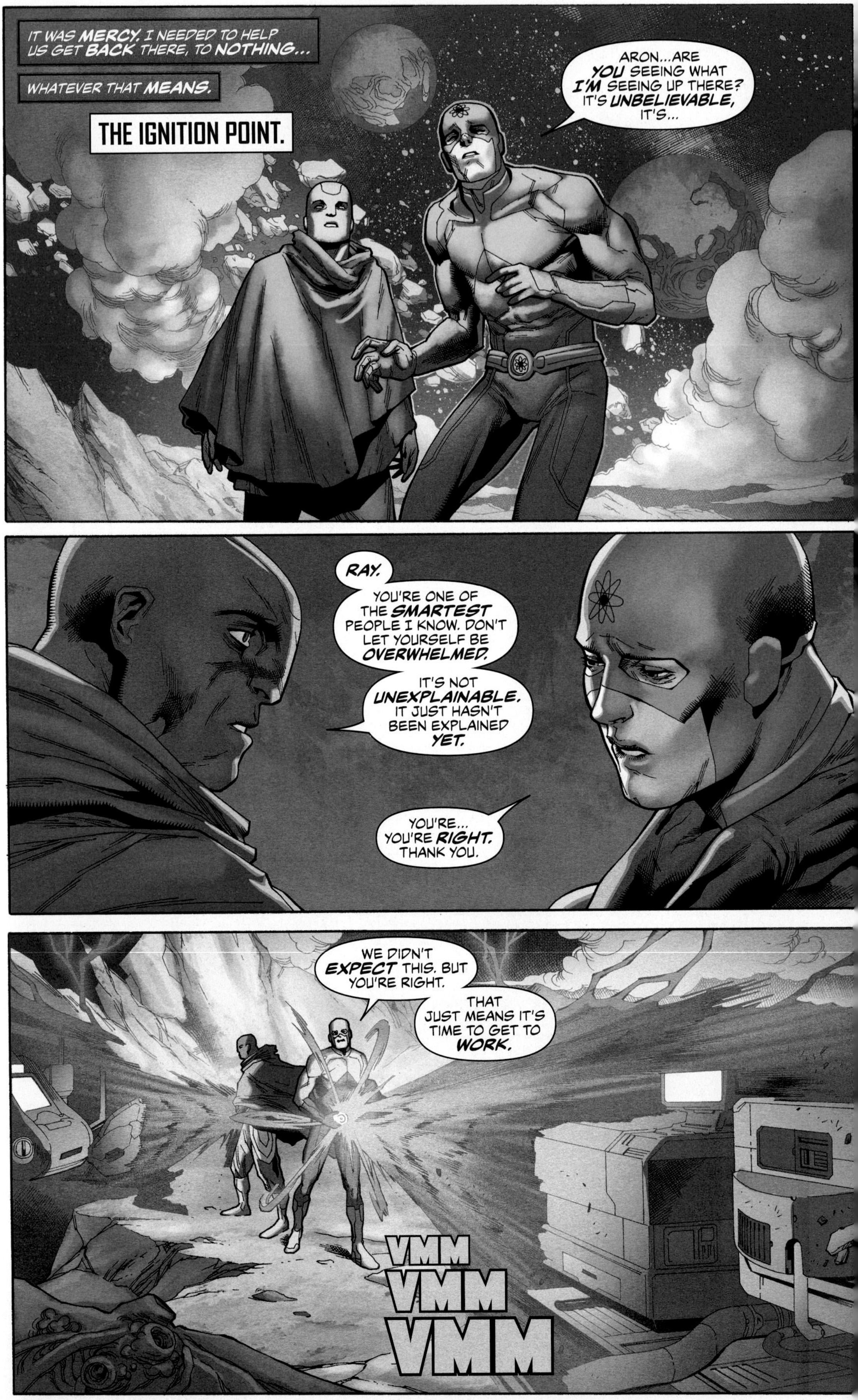
IT WAS MERCY. I NEEDED TO HELP US GET BACK THERE, TO NOTHING...
WHATEVER THAT MEANS.
THE IGNITION POINT.
ARON...ARE YOU SEEING WHAT I'M SEEING UP THERE? IT'S UNBELIEVABLE, IT'S...
RAY.
YOU'RE ONE OF THE SMARTEST PEOPLE I KNOW. DON'T LET YOURSELF BE OVERWHELMED.
IT'S NOT UNEXPLAINABLE. IT JUST HASN'T BEEN EXPLAINED YET.
YOU'RE... YOU'RE RIGHT. THANK YOU.
WE DIDN'T EXPECT THIS. BUT YOU'RE RIGHT.
THAT JUST MEANS IT'S TIME TO GET TO WORK.
VMM
VMM
VMM

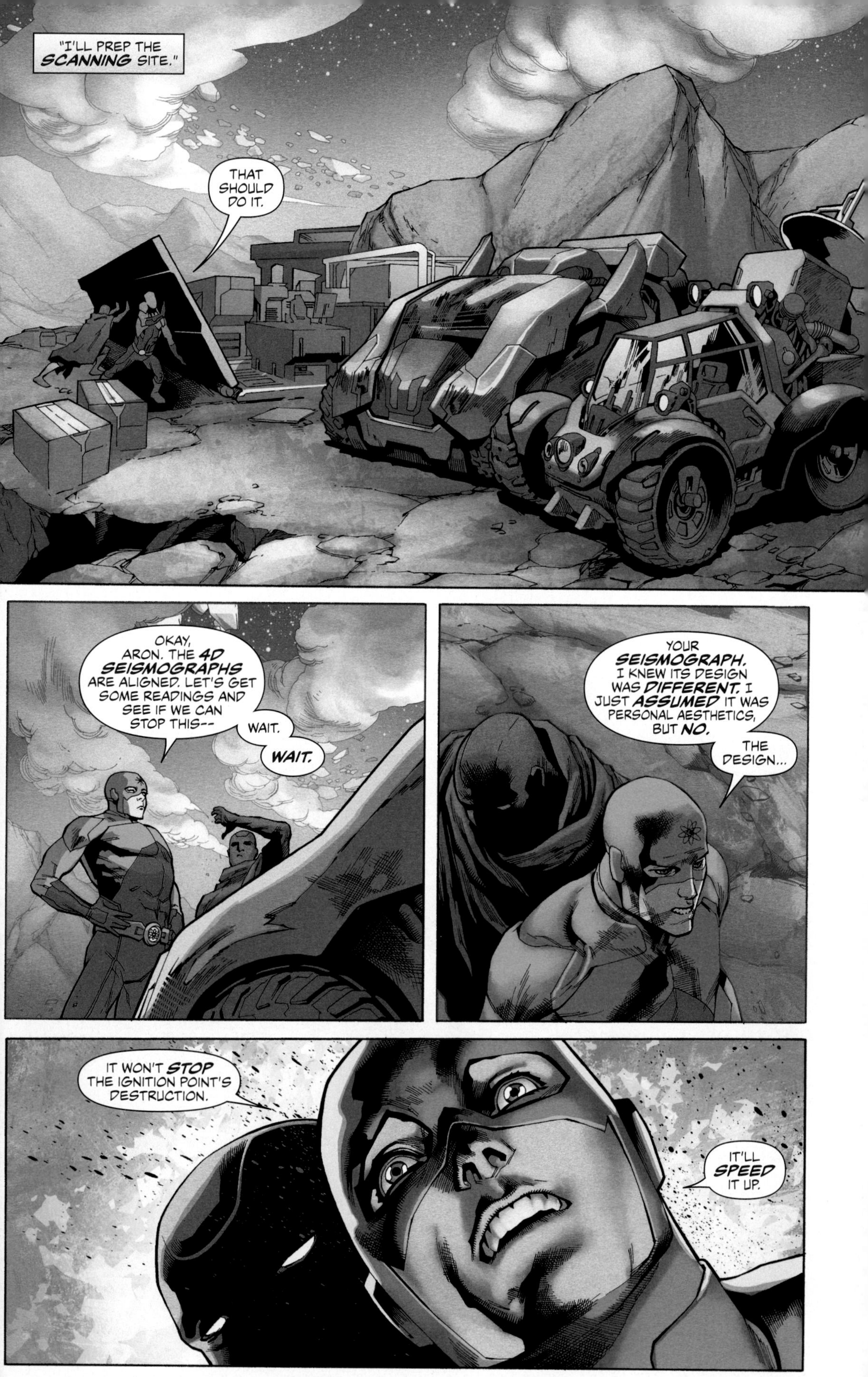
"I'LL PREP THE SCANNING SITE."
THAT SHOULD DO IT.
OKAY, ARON. THE 4D SEISMOGRAPHS ARE ALIGNED. LET'S GET SOME READINGS AND SEE IF WE CAN STOP THIS--
WAIT.
WAIT.
YOUR SEISMOGRAPH. I KNEW ITS DESIGN WAS DIFFERENT. I JUST ASSUMED IT WAS PERSONAL AESTHETICS, BUT NO.
THE DESIGN...
IT WON'T STOP THE IGNITION POINT'S DESTRUCTION.
IT'LL SPEED IT UP.

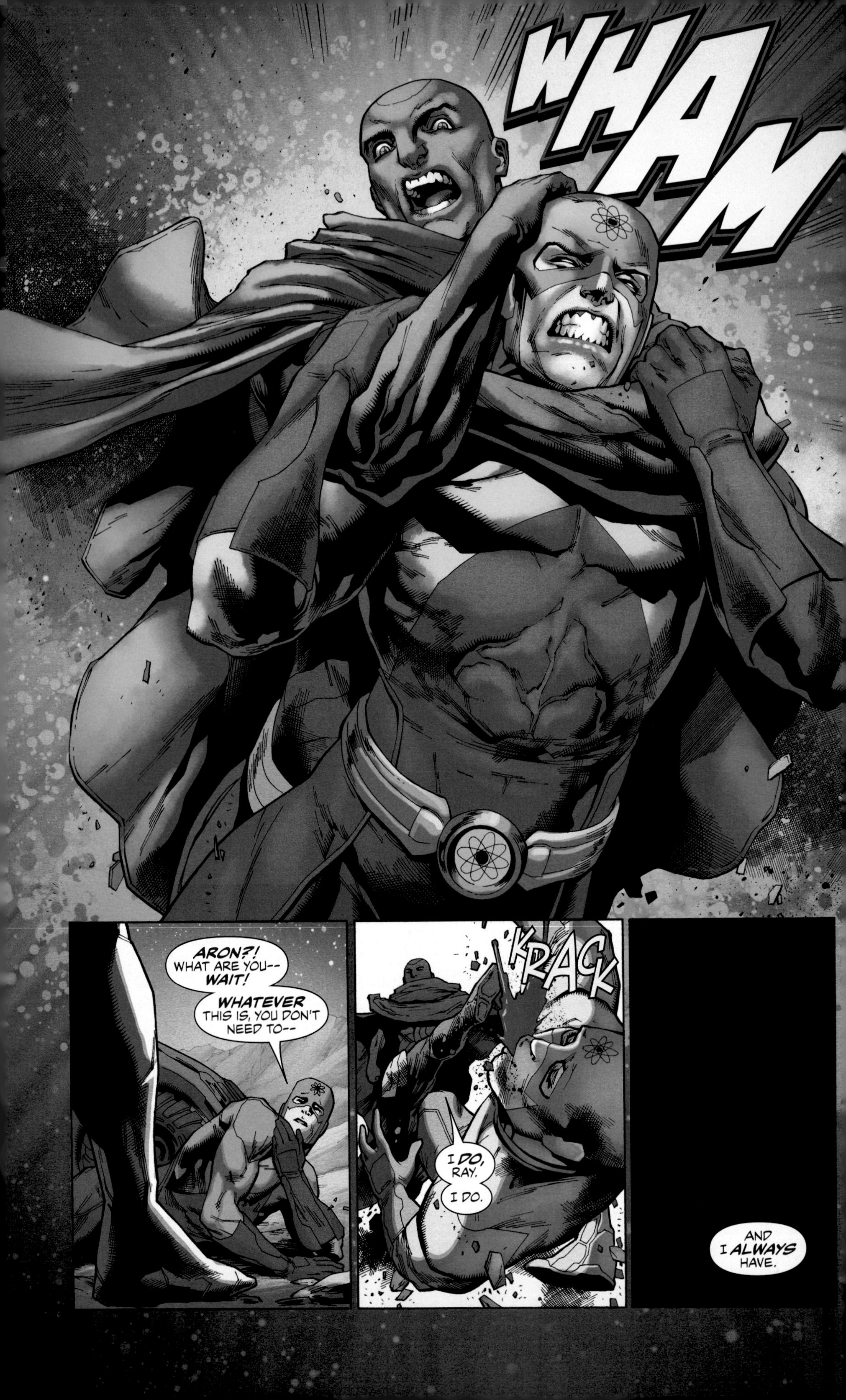
WHAM
ARON?! WHAT ARE YOU-- WAIT!
WHATEVER THIS IS, YOU DON'T NEED TO--
KRACK
I DO, RAY.
I DO.
AND I ALWAYS HAVE.

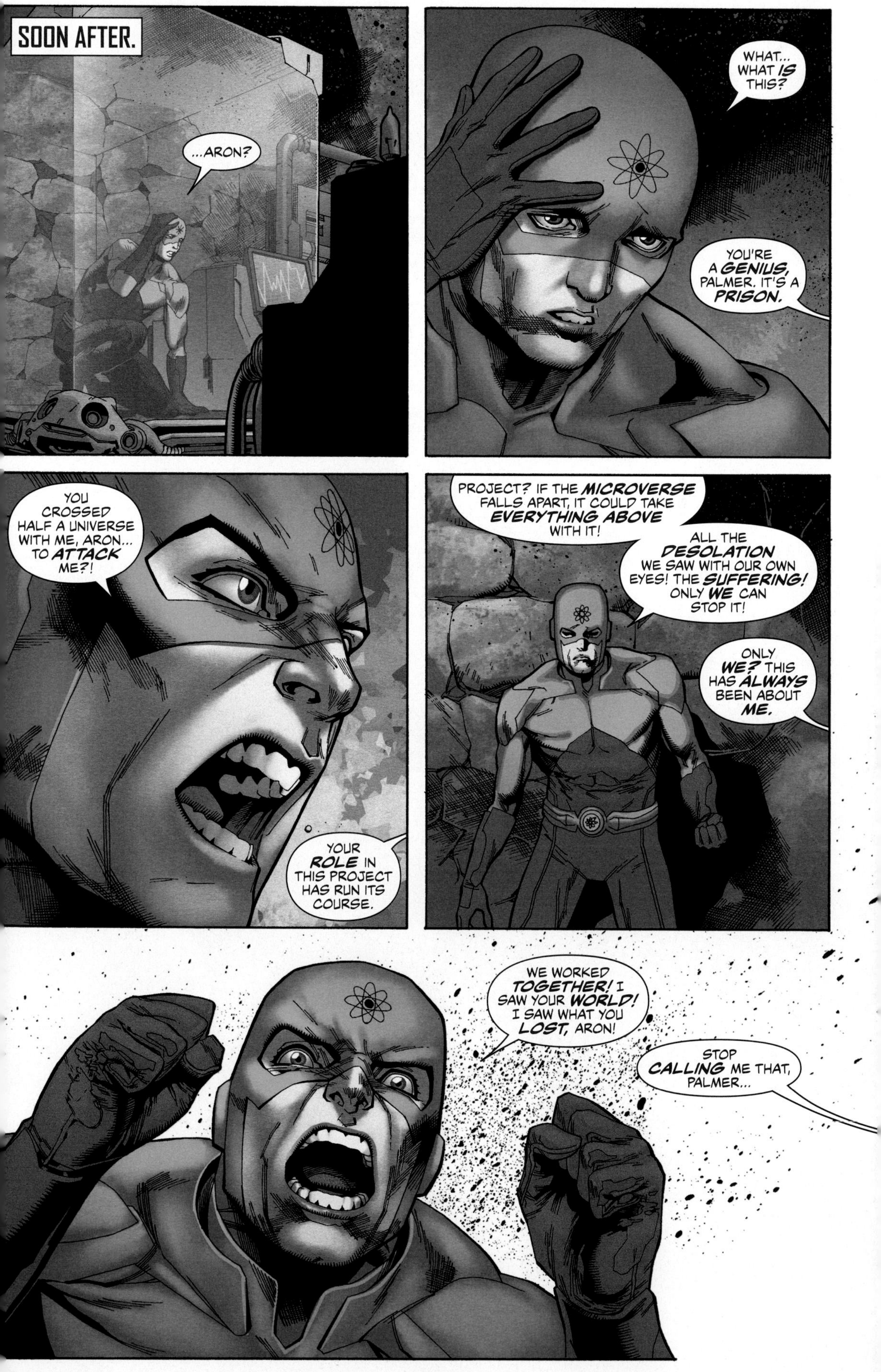
SOON AFTER.
...ARON?
WHAT... WHAT IS THIS?
YOU'RE A GENIUS, PALMER. IT'S A PRISON.
YOU CROSSED HALF A UNIVERSE WITH ME, ARON... TO ATTACK ME?!
YOUR ROLE IN THIS PROJECT HAS RUN ITS COURSE.
PROJECT? IF THE MICROVERSE FALLS APART, IT COULD TAKE EVERYTHING ABOVE WITH IT!
ALL THE DESOLATION WE SAW WITH OUR OWN EYES! THE SUFFERING! ONLY WE CAN STOP IT!
ONLY WE? THIS HAS ALWAYS BEEN ABOUT ME.
WE WORKED TOGETHER! I SAW YOUR WORLD! I SAW WHAT YOU LOST, ARON!
STOP CALLING ME THAT, PALMER...

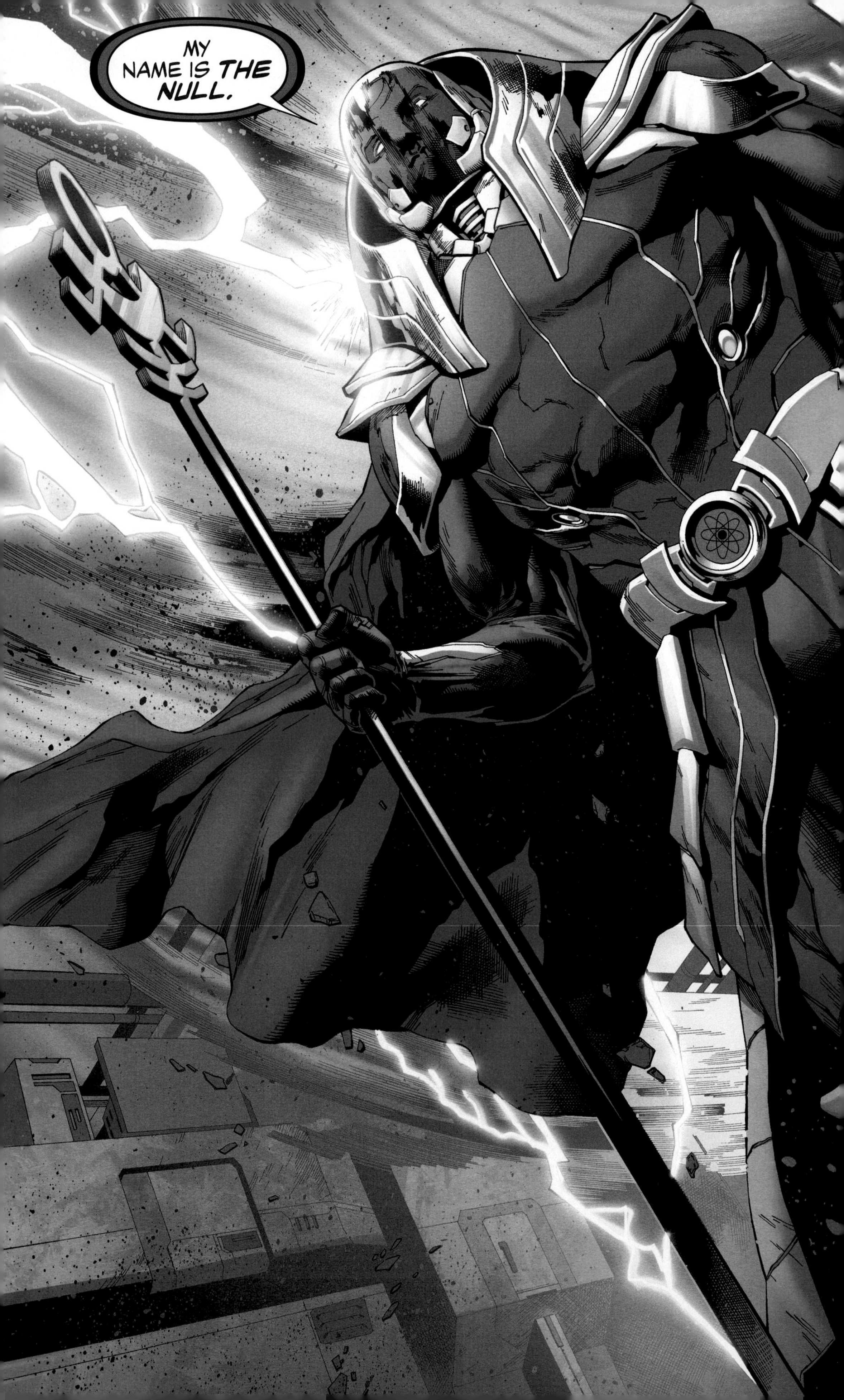
MY NAME IS THE NULL.

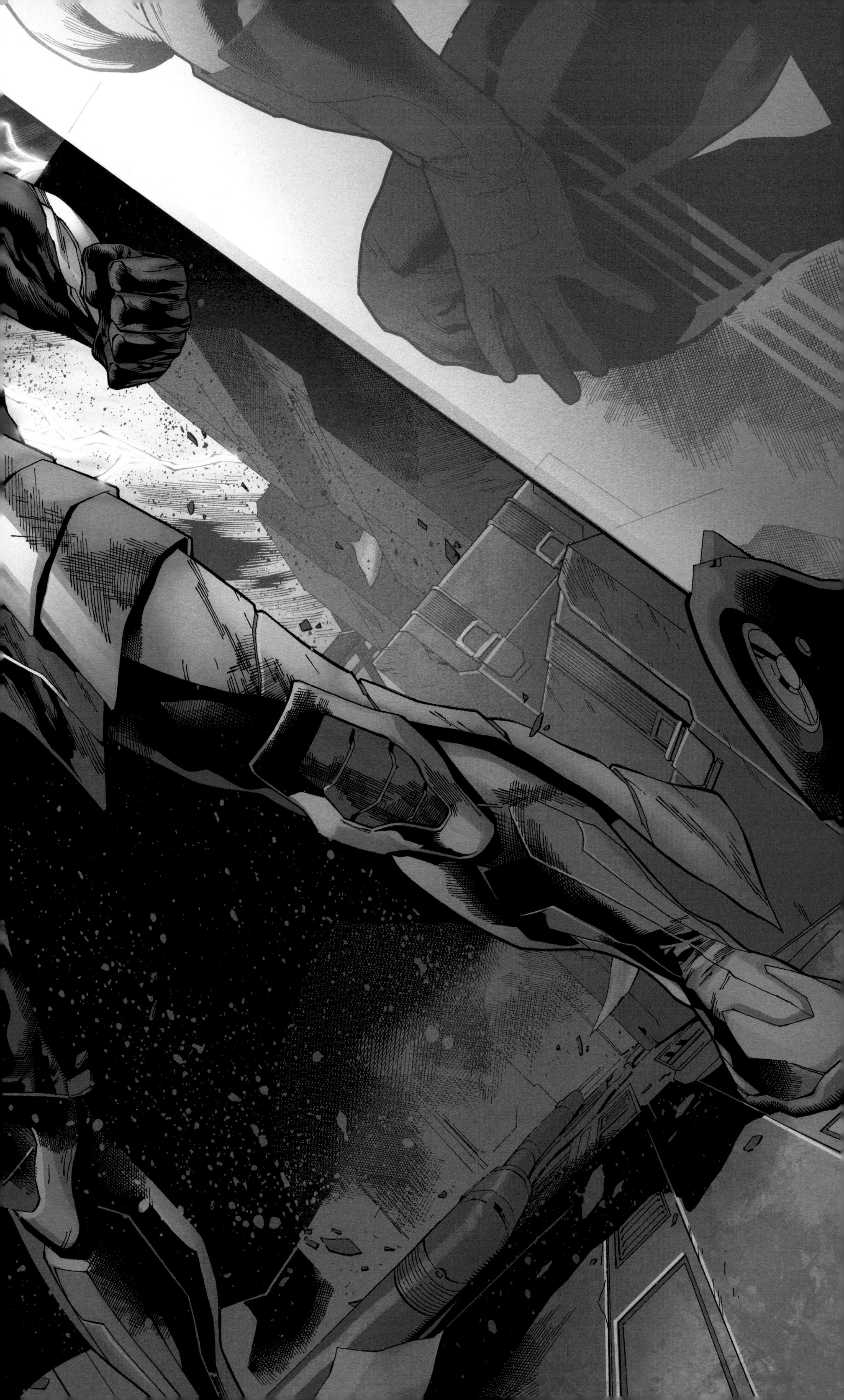

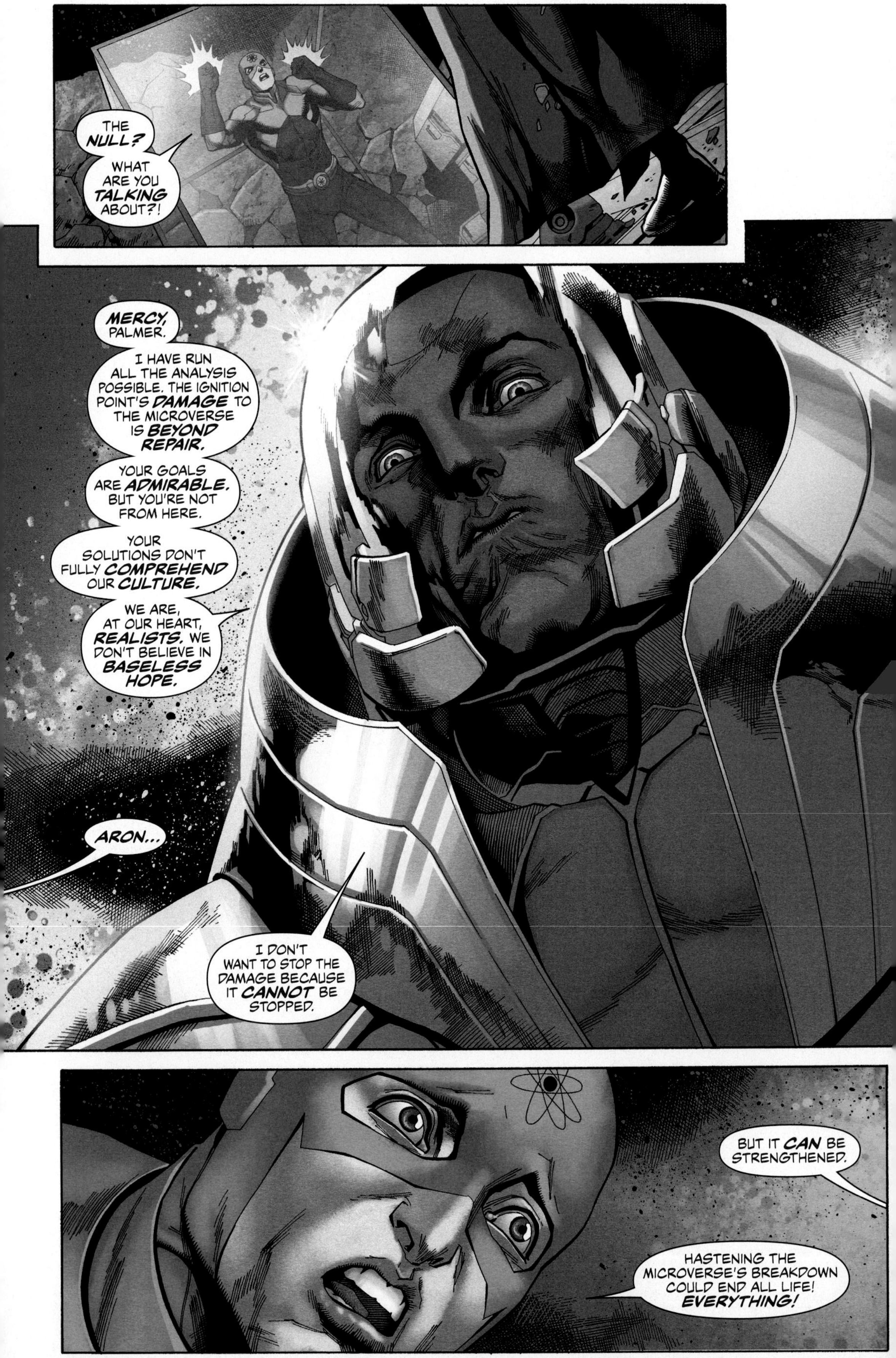
THE NULL? WHAT ARE YOU TALKING ABOUT?!
MERCY, PALMER.
I HAVE RUN ALL THE ANALYSIS POSSIBLE. THE IGNITION POINT'S DAMAGE TO THE MICROVERSE IS BEYOND REPAIR.
YOUR GOALS ARE ADMIRABLE. BUT YOU'RE NOT FROM HERE.
YOUR SOLUTIONS DON'T FULLY COMPREHEND OUR CULTURE.
WE ARE, AT OUR HEART, REALISTS. WE DON'T BELIEVE IN BASELESS HOPE.
ARON...
I DON'T WANT TO STOP THE DAMAGE BECAUSE IT CANNOT BE STOPPED.
BUT IT CAN BE STRENGTHENED.
HASTENING THE MICROVERSE'S BREAKDOWN COULD END ALL LIFE! EVERYTHING!

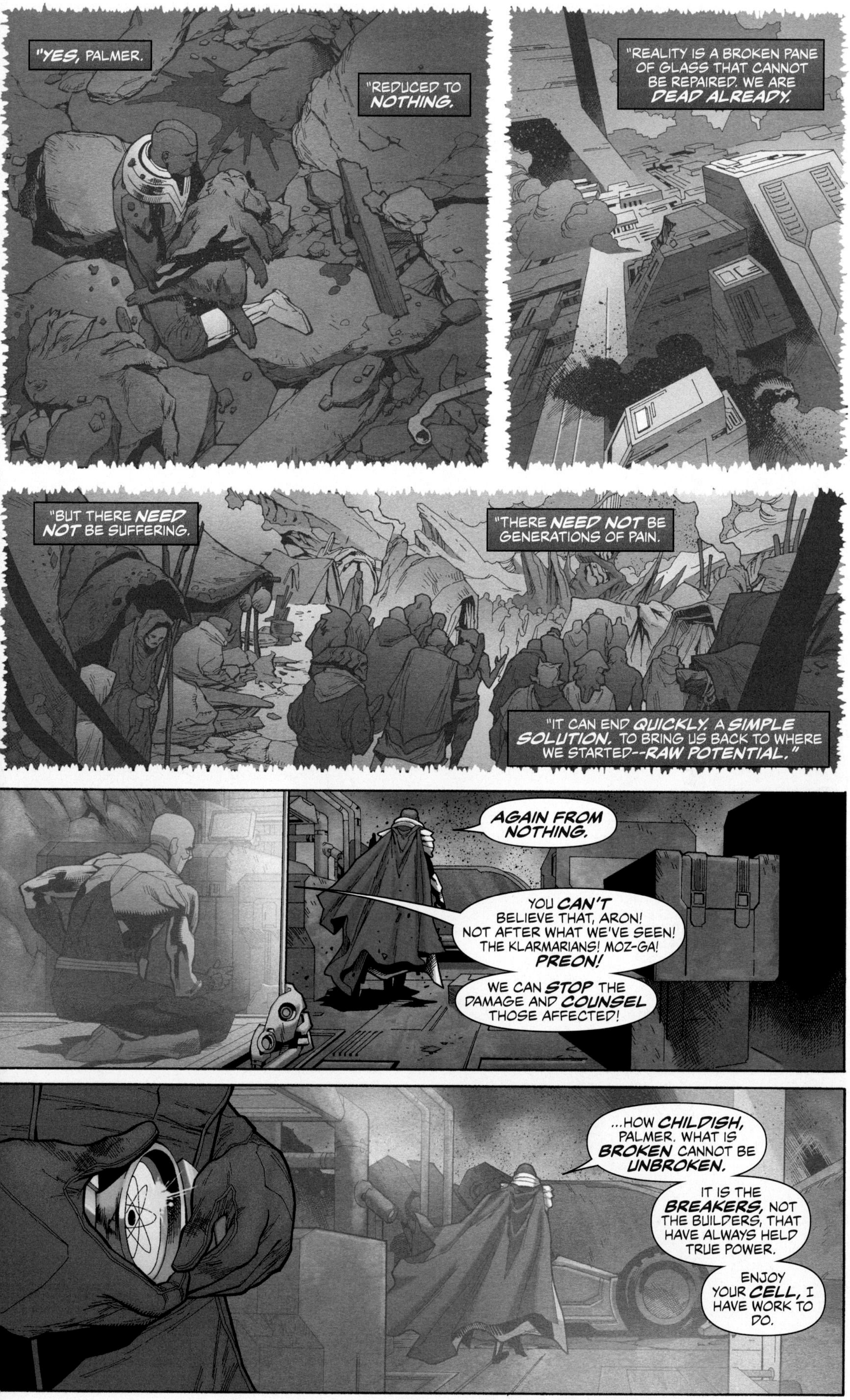

"YES, PALMER.
"REDUCED TO NOTHING.
"REALITY IS A BROKEN PANE OF GLASS THAT CANNOT BE REPAIRED. WE ARE DEAD ALREADY.
"BUT THERE NEED NOT BE SUFFERING.
"THERE NEED NOT BE GENERATIONS OF PAIN.
"IT CAN END QUICKLY. A SIMPLE SOLUTION. TO BRING US BACK TO WHERE WE STARTED--RAW POTENTIAL."
AGAIN FROM NOTHING.
YOU CAN'T BELIEVE THAT, ARON! NOT AFTER WHAT WE'VE SEEN! THE KLARMARIANS! MOZ-GA! PREON!
WE CAN STOP THE DAMAGE AND COUNSEL THOSE AFFECTED!
...HOW CHILDISH, PALMER. WHAT IS BROKEN CANNOT BE UNBROKEN.
IT IS THE BREAKERS, NOT THE BUILDERS, THAT HAVE ALWAYS HELD TRUE POWER.
ENJOY YOUR CELL, I HAVE WORK TO DO.

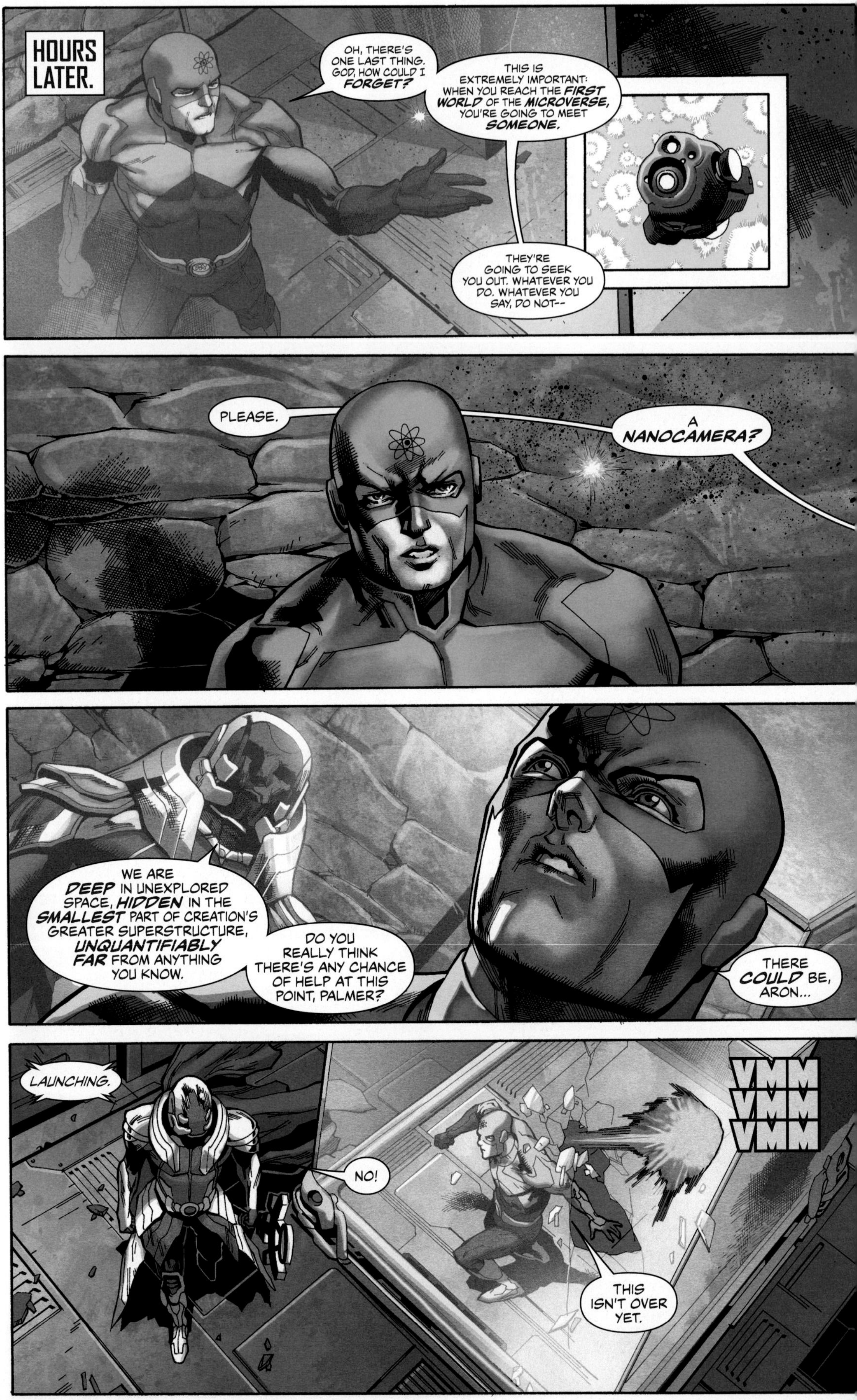
HOURS LATER.
OH, THERE'S ONE LAST THING. GOD, HOW COULD I FORGET?
THIS IS EXTREMELY IMPORTANT: WHEN YOU REACH THE FIRST WORLD OF THE MICROVERSE, YOU'RE GOING TO MEET SOMEONE.
THEY'RE GOING TO SEEK YOU OUT. WHATEVER YOU DO. WHATEVER YOU SAY, DO NOT--
PLEASE.
A NANOCAMERA?
WE ARE DEEP IN UNEXPLORED SPACE, HIDDEN IN THE SMALLEST PART OF CREATION'S GREATER SUPERSTRUCTURE, UNQUANTIFIABLY FAR FROM ANYTHING YOU KNOW.
DO YOU REALLY THINK THERE'S ANY CHANCE OF HELP AT THIS POINT, PALMER?
THERE COULD BE, ARON...
LAUNCHING.
VMM VMM VMM
NO!
THIS ISN'T OVER YET.

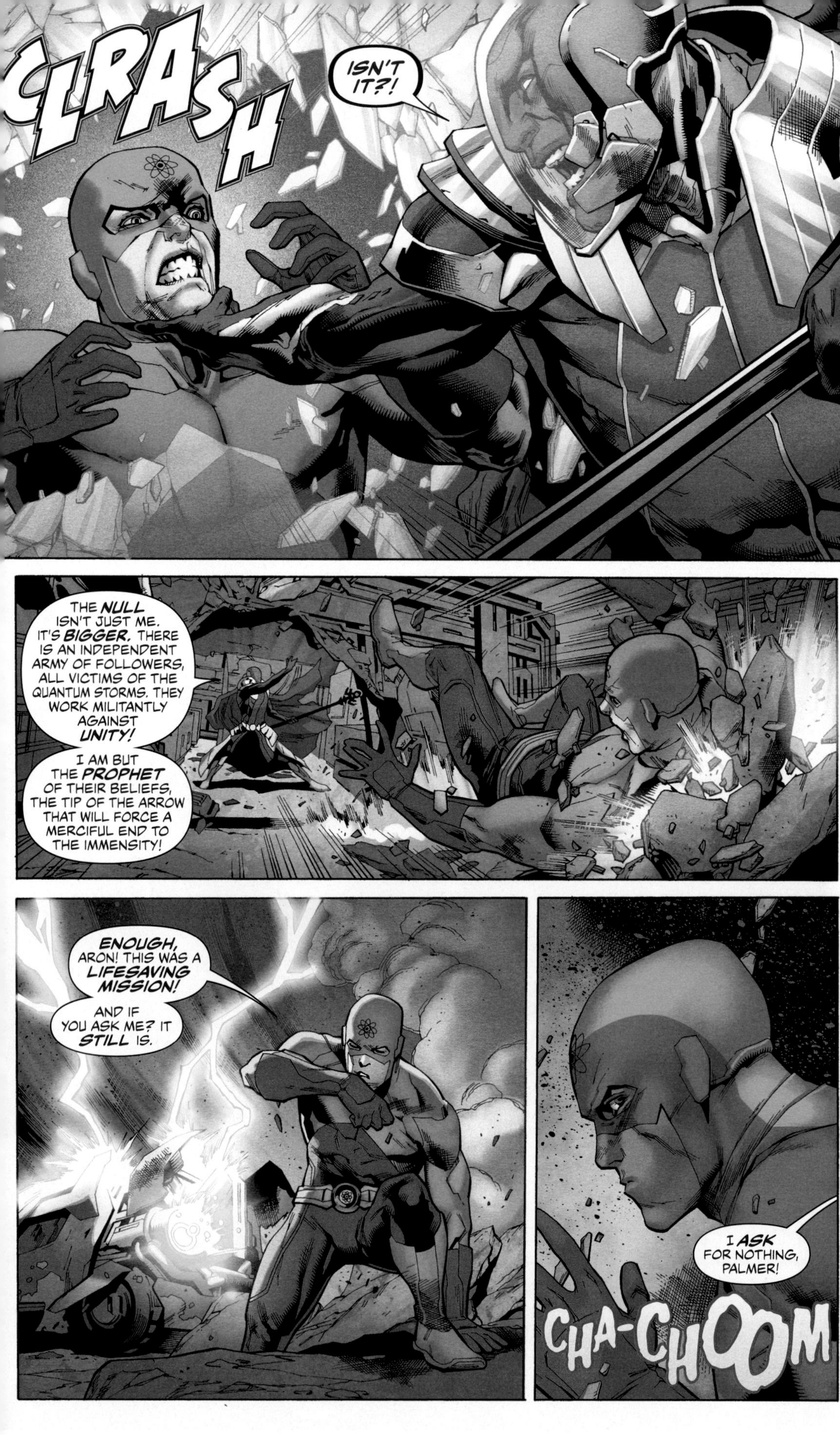
CLRASH
ISN'T IT?!
THE NULL ISN'T JUST ME. IT'S BIGGER. THERE IS AN INDEPENDENT ARMY OF FOLLOWERS, ALL VICTIMS OF THE QUANTUM STORMS. THEY WORK MILITANTLY AGAINST UNITY!
I AM BUT THE PROPHET OF THEIR BELIEFS, THE TIP OF THE ARROW THAT WILL FORCE A MERCIFUL END TO THE IMMENSITY!
ENOUGH, ARON! THIS WAS A LIFESAVING MISSION!
AND IF YOU ASK ME? IT STILL IS.
I ASK FOR NOTHING, PALMER!
CHA-CHOOM

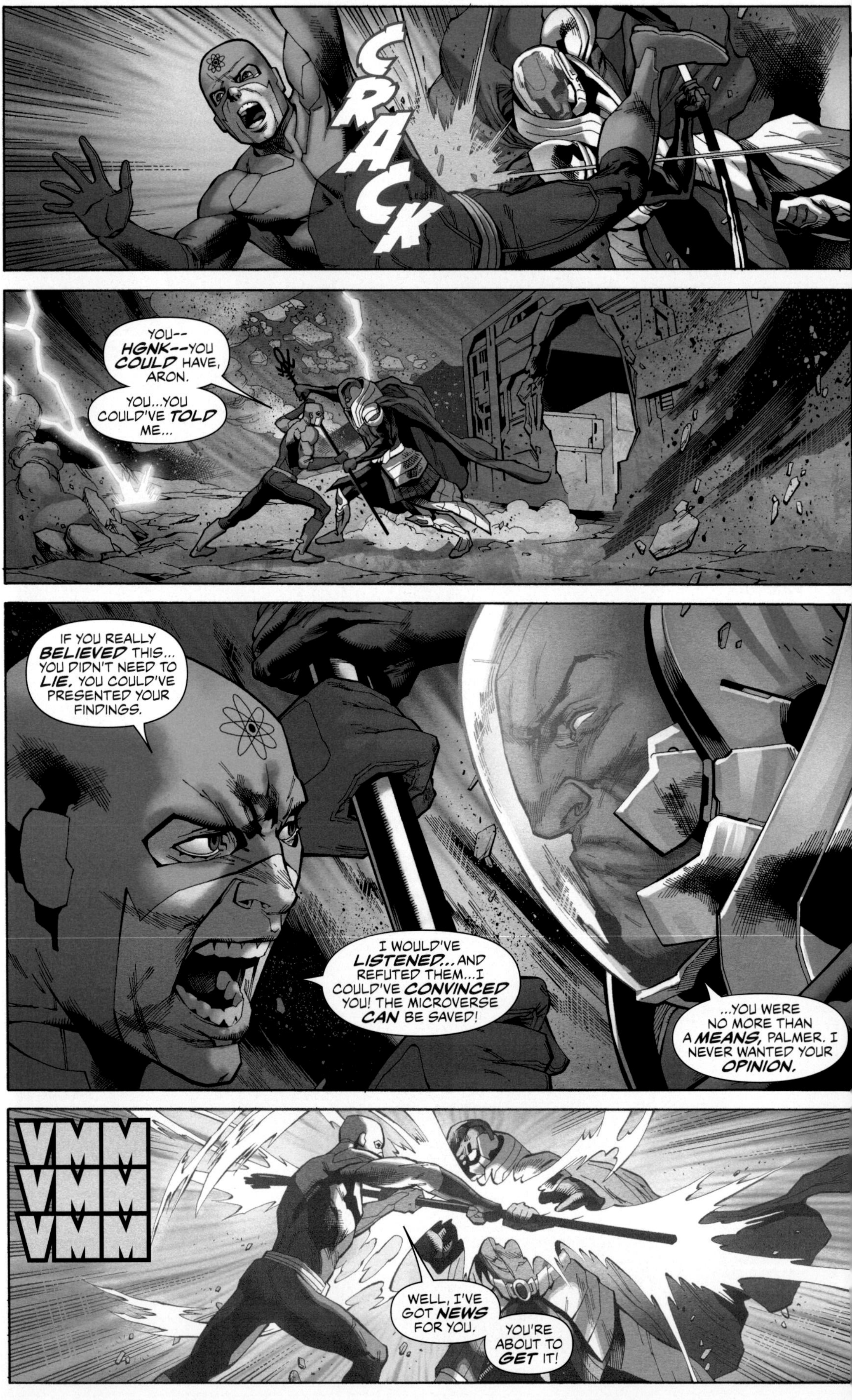
CRACK
YOU-- HGNK--YOU COULD HAVE, ARON.
YOU...YOU COULD'VE TOLD ME...
IF YOU REALLY BELIEVED THIS... YOU DIDN'T NEED TO LIE. YOU COULD'VE PRESENTED YOUR FINDINGS.
I WOULD'VE LISTENED...AND REFUTED THEM...I COULD'VE CONVINCED YOU! THE MICROVERSE CAN BE SAVED!
...YOU WERE NO MORE THAN A MEANS, PALMER. I NEVER WANTED YOUR OPINION.
VMM VMM VMM
WELL, I'VE GOT NEWS FOR YOU.
YOU'RE ABOUT TO GET IT!

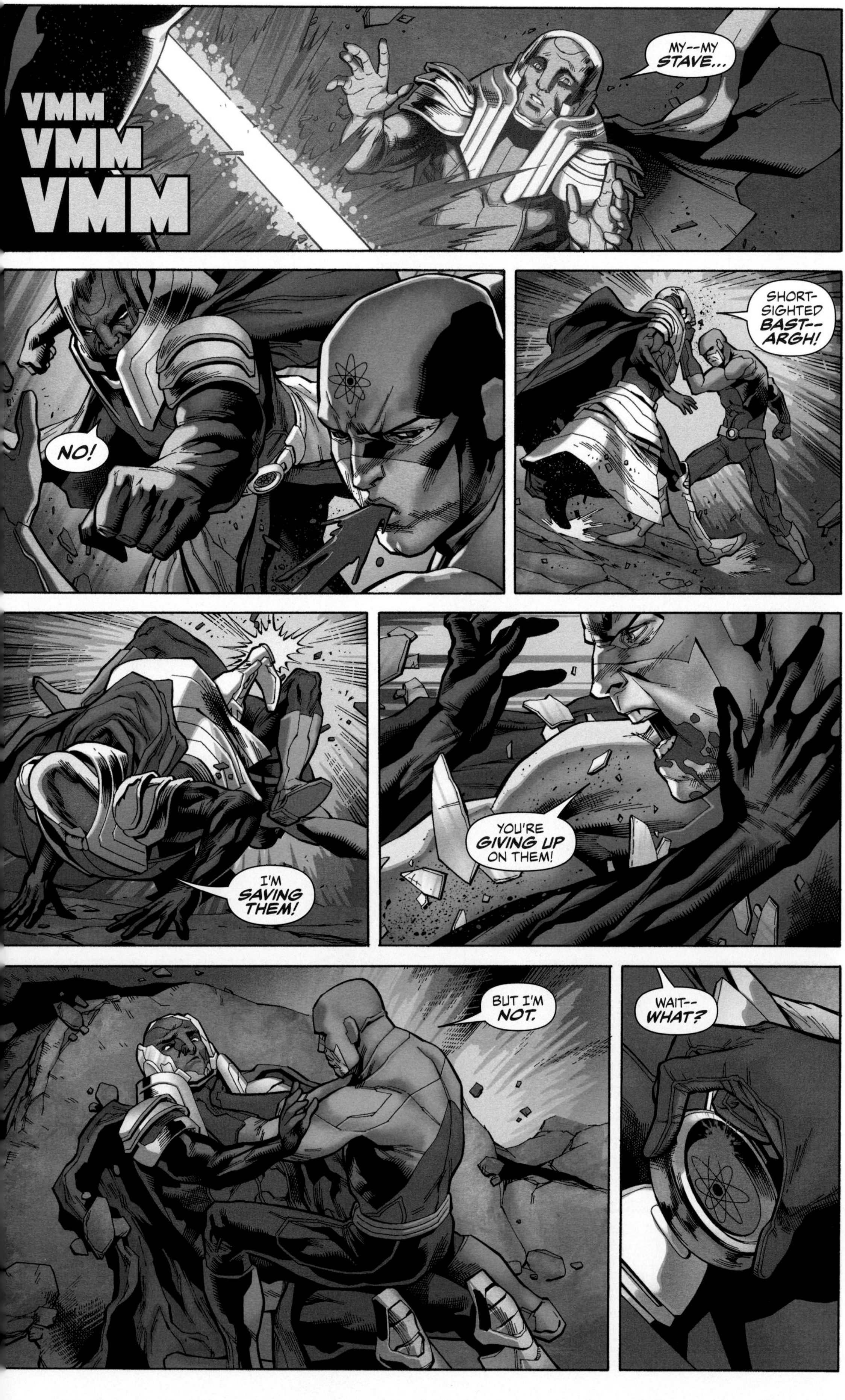

VMM VMM VMM
MY--MY STAVE...
NO!
SHORT-SIGHTED BAST--ARGH!
I'M SAVING THEM!
YOU'RE GIVING UP ON THEM!
BUT I'M NOT.
WAIT--WHAT?

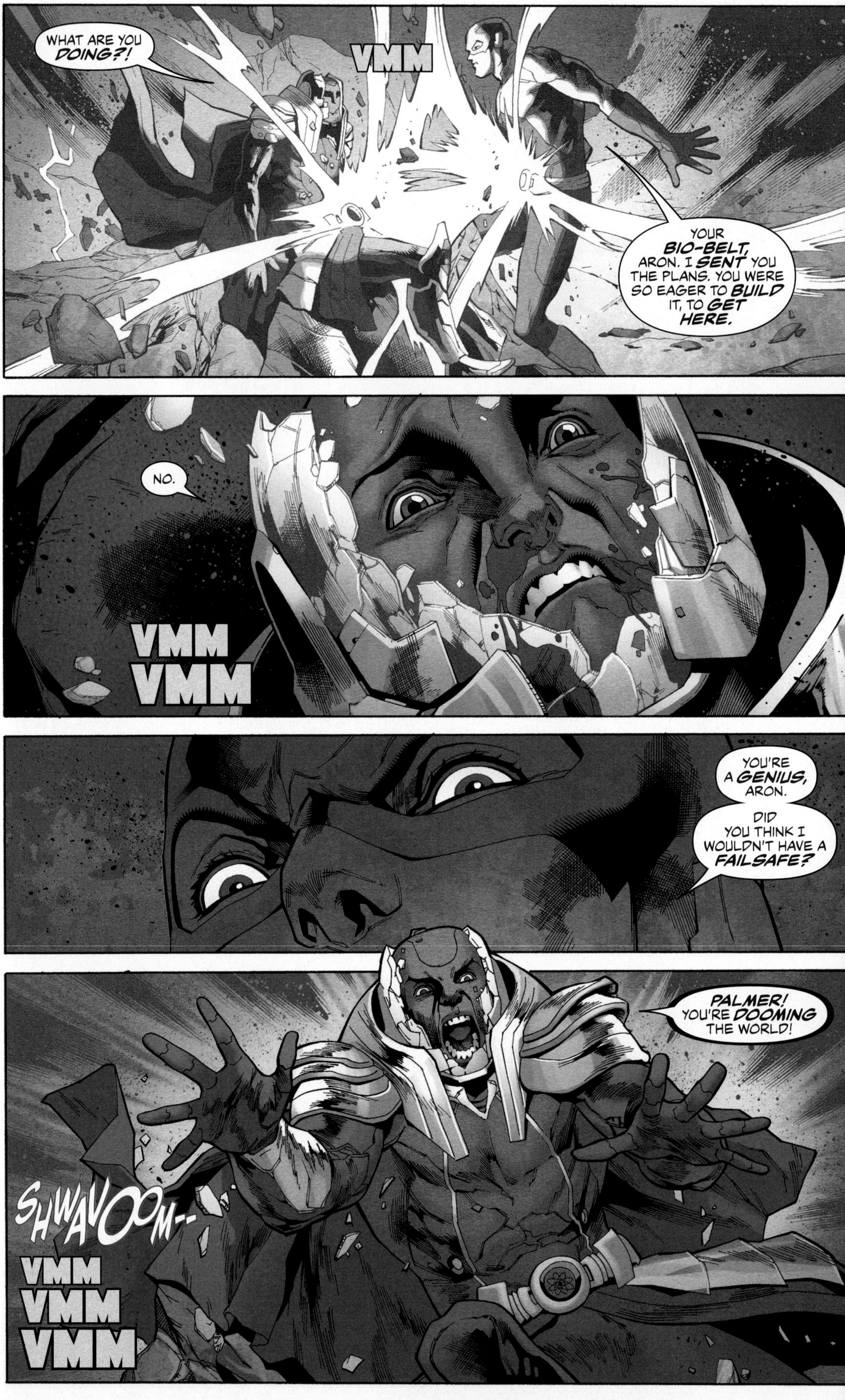

WHAT ARE YOU DOING?!
VMM
YOUR BIO-BELT, ARON. I SENT YOU THE PLANS. YOU WERE SO EAGER TO BUILD IT, TO GET HERE.
NO.
VMM VMM
YOU'RE A GENIUS, ARON.
DID YOU THINK I WOULDN'T HAVE A FAILSAFE?
PALMER! YOU'RE DOOMING THE WORLD!
SHWAVOOM--
VMM VMM VMM

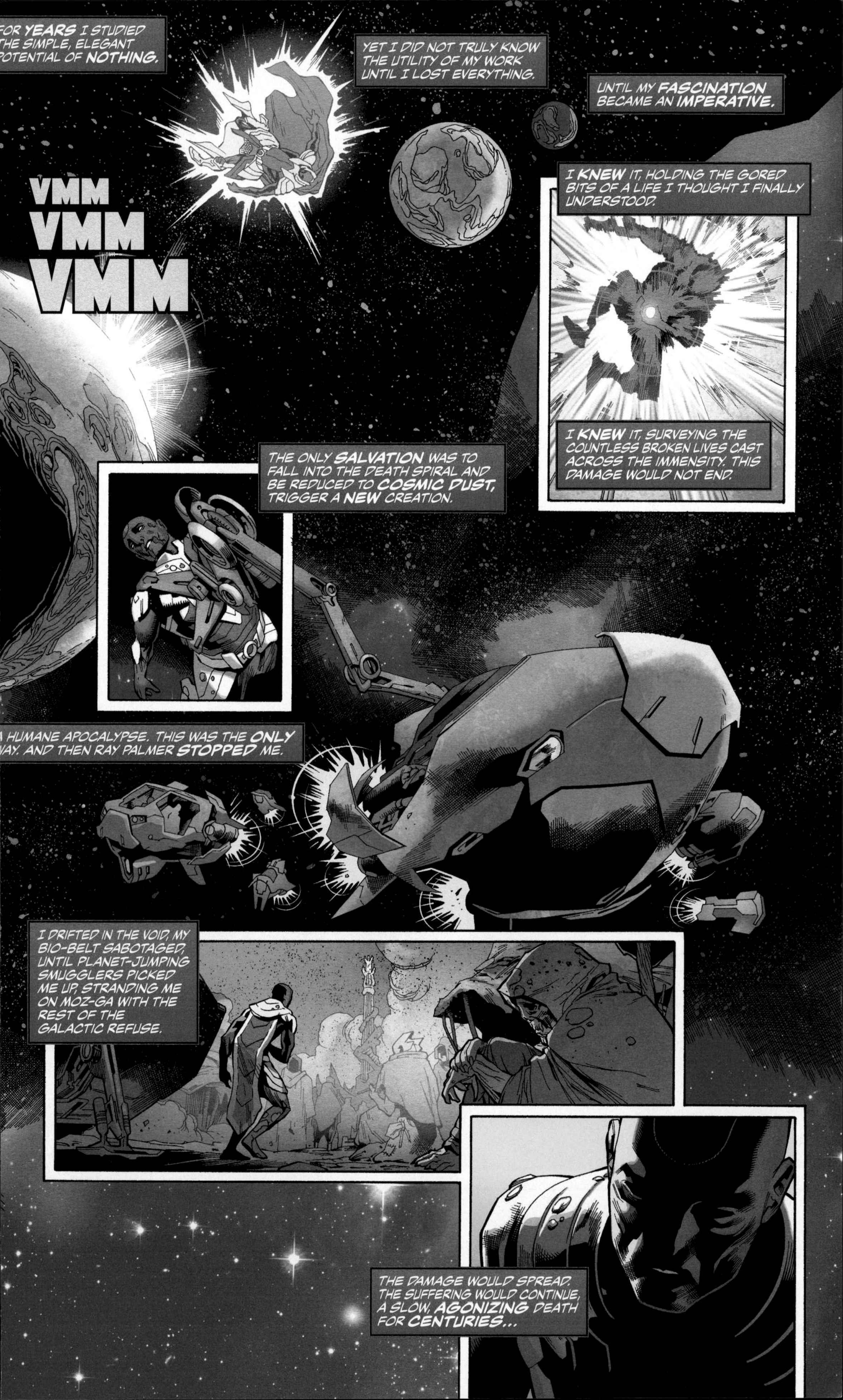

FOR YEARS I STUDIED THE SIMPLE, ELEGANT POTENTIAL OF NOTHING.
YET I DID NOT TRULY KNOW THE UTILITY OF MY WORK UNTIL I LOST EVERYTHING.
UNTIL MY FASCINATION BECAME AN IMPERATIVE.
VMM VMM VMM
I KNEW IT, HOLDING THE GORED BITS OF A LIFE I THOUGHT I FINALLY UNDERSTOOD.
I KNEW IT, SURVEYING THE COUNTLESS BROKEN LIVES CAST ACROSS THE IMMENSITY. THIS DAMAGE WOULD NOT END.
THE ONLY SALVATION WAS TO FALL INTO THE DEATH SPIRAL AND BE REDUCED TO COSMIC DUST, TRIGGER A NEW CREATION.
A HUMANE APOCALYPSE. THIS WAS THE ONLY WAY. AND THEN RAY PALMER STOPPED ME.
I DRIFTED IN THE VOID, MY BIO-BELT SABOTAGED, UNTIL PLANET-JUMPING SMUGGLERS PICKED ME UP, STRANDING ME ON MOZ-GA WITH THE REST OF THE GALACTIC REFUSE.
THE DAMAGE WOULD SPREAD. THE SUFFERING WOULD CONTINUE, A SLOW, AGONIZING DEATH FOR CENTURIES...

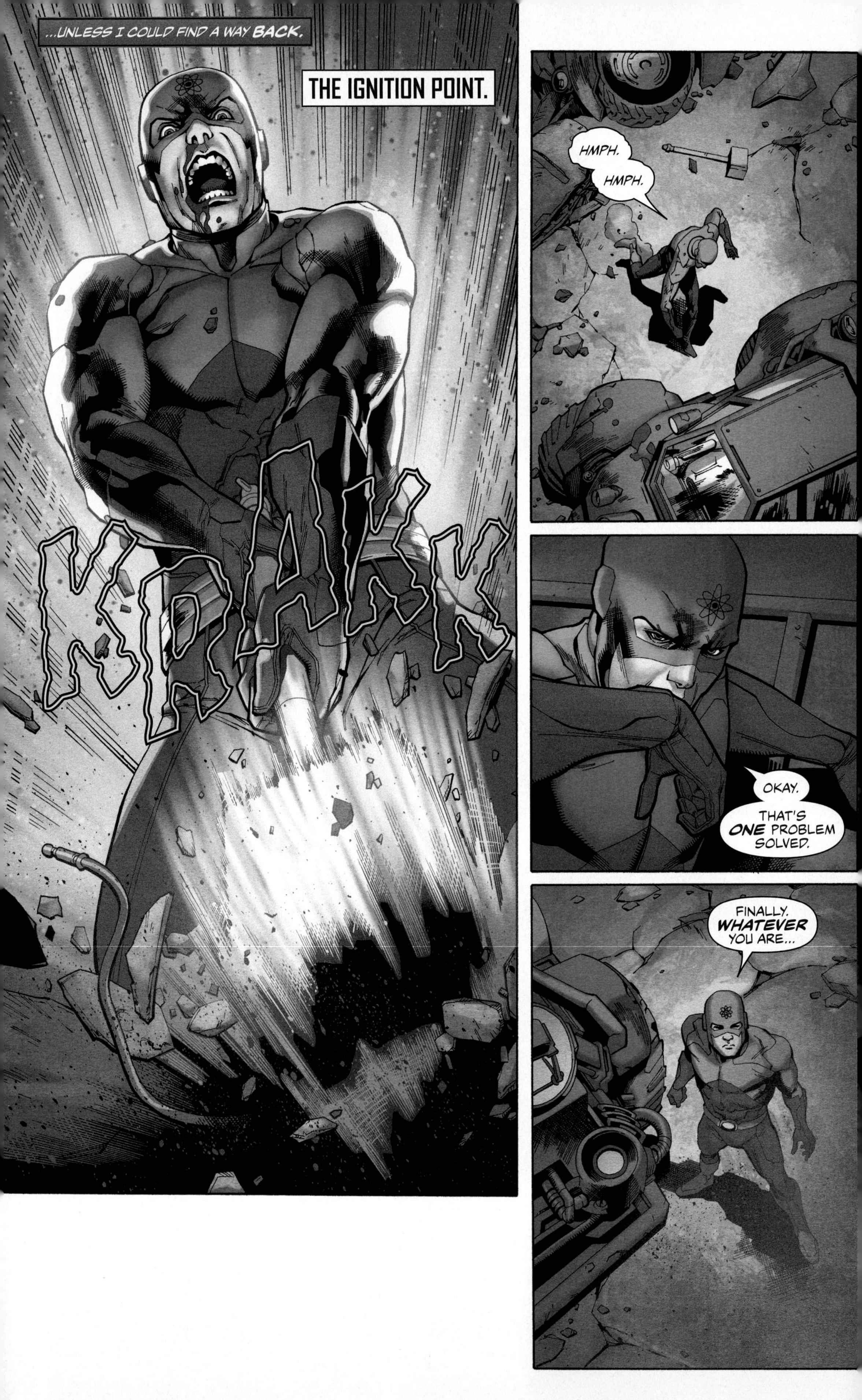
...UNLESS I COULD FIND A WAY BACK.
THE IGNITION POINT.
KRAKK
HMPH.
HMPH.
OKAY.
THAT'S ONE PROBLEM SOLVED.
FINALLY. WHATEVER YOU ARE...

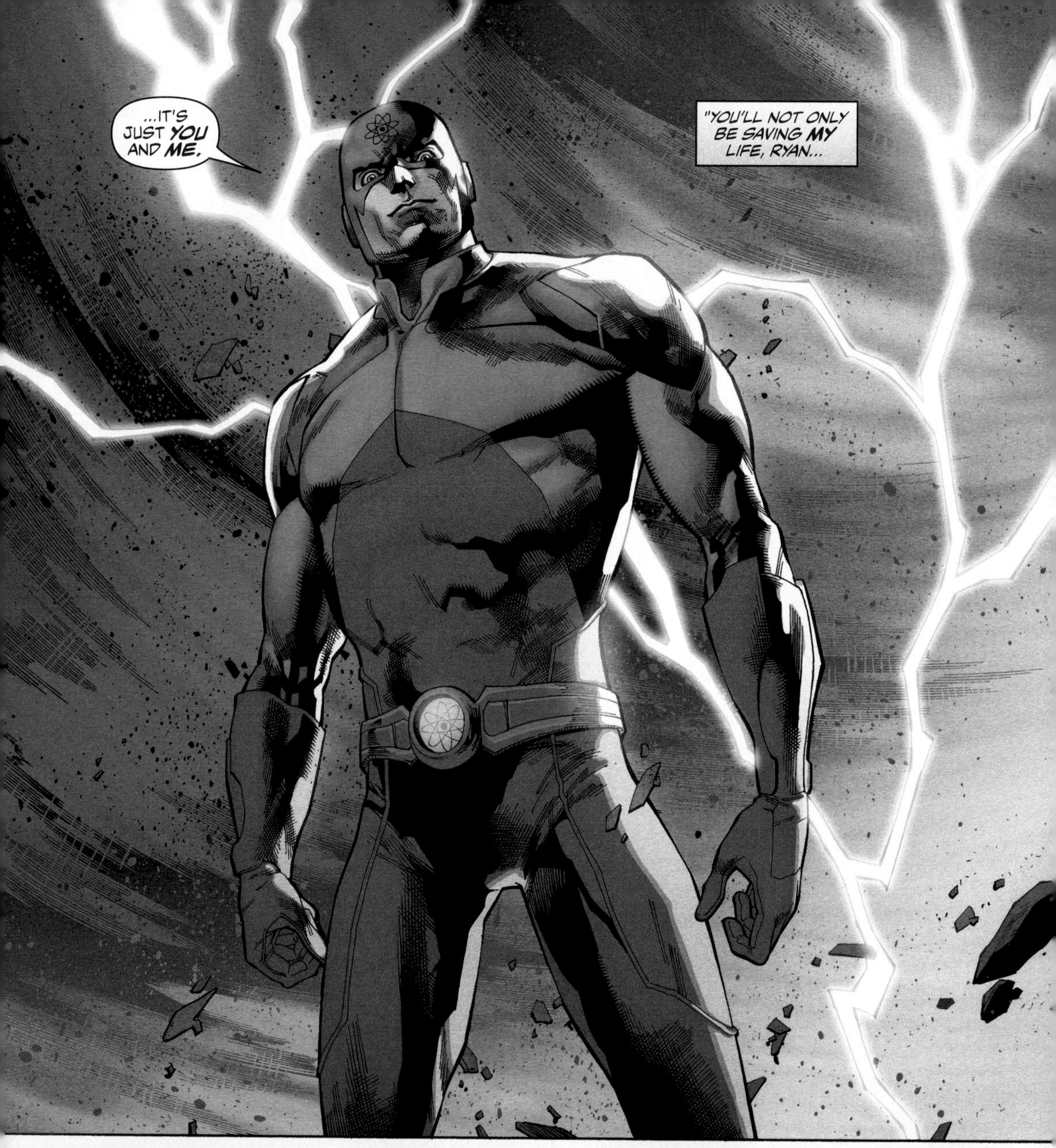
...IT'S JUST YOU AND ME.
"YOU'LL NOT ONLY BE SAVING MY LIFE, RYAN...

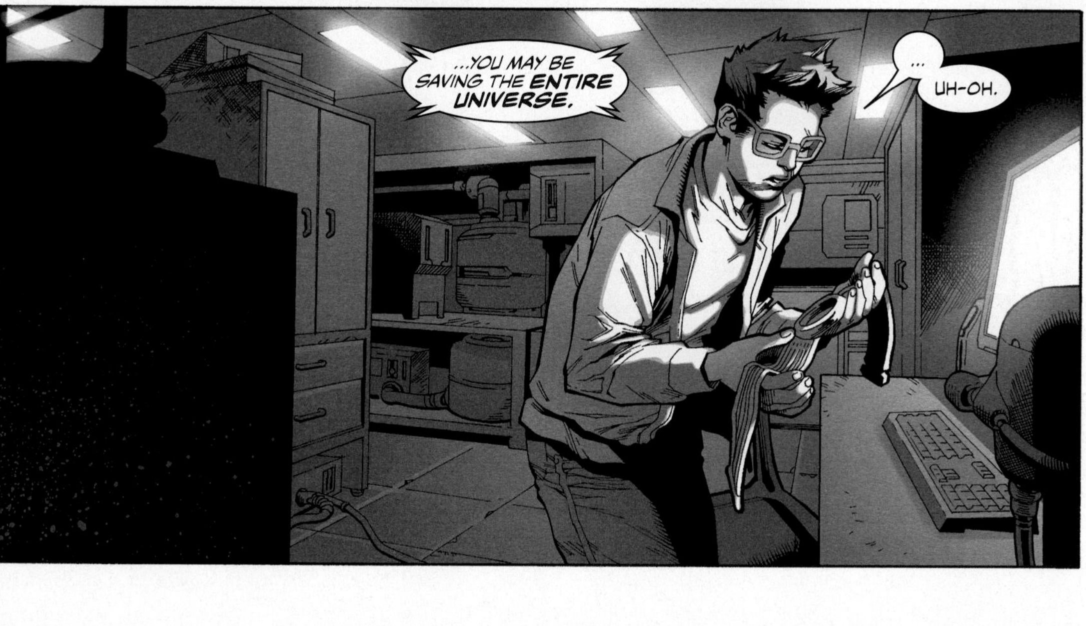
...YOU MAY BE SAVING THE ENTIRE UNIVERSE.
...
UH-OH.

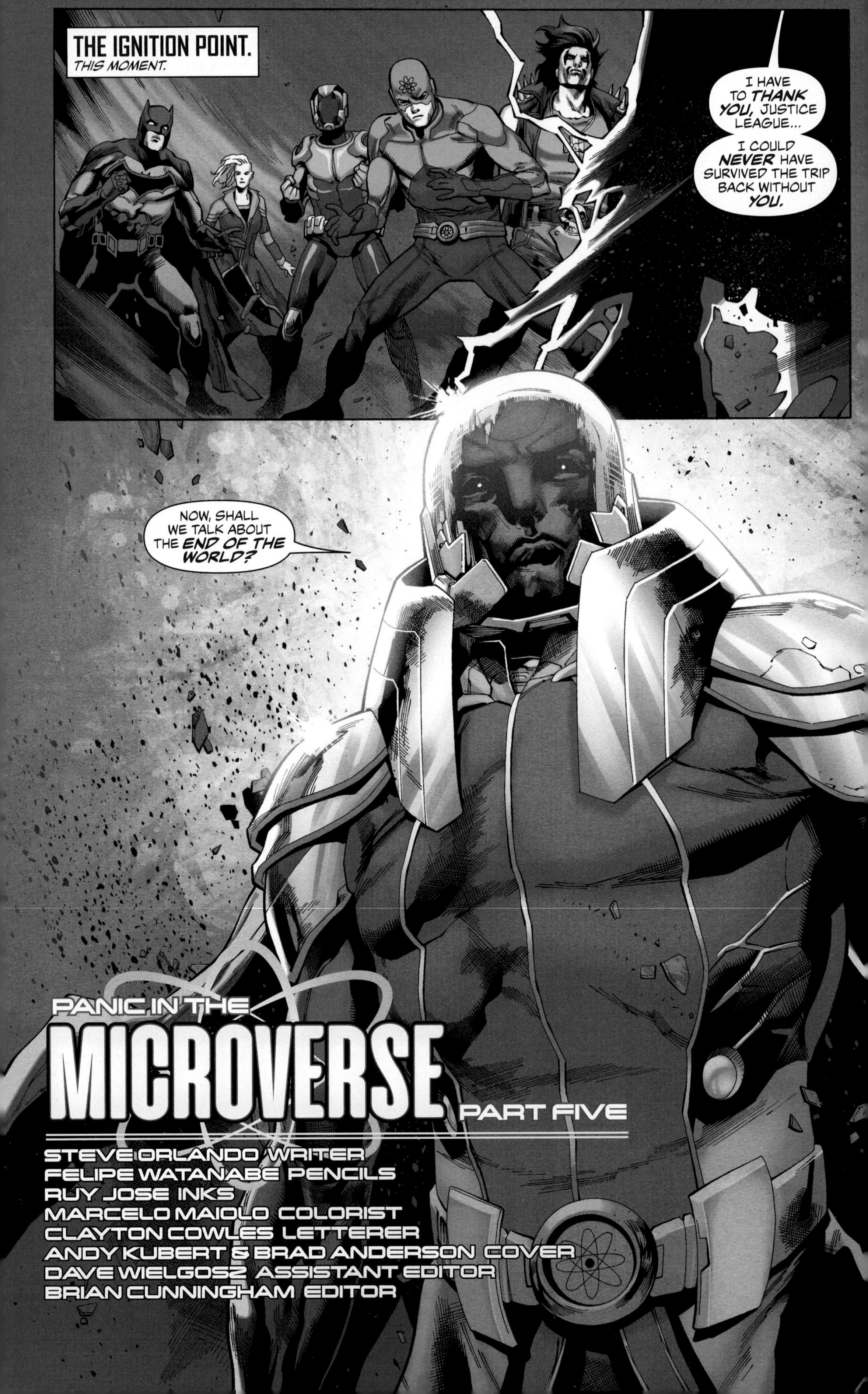
THE IGNITION POINT.
THIS MOMENT.
I HAVE TO THANK YOU, JUSTICE LEAGUE...
I COULD NEVER HAVE SURVIVED THE TRIP BACK WITHOUT YOU.
NOW, SHALL WE TALK ABOUT THE END OF THE WORLD?
PANIC IN THE MICROVERSE PART FIVE
STEVE ORLANDO WRITER
FELIPE WATANABE PENCILS
RUY JOSE INKS
MARCELO MAIOLO COLORIST
CLAYTON COWLES LETTERER
ANDY KUBERT & BRAD ANDERSON COVER
DAVE WIELGOSZ ASSISTANT EDITOR
BRIAN CUNNINGHAM EDITOR

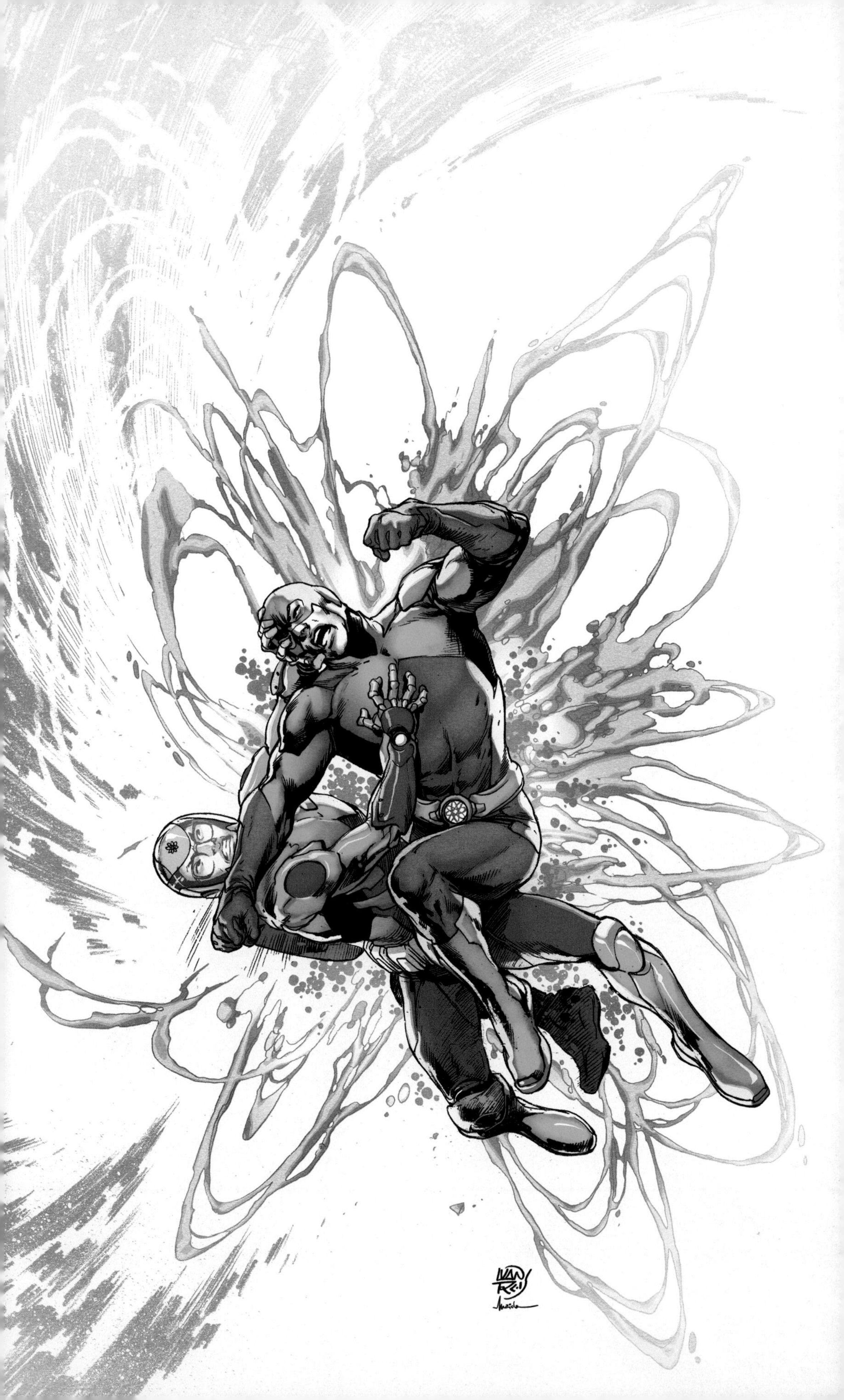

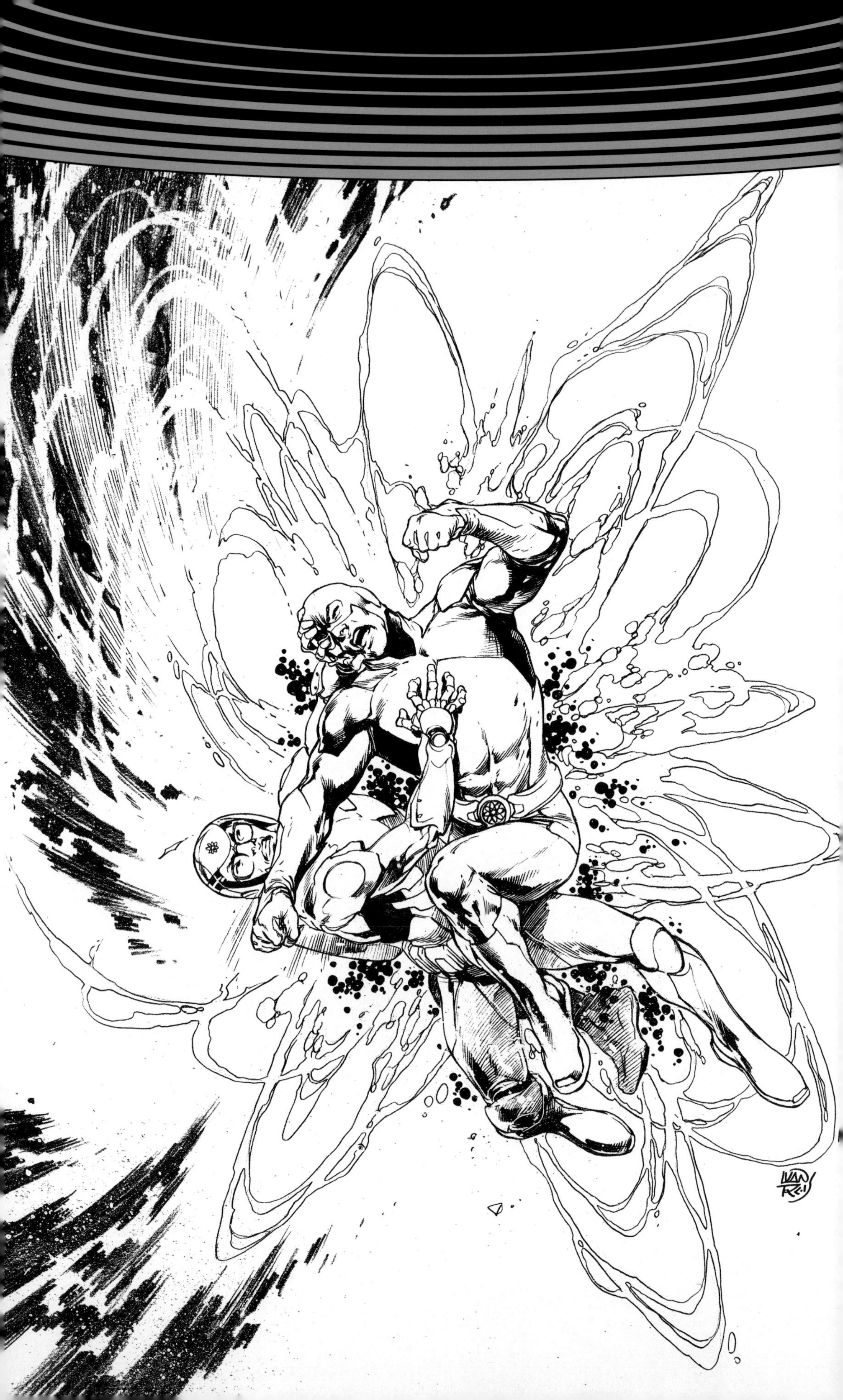

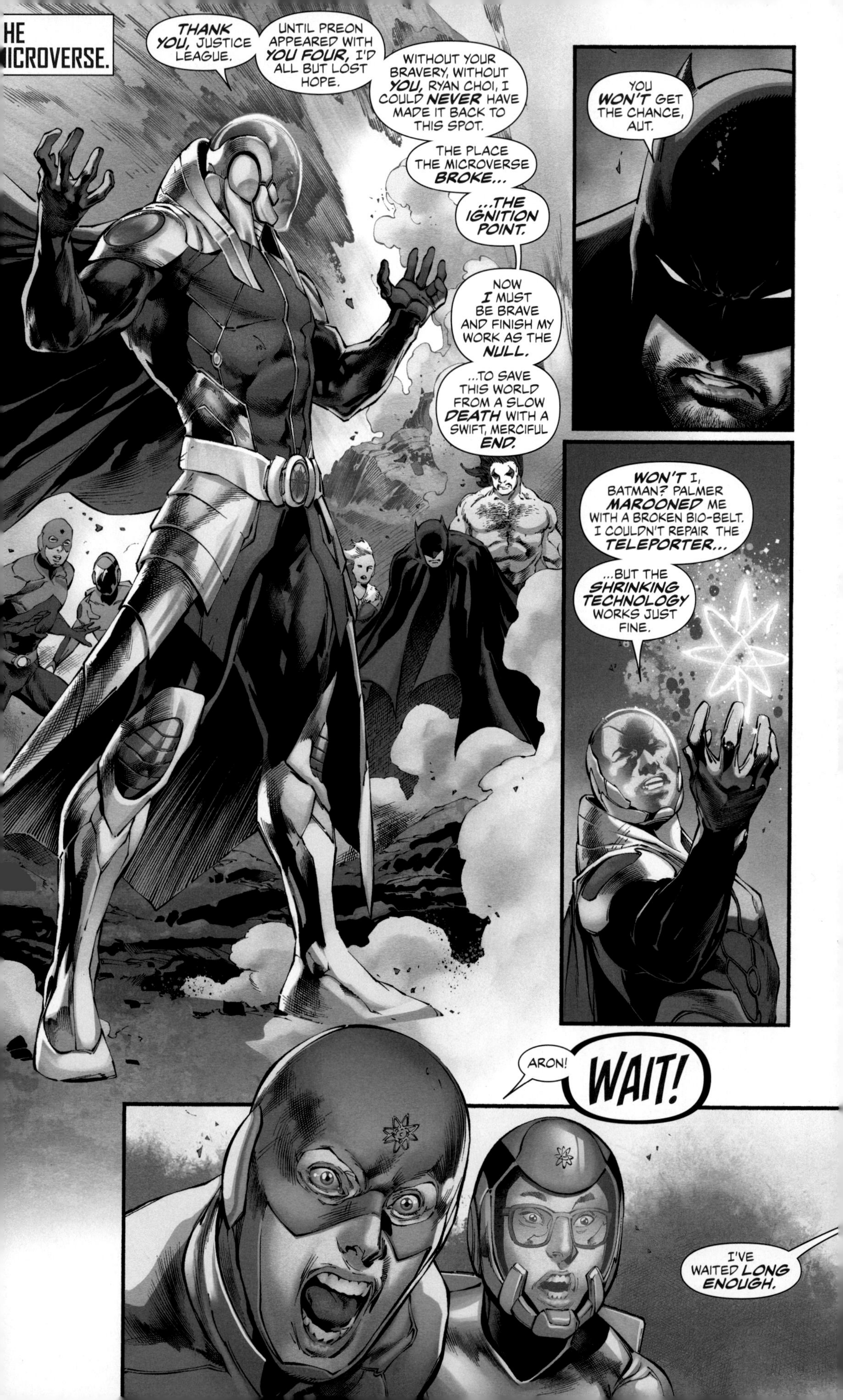
HE
ICROVERSE.
THANK YOU, JUSTICE LEAGUE.
UNTIL PREON APPEARED WITH YOU FOUR, I'D ALL BUT LOST HOPE.
WITHOUT YOUR BRAVERY, WITHOUT YOU, RYAN CHOI, I COULD NEVER HAVE MADE IT BACK TO THIS SPOT.
THE PLACE THE MICROVERSE BROKE...
...THE IGNITION POINT.
NOW I MUST BE BRAVE AND FINISH MY WORK AS THE NULL.
...TO SAVE THIS WORLD FROM A SLOW DEATH WITH A SWIFT, MERCIFUL END.
YOU WON'T GET THE CHANCE, AUT.
WON'T I, BATMAN? PALMER MAROONED ME WITH A BROKEN BIO-BELT. I COULDN'T REPAIR THE TELEPORTER...
...BUT THE SHRINKING TECHNOLOGY WORKS JUST FINE.
ARON!
WAIT!
I'VE WAITED LONG ENOUGH.

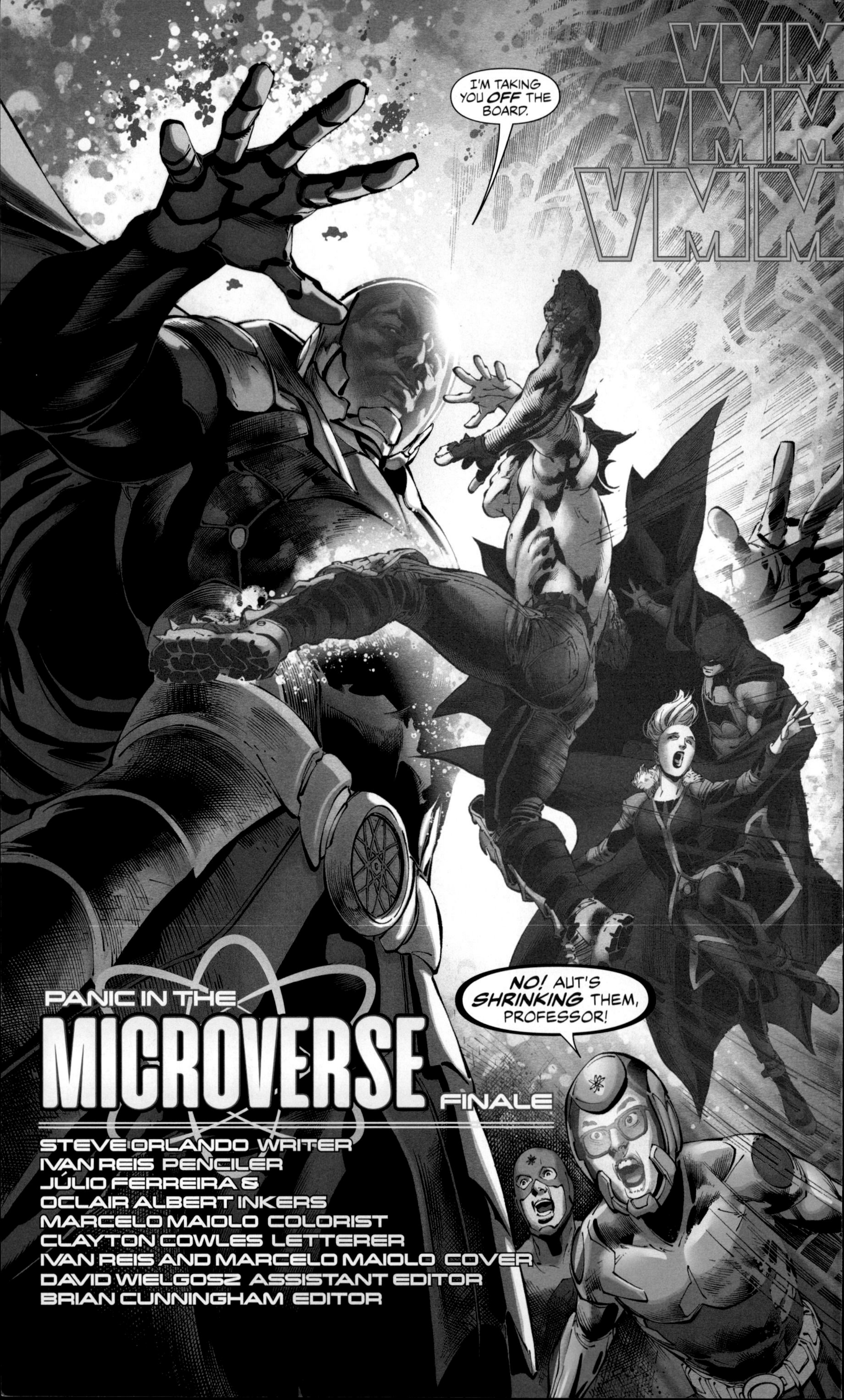
VMM
VMM
VMM
I'M TAKING YOU OFF THE BOARD.
NO! AUT'S SHRINKING THEM, PROFESSOR!
PANIC IN THE
MICROVERSE
FINALE
STEVE ORLANDO WRITER
IVAN REIS PENCILER
JÚLIO FERREIRA &
OCLAIR ALBERT INKERS
MARCELO MAIOLO COLORIST
CLAYTON COWLES LETTERER
IVAN REIS AND MARCELO MAIOLO COVER
DAVID WIELGOSZ ASSISTANT EDITOR
BRIAN CUNNINGHAM EDITOR

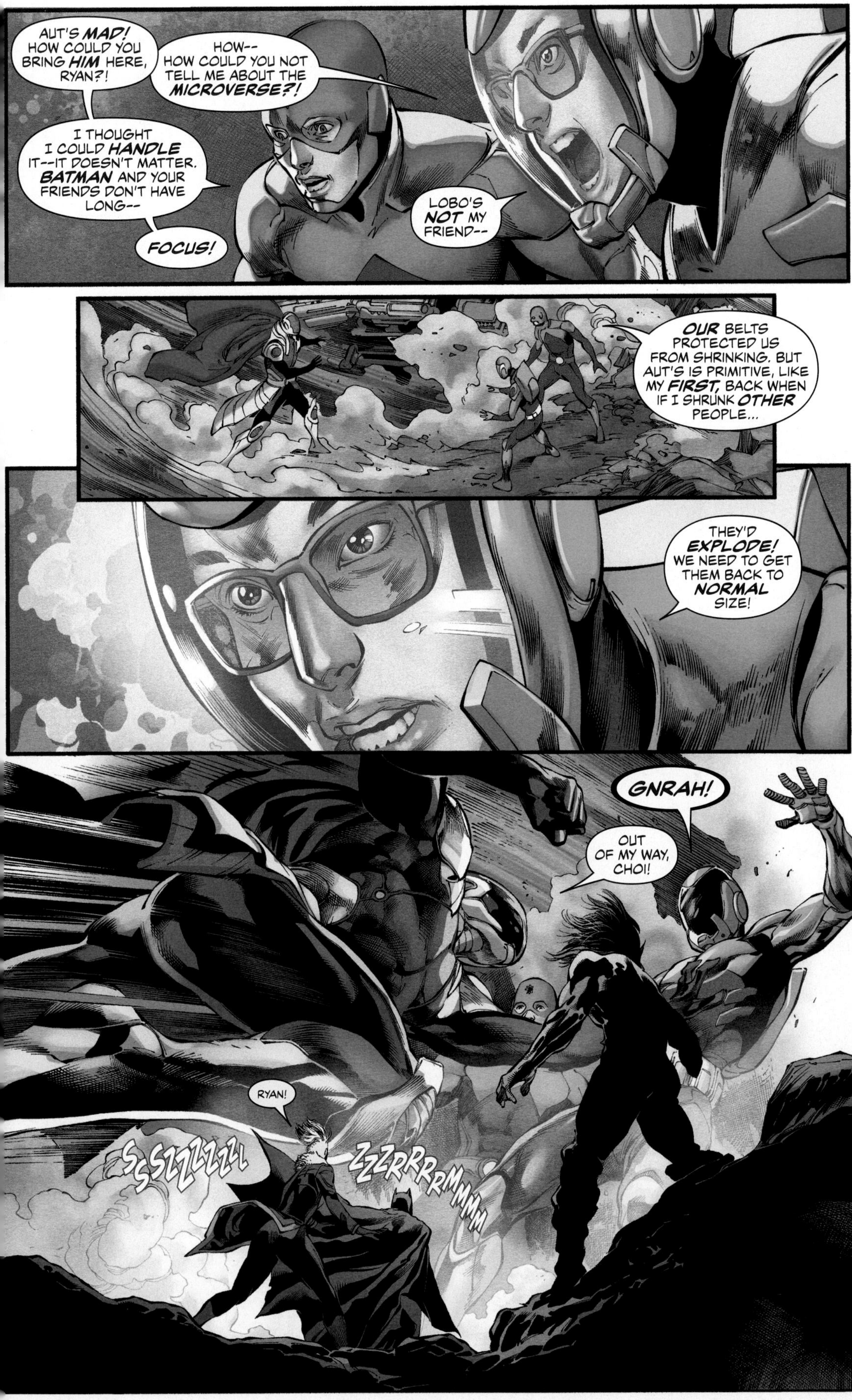
AUT'S MAD! HOW COULD YOU BRING HIM HERE, RYAN?!
HOW-- HOW COULD YOU NOT TELL ME ABOUT THE MICROVERSE?!
I THOUGHT I COULD HANDLE IT--IT DOESN'T MATTER. BATMAN AND YOUR FRIENDS DON'T HAVE LONG--
LOBO'S NOT MY FRIEND--
FOCUS!
OUR BELTS PROTECTED US FROM SHRINKING. BUT AUT'S IS PRIMITIVE, LIKE MY FIRST, BACK WHEN IF I SHRUNK OTHER PEOPLE...
THEY'D EXPLODE! WE NEED TO GET THEM BACK TO NORMAL SIZE!
GNRAH!
OUT OF MY WAY, CHOI!
RYAN!
SSSZZZZZZ
ZZZRRRRRMMMM

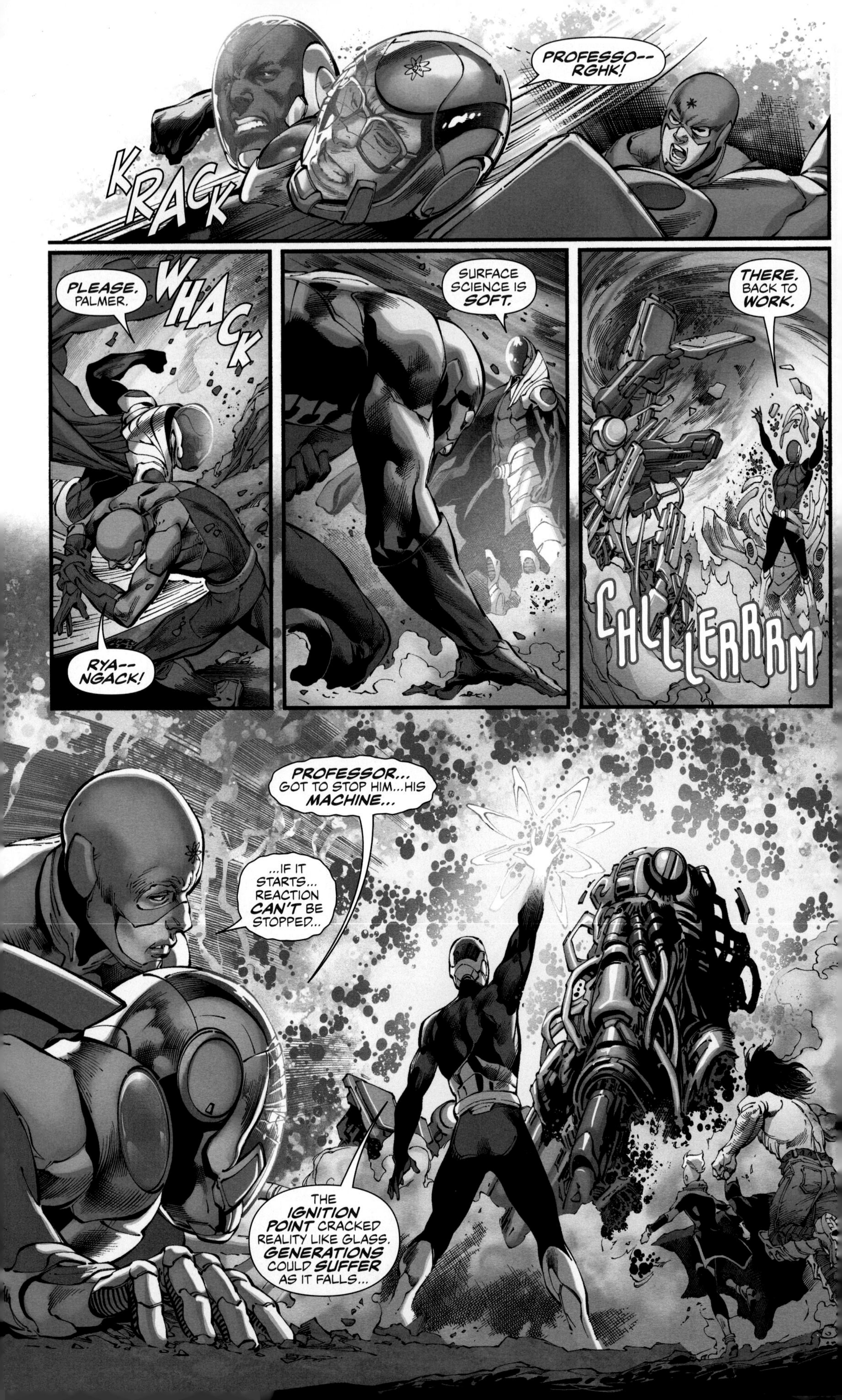
PROFESSO-- RGHK!
KRACK
PLEASE. PALMER.
WHACK
RYA-- NGACK!
SURFACE SCIENCE IS SOFT.
THERE. BACK TO WORK.
CHLLLERRRRM
PROFESSOR... GOT TO STOP HIM...HIS MACHINE...
...IF IT STARTS... REACTION CAN'T BE STOPPED...
THE IGNITION POINT CRACKED REALITY LIKE GLASS. GENERATIONS COULD SUFFER AS IT FALLS...

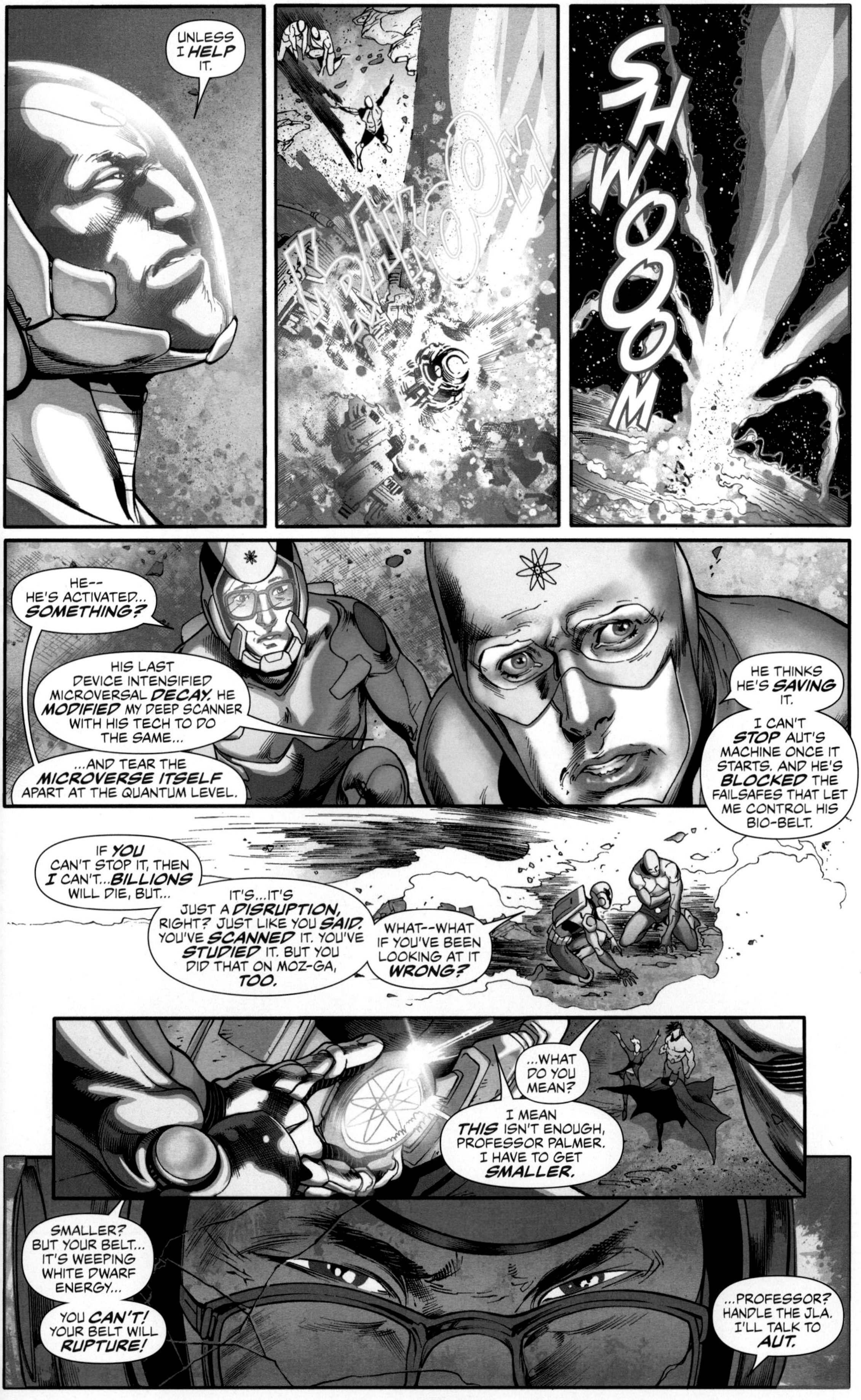

UNLESS I HELP IT.
KRAKOOOM
SHWOOOM
HE-- HE'S ACTIVATED... SOMETHING?
HIS LAST DEVICE INTENSIFIED MICROVERSAL DECAY. HE MODIFIED MY DEEP SCANNER WITH HIS TECH TO DO THE SAME...
...AND TEAR THE MICROVERSE ITSELF APART AT THE QUANTUM LEVEL.
HE THINKS HE'S SAVING IT.
I CAN'T STOP AUT'S MACHINE ONCE IT STARTS. AND HE'S BLOCKED THE FAILSAFES THAT LET ME CONTROL HIS BIO-BELT.
IF YOU CAN'T STOP IT, THEN I CAN'T...BILLIONS WILL DIE, BUT...
IT'S...IT'S JUST A DISRUPTION, RIGHT? JUST LIKE YOU SAID. YOU'VE SCANNED IT. YOU'VE STUDIED IT. BUT YOU DID THAT ON MOZ-GA, TOO.
WHAT--WHAT IF YOU'VE BEEN LOOKING AT IT WRONG?
...WHAT DO YOU MEAN?
I MEAN THIS ISN'T ENOUGH, PROFESSOR PALMER. I HAVE TO GET SMALLER.
SMALLER? BUT YOUR BELT... IT'S WEEPING WHITE DWARF ENERGY...
YOU CAN'T! YOUR BELT WILL RUPTURE!
...PROFESSOR? HANDLE THE JLA. I'LL TALK TO AUT.

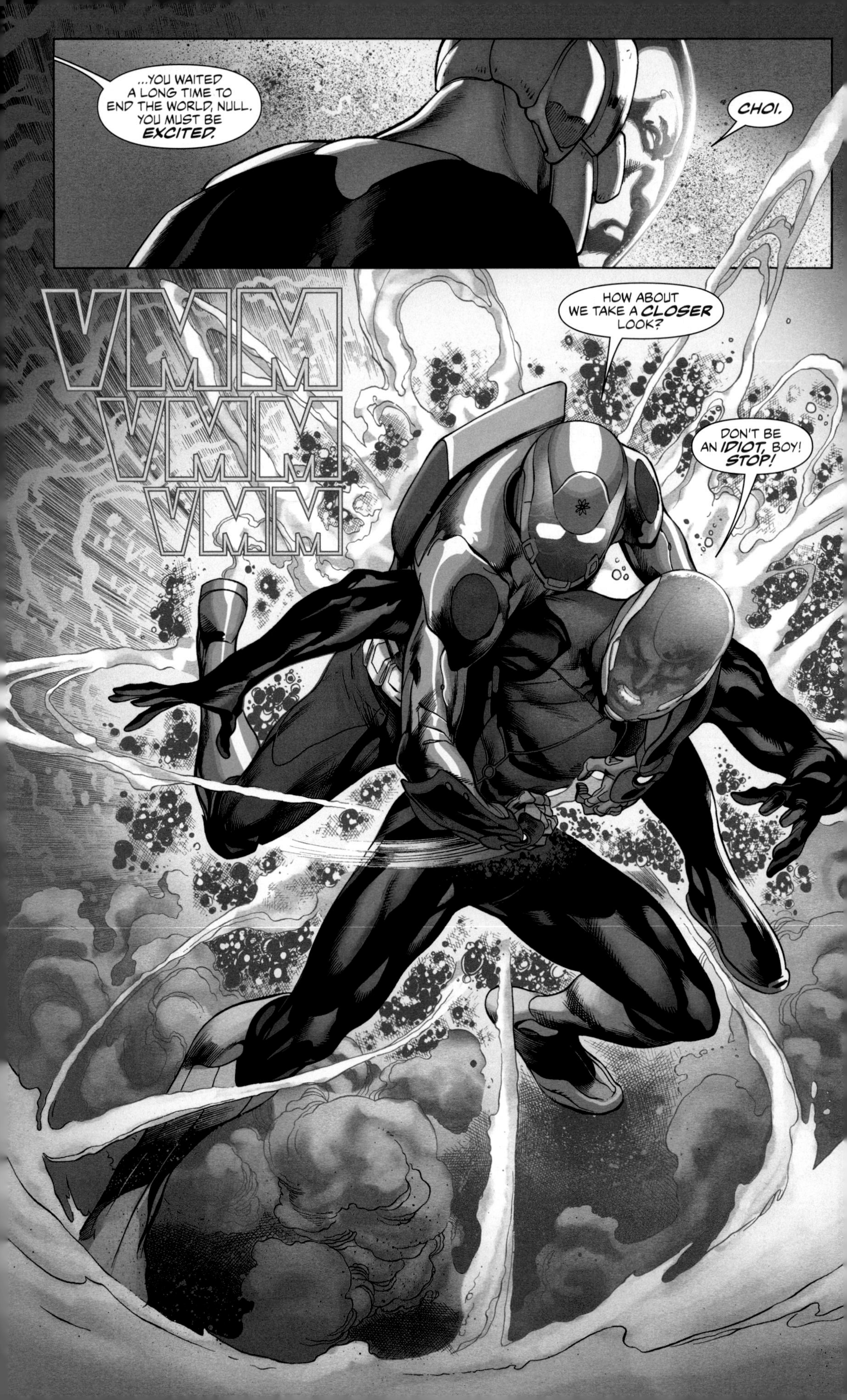

...YOU WAITED A LONG TIME TO END THE WORLD, NULL. YOU MUST BE EXCITED.
CHOI.
VMMM VMMM VMMM
HOW ABOUT WE TAKE A CLOSER LOOK?
DON'T BE AN IDIOT, BOY! STOP!

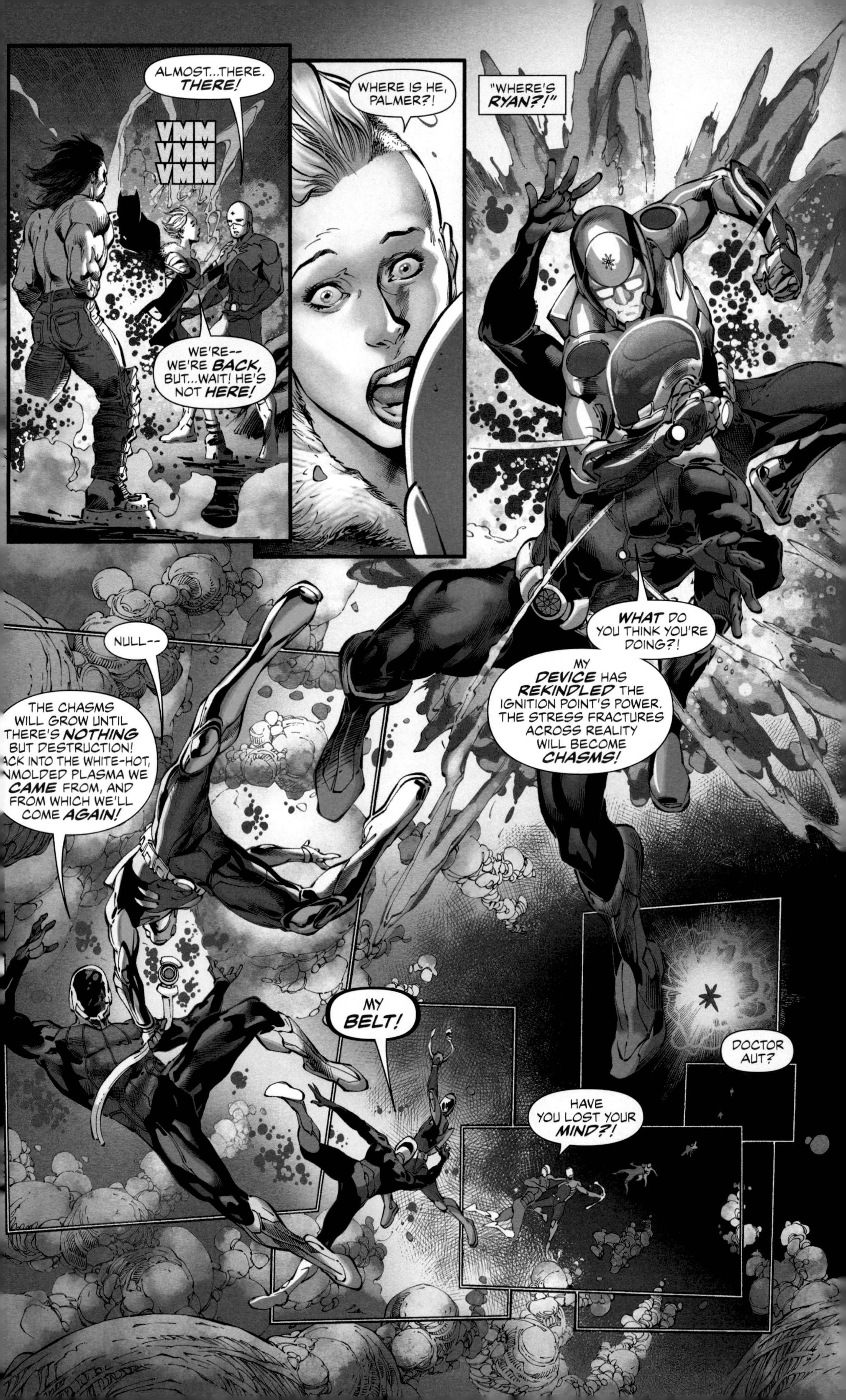
ALMOST...THERE. THERE!
VMM VMM VMM
WE'RE-- WE'RE BACK, BUT...WAIT! HE'S NOT HERE!
WHERE IS HE, PALMER?!
"WHERE'S RYAN?!"
WHAT DO YOU THINK YOU'RE DOING?!
MY DEVICE HAS REKINDLED THE IGNITION POINT'S POWER. THE STRESS FRACTURES ACROSS REALITY WILL BECOME CHASMS!
NULL--
THE CHASMS WILL GROW UNTIL THERE'S NOTHING BUT DESTRUCTION!
ACK INTO THE WHITE-HOT, NMOLDED PLASMA WE CAME FROM, AND FROM WHICH WE'LL COME AGAIN!
MY BELT!
DOCTOR AUT?
HAVE YOU LOST YOUR MIND?!

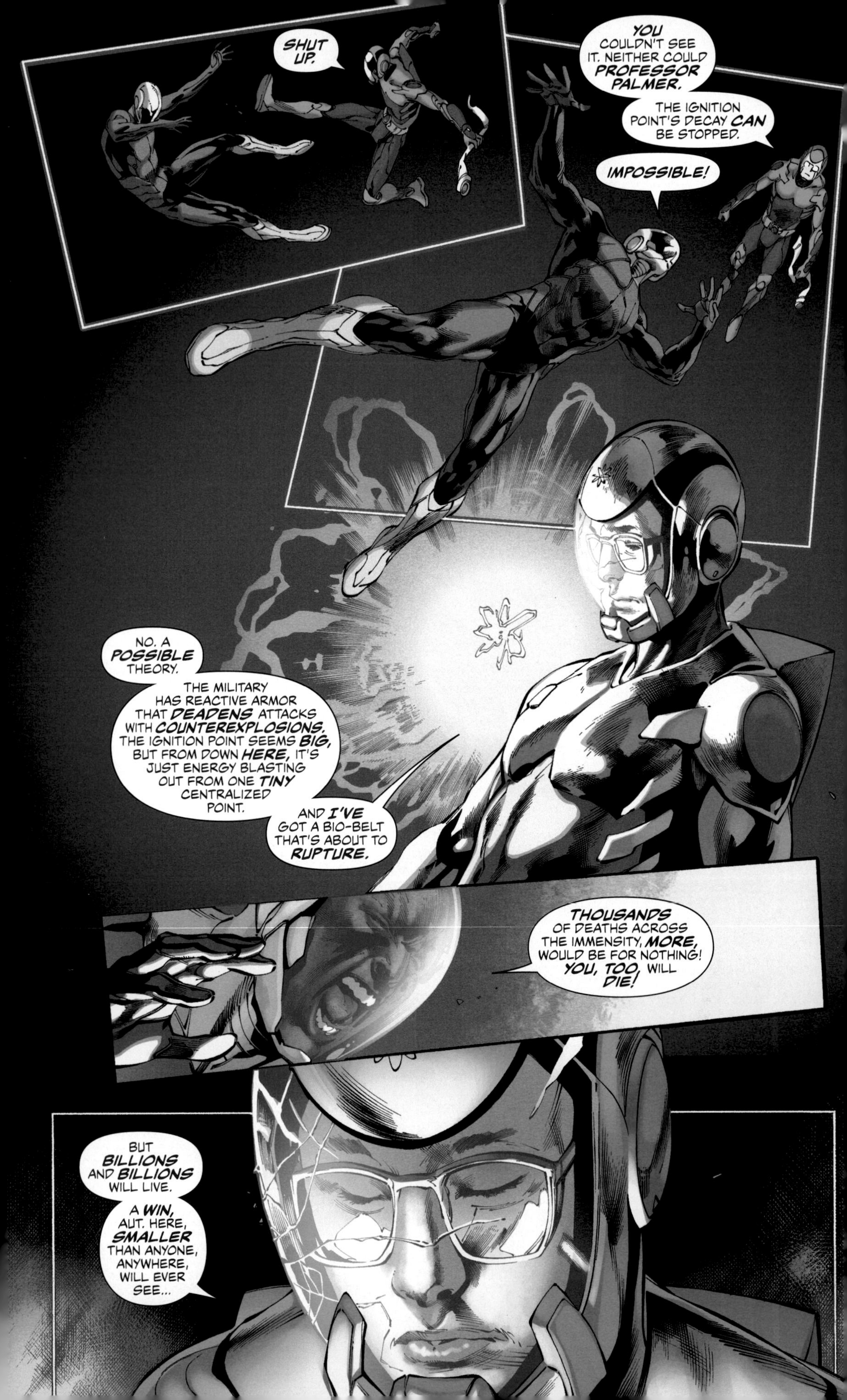
SHUT UP.
YOU COULDN'T SEE IT. NEITHER COULD PROFESSOR PALMER.
THE IGNITION POINT'S DECAY CAN BE STOPPED.
IMPOSSIBLE!
NO. A POSSIBLE THEORY.
THE MILITARY HAS REACTIVE ARMOR THAT DEADENS ATTACKS WITH COUNTEREXPLOSIONS. THE IGNITION POINT SEEMS BIG, BUT FROM DOWN HERE, IT'S JUST ENERGY BLASTING OUT FROM ONE TINY CENTRALIZED POINT.
AND I'VE GOT A BIO-BELT THAT'S ABOUT TO RUPTURE.
THOUSANDS OF DEATHS ACROSS THE IMMENSITY, MORE, WOULD BE FOR NOTHING! YOU, TOO, WILL DIE!
BUT BILLIONS AND BILLIONS WILL LIVE.
A WIN, AUT. HERE, SMALLER THAN ANYONE, ANYWHERE, WILL EVER SEE...

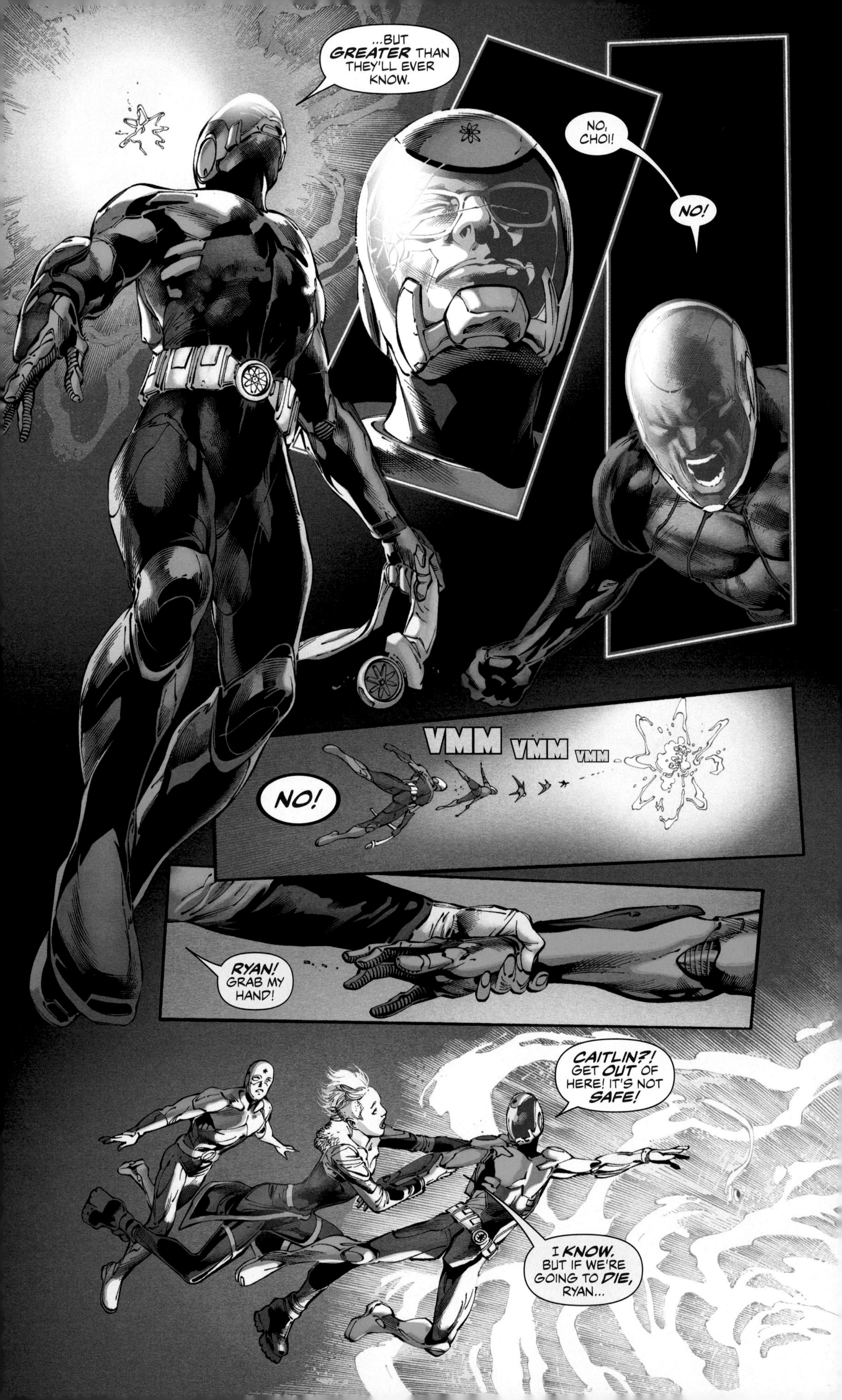
...BUT GREATER THAN THEY'LL EVER KNOW.
NO, CHOI!
NO!
VMM VMM VMM
NO!
RYAN! GRAB MY HAND!
CAITLIN?! GET OUT OF HERE! IT'S NOT SAFE!
I KNOW. BUT IF WE'RE GOING TO DIE, RYAN...

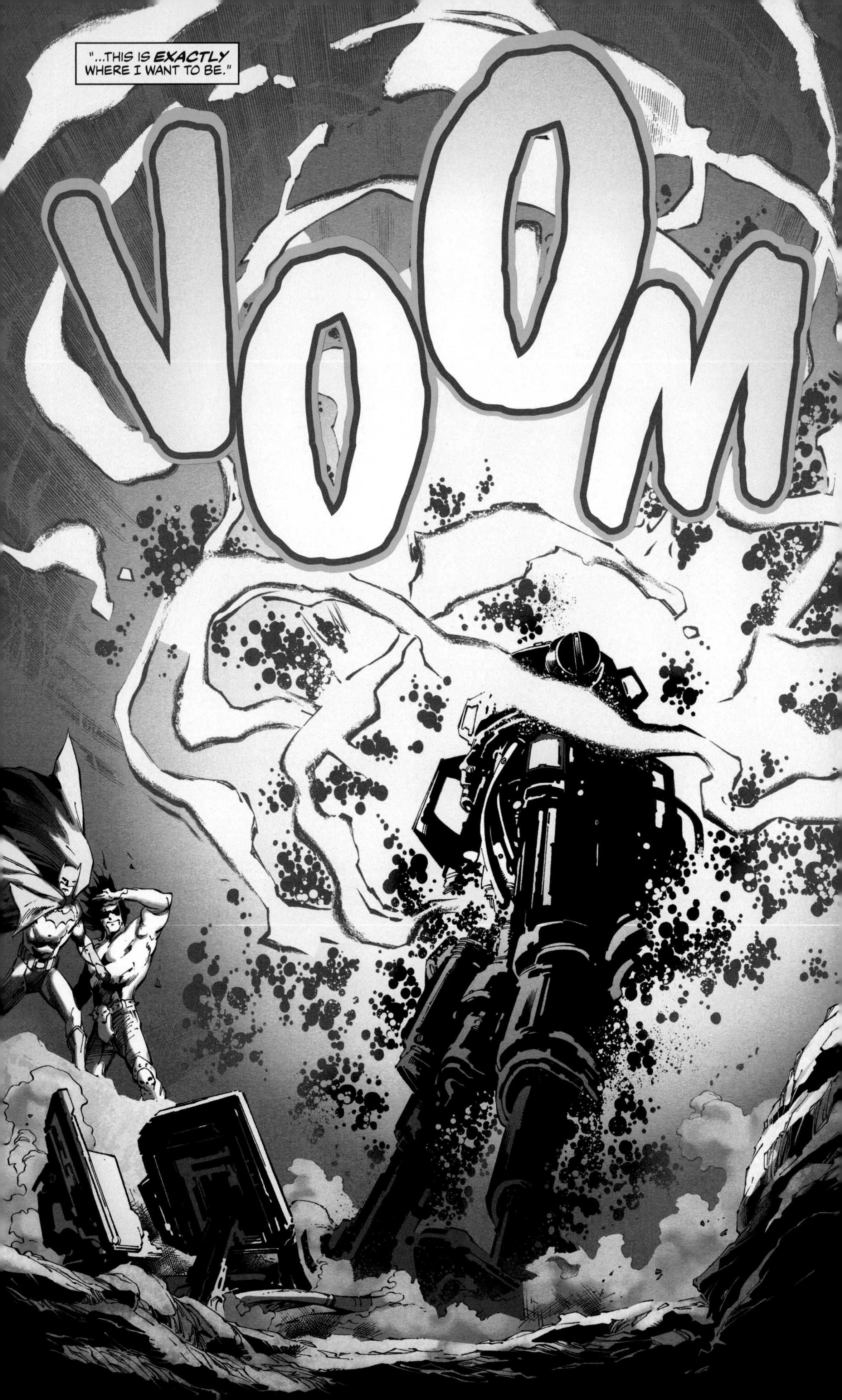
"...THIS IS EXACTLY WHERE I WANT TO BE."
VOOM

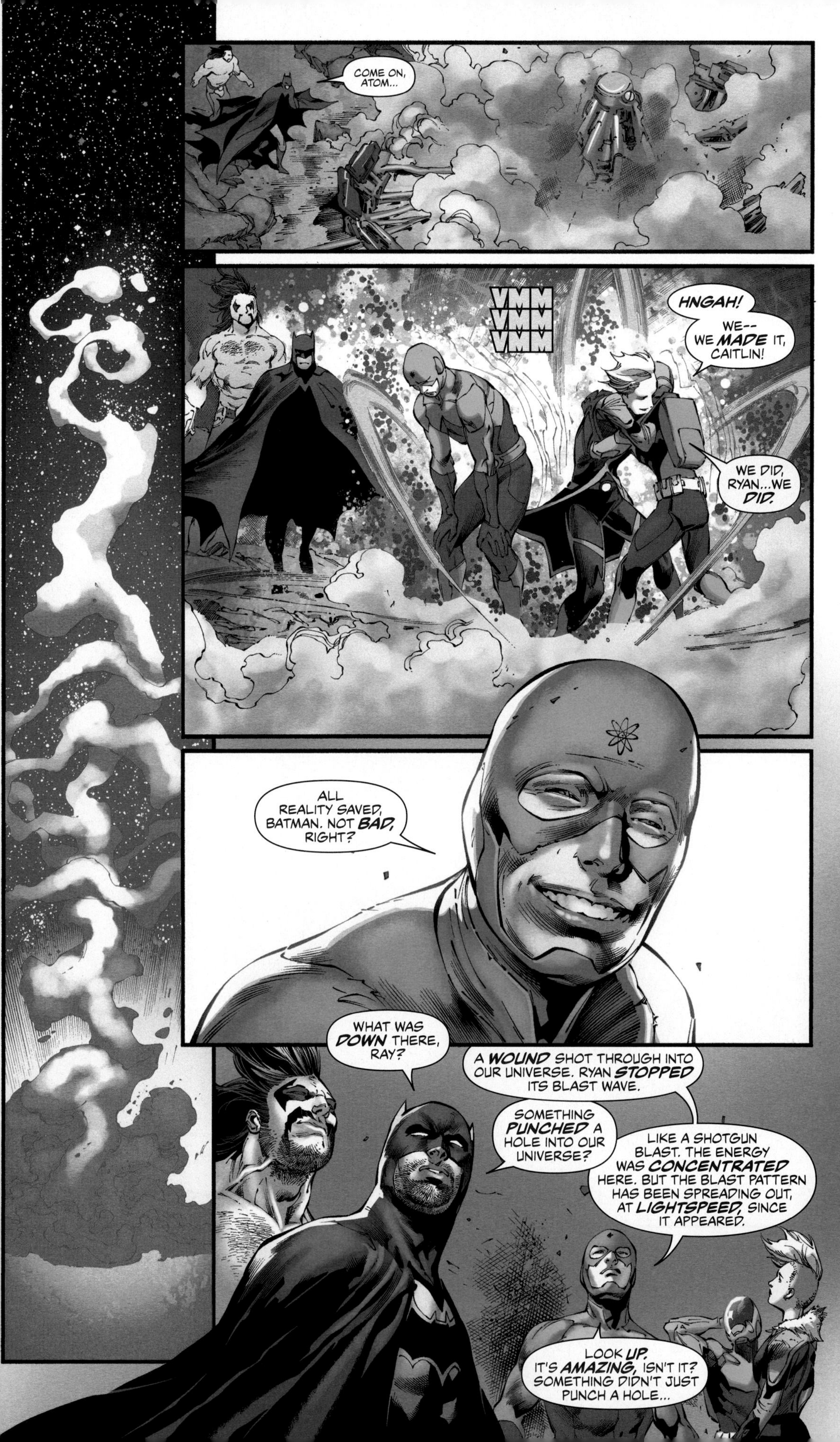
COME ON, ATOM...
VMM VMM VMM
HNGAH!
WE-- WE MADE IT, CAITLIN!
WE DID, RYAN...WE DID.
ALL REALITY SAVED, BATMAN. NOT BAD, RIGHT?
WHAT WAS DOWN THERE, RAY?
A WOUND SHOT THROUGH INTO OUR UNIVERSE. RYAN STOPPED ITS BLAST WAVE.
SOMETHING PUNCHED A HOLE INTO OUR UNIVERSE?
LIKE A SHOTGUN BLAST. THE ENERGY WAS CONCENTRATED HERE. BUT THE BLAST PATTERN HAS BEEN SPREADING OUT, AT LIGHTSPEED, SINCE IT APPEARED.
LOOK UP. IT'S AMAZING, ISN'T IT? SOMETHING DIDN'T JUST PUNCH A HOLE...

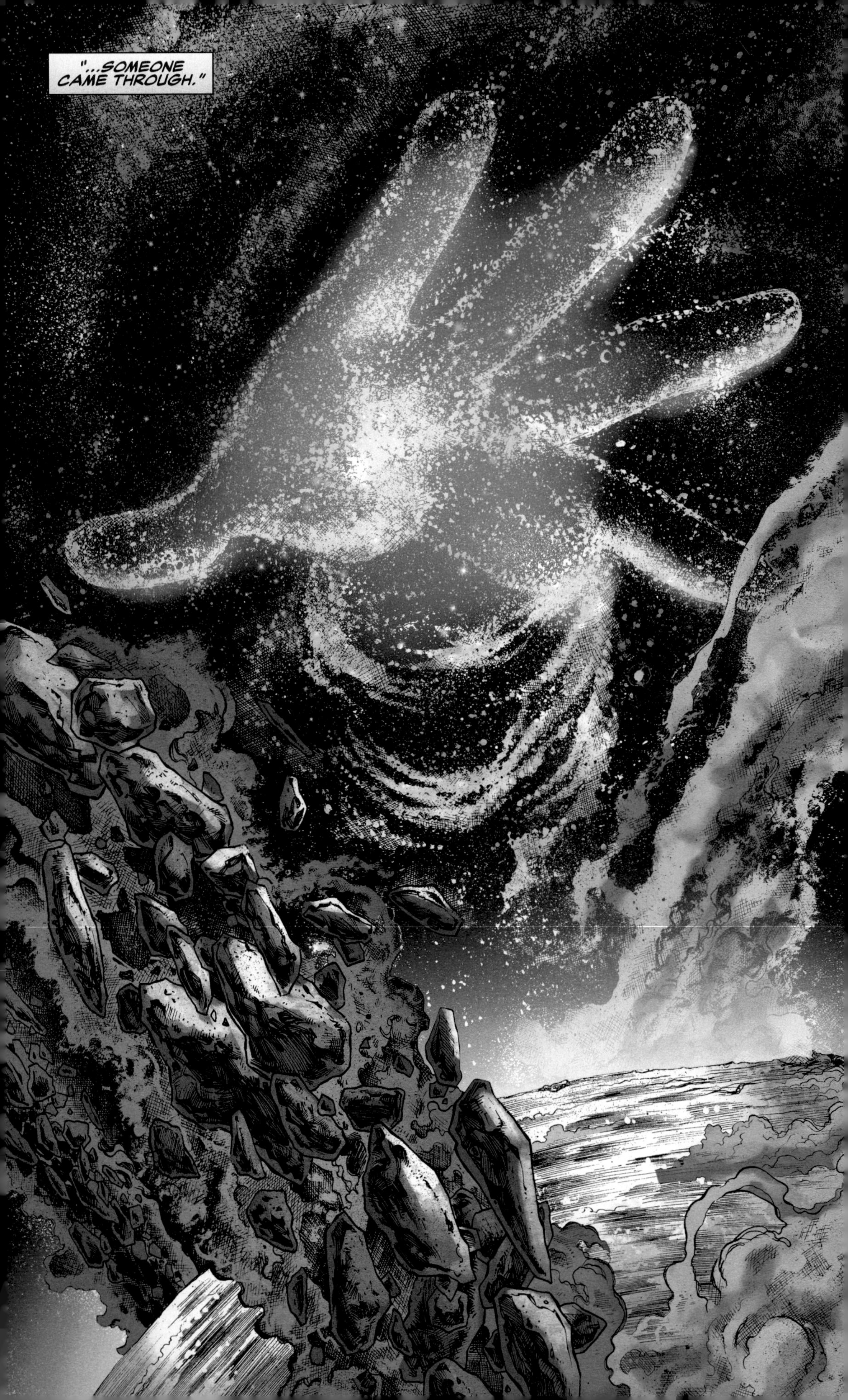
"...SOMEONE CAME THROUGH."

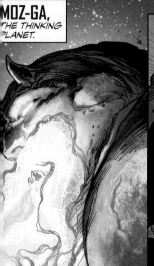

MOZ-GA, THE THINKING PLANET.

PREON!

CAREFUL, RAYMOND PALMER. I *JUST* SURVIVED A *STASIS BLAST.* I'M NOT *UNSORE.*

I THINK I CAN *CURE* THAT.

PROFESSOR PALMER... I'M *SORRY* IT TOOK SO LONG. I *LOOKED* FOR YOU. I *DID.* I COULDN'T FIND THE *TETHER SIGNAL* UNTIL PREON'S *BIO-BELT* WAS IN RANGE.

NO, RYAN... I SHOULD HAVE *TOLD* YOU.

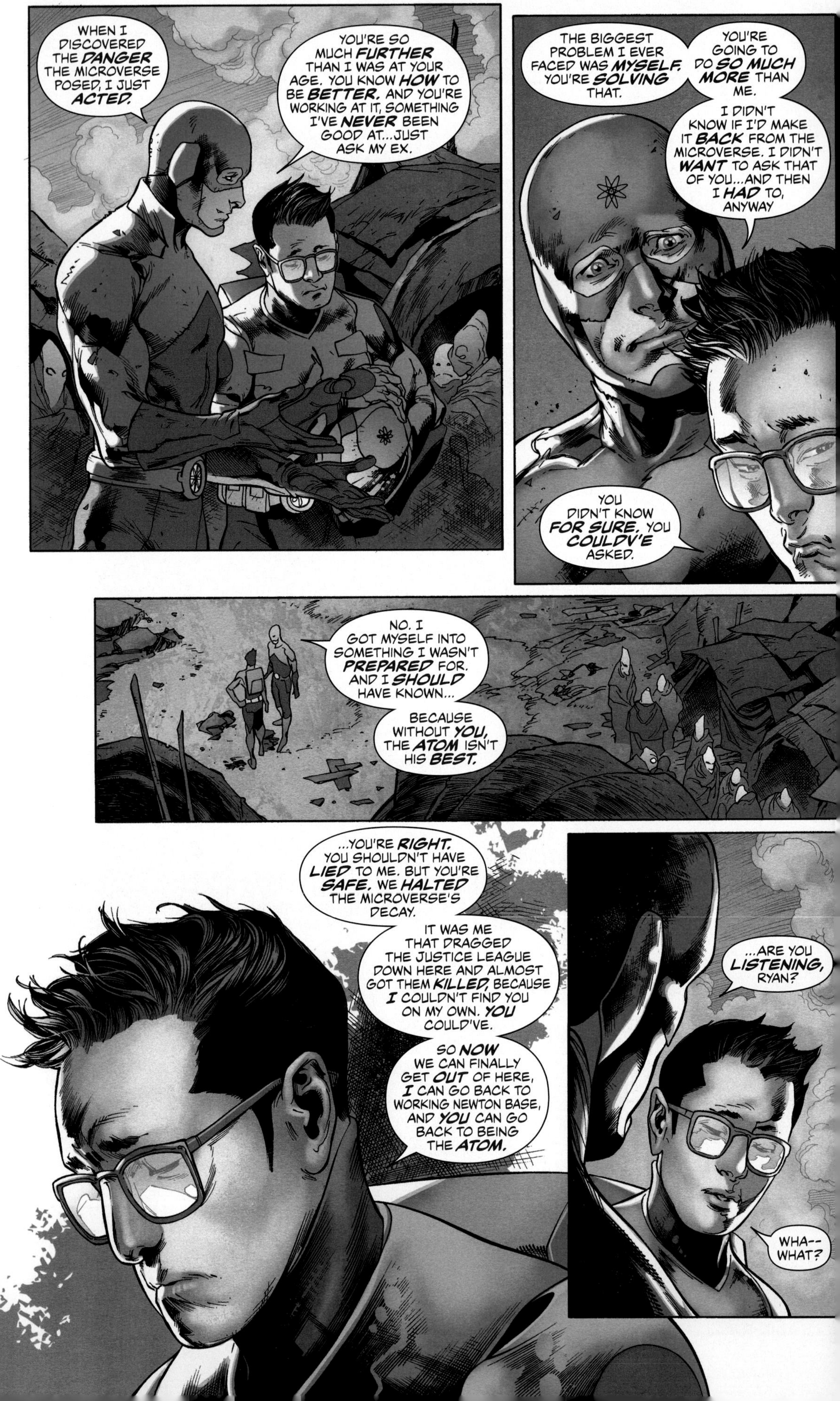
WHEN I DISCOVERED THE DANGER THE MICROVERSE POSED, I JUST ACTED.
YOU'RE SO MUCH FURTHER THAN I WAS AT YOUR AGE. YOU KNOW HOW TO BE BETTER. AND YOU'RE WORKING AT IT, SOMETHING I'VE NEVER BEEN GOOD AT...JUST ASK MY EX.
THE BIGGEST PROBLEM I EVER FACED WAS MYSELF. YOU'RE SOLVING THAT.
YOU'RE GOING TO DO SO MUCH MORE THAN ME.
I DIDN'T KNOW IF I'D MAKE IT BACK FROM THE MICROVERSE. I DIDN'T WANT TO ASK THAT OF YOU...AND THEN I HAD TO, ANYWAY
YOU DIDN'T KNOW FOR SURE. YOU COULDV'E ASKED.
NO. I GOT MYSELF INTO SOMETHING I WASN'T PREPARED FOR. AND I SHOULD HAVE KNOWN...
BECAUSE WITHOUT YOU, THE ATOM ISN'T HIS BEST.
...YOU'RE RIGHT. YOU SHOULDN'T HAVE LIED TO ME. BUT YOU'RE SAFE. WE HALTED THE MICROVERSE'S DECAY.
IT WAS ME THAT DRAGGED THE JUSTICE LEAGUE DOWN HERE AND ALMOST GOT THEM KILLED, BECAUSE I COULDN'T FIND YOU ON MY OWN. YOU COULD'VE.
SO NOW WE CAN FINALLY GET OUT OF HERE, I CAN GO BACK TO WORKING NEWTON BASE, AND YOU CAN GO BACK TO BEING THE ATOM.
...ARE YOU LISTENING, RYAN?
WHA-- WHAT?

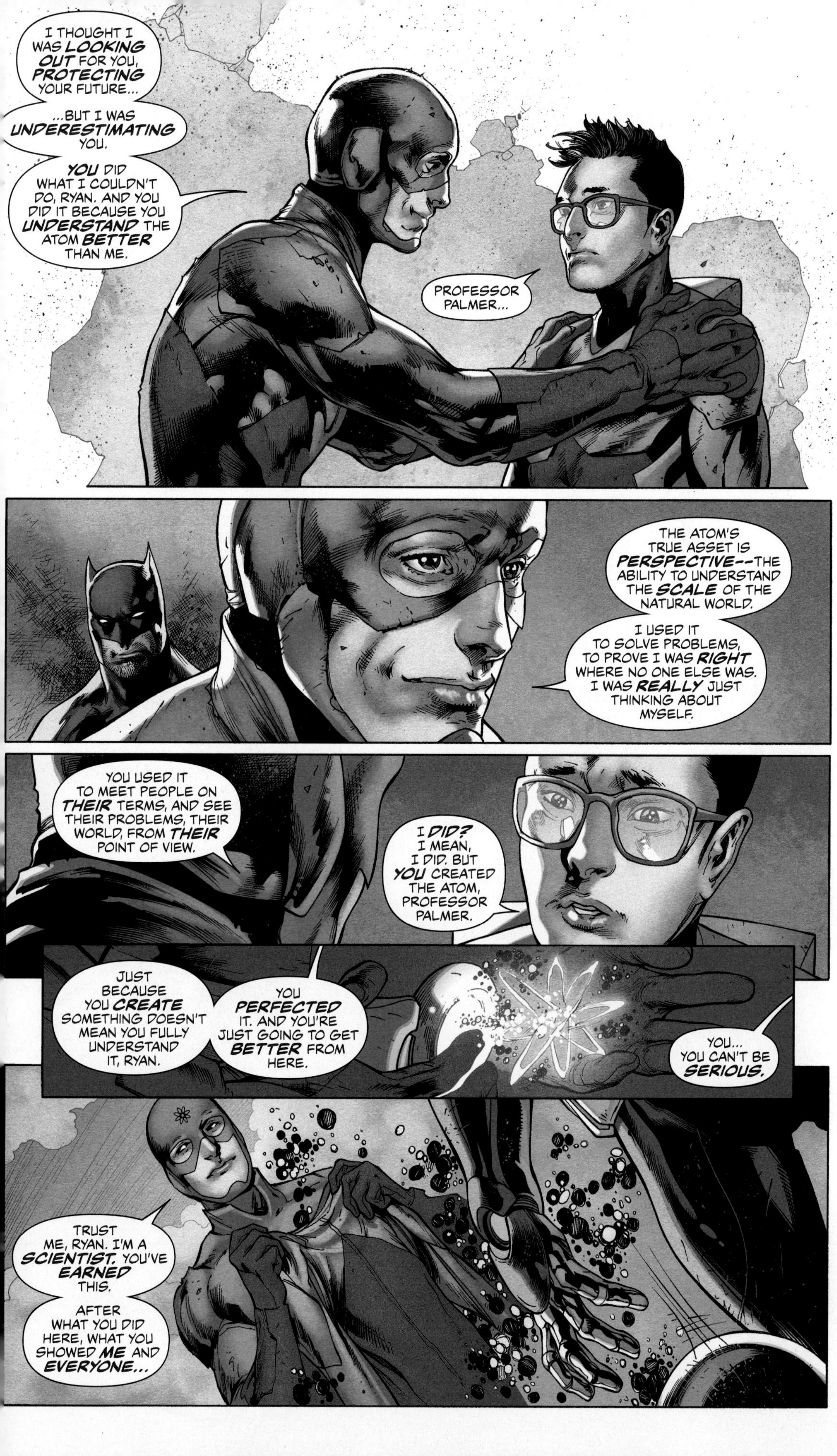
I THOUGHT I WAS LOOKING OUT FOR YOU, PROTECTING YOUR FUTURE...
...BUT I WAS UNDERESTIMATING YOU.
YOU DID WHAT I COULDN'T DO, RYAN. AND YOU DID IT BECAUSE YOU UNDERSTAND THE ATOM BETTER THAN ME.
PROFESSOR PALMER...
THE ATOM'S TRUE ASSET IS PERSPECTIVE--THE ABILITY TO UNDERSTAND THE SCALE OF THE NATURAL WORLD.
I USED IT TO SOLVE PROBLEMS, TO PROVE I WAS RIGHT WHERE NO ONE ELSE WAS. I WAS REALLY JUST THINKING ABOUT MYSELF.
YOU USED IT TO MEET PEOPLE ON THEIR TERMS, AND SEE THEIR PROBLEMS, THEIR WORLD, FROM THEIR POINT OF VIEW.
I DID? I MEAN, I DID. BUT YOU CREATED THE ATOM, PROFESSOR PALMER.
JUST BECAUSE YOU CREATE SOMETHING DOESN'T MEAN YOU FULLY UNDERSTAND IT, RYAN.
YOU PERFECTED IT. AND YOU'RE JUST GOING TO GET BETTER FROM HERE.
YOU... YOU CAN'T BE SERIOUS.
TRUST ME, RYAN. I'M A SCIENTIST. YOU'VE EARNED THIS.
AFTER WHAT YOU DID HERE, WHAT YOU SHOWED ME AND EVERYONE...

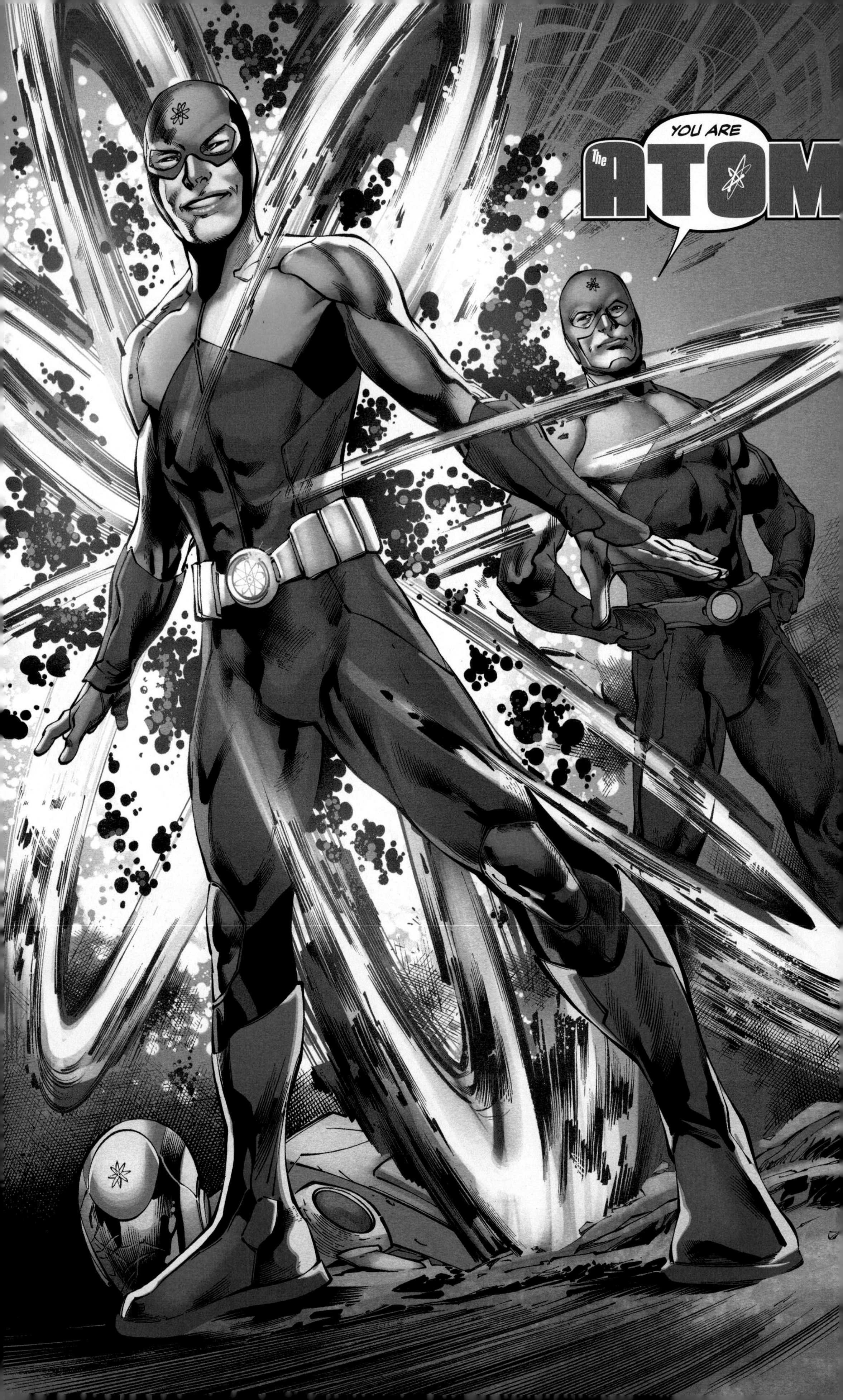
YOU ARE
The ATOM

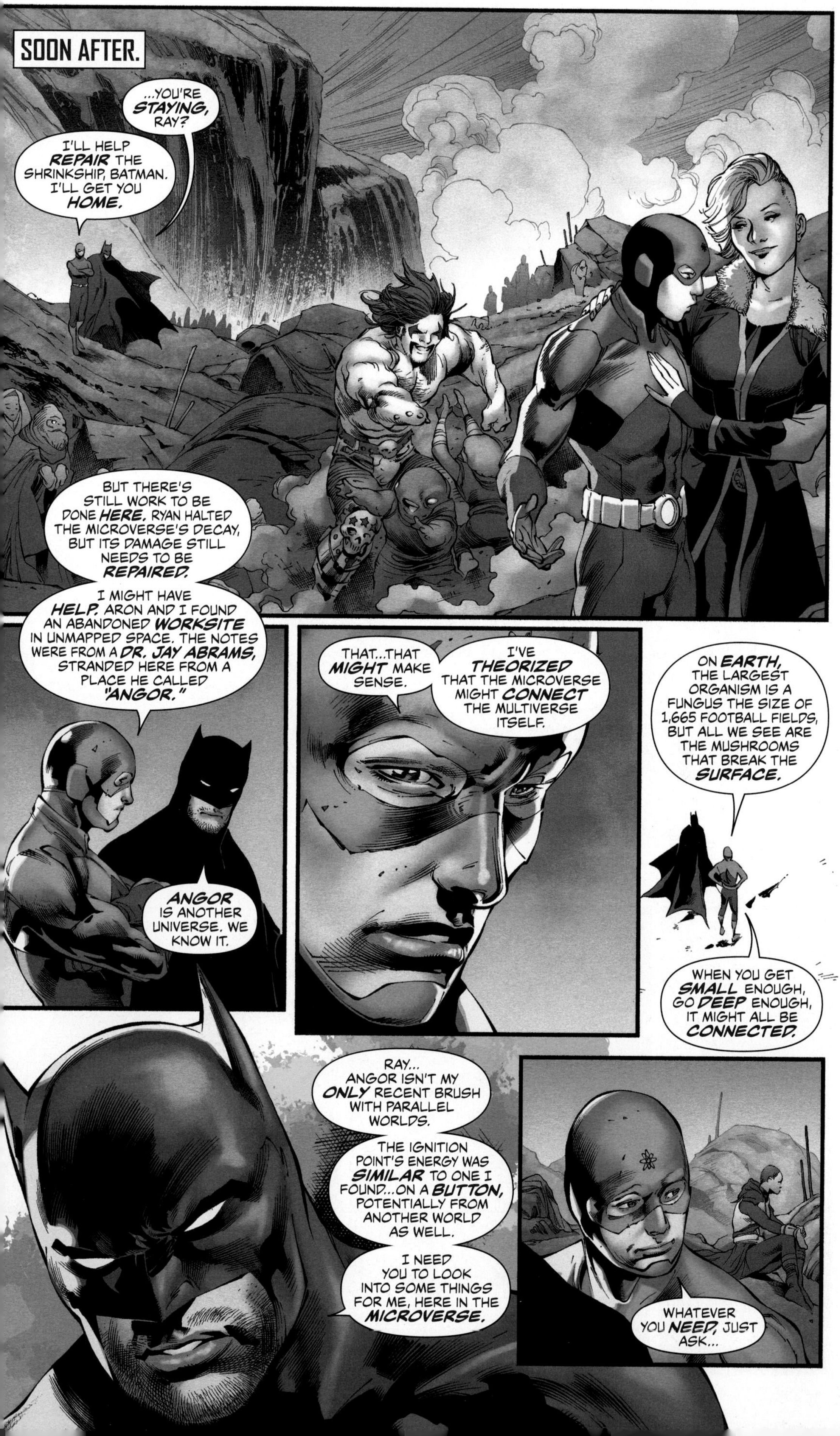
SOON AFTER.
...YOU'RE STAYING, RAY?
I'LL HELP REPAIR THE SHRINKSHIP, BATMAN. I'LL GET YOU HOME.
BUT THERE'S STILL WORK TO BE DONE HERE. RYAN HALTED THE MICROVERSE'S DECAY, BUT ITS DAMAGE STILL NEEDS TO BE REPAIRED.
I MIGHT HAVE HELP. ARON AND I FOUND AN ABANDONED WORKSITE IN UNMAPPED SPACE. THE NOTES WERE FROM A DR. JAY ABRAMS, STRANDED HERE FROM A PLACE HE CALLED "ANGOR."
ANGOR IS ANOTHER UNIVERSE. WE KNOW IT.
THAT...THAT MIGHT MAKE SENSE.
I'VE THEORIZED THAT THE MICROVERSE MIGHT CONNECT THE MULTIVERSE ITSELF.
ON EARTH, THE LARGEST ORGANISM IS A FUNGUS THE SIZE OF 1,665 FOOTBALL FIELDS, BUT ALL WE SEE ARE THE MUSHROOMS THAT BREAK THE SURFACE.
WHEN YOU GET SMALL ENOUGH, GO DEEP ENOUGH, IT MIGHT ALL BE CONNECTED.
RAY... ANGOR ISN'T MY ONLY RECENT BRUSH WITH PARALLEL WORLDS.
THE IGNITION POINT'S ENERGY WAS SIMILAR TO ONE I FOUND...ON A BUTTON, POTENTIALLY FROM ANOTHER WORLD AS WELL.
I NEED YOU TO LOOK INTO SOME THINGS FOR ME, HERE IN THE MICROVERSE.
WHATEVER YOU NEED, JUST ASK...

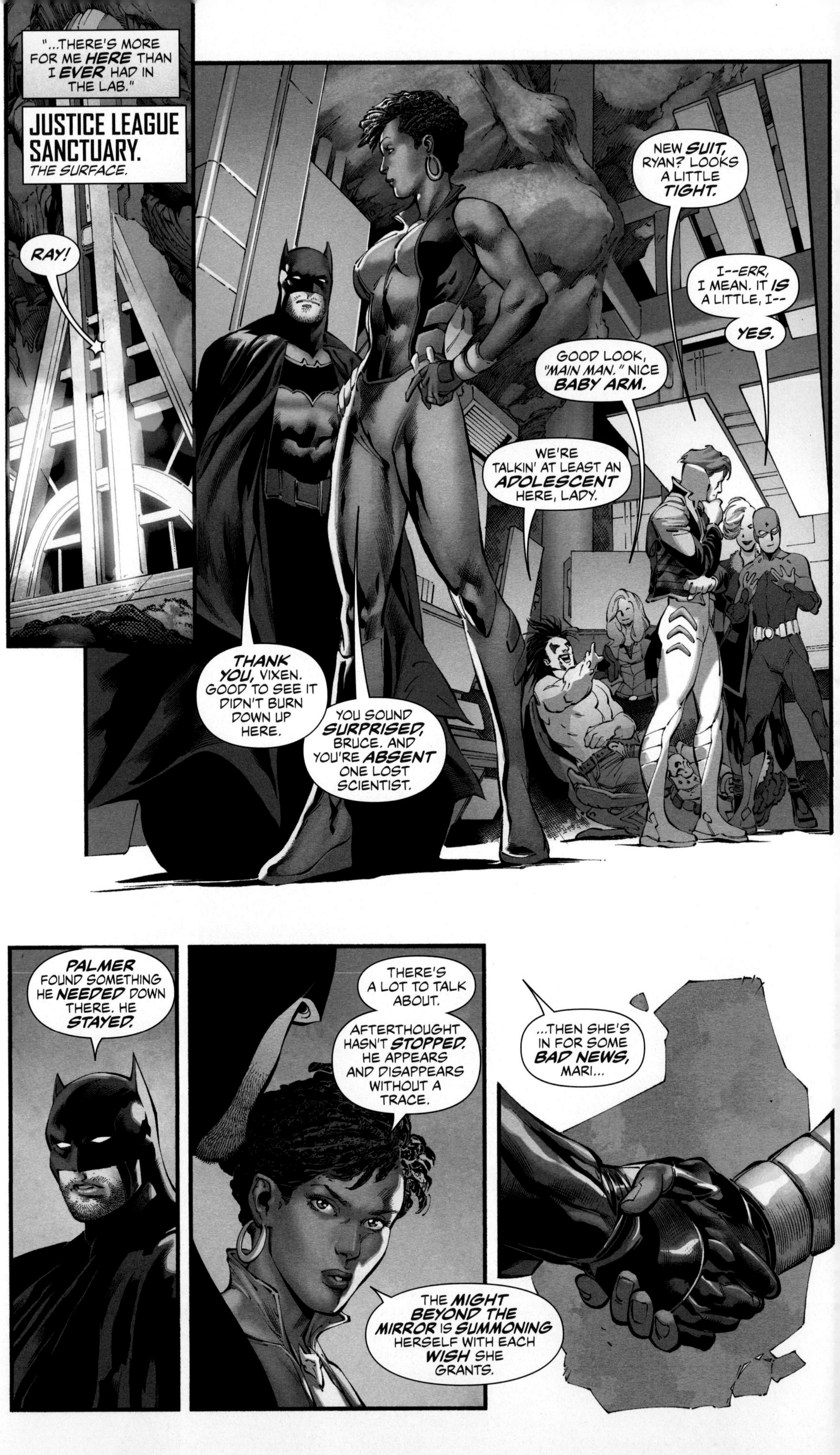
"...THERE'S MORE FOR ME HERE THAN I EVER HAD IN THE LAB."
JUSTICE LEAGUE SANCTUARY.
THE SURFACE.
RAY!
NEW SUIT, RYAN? LOOKS A LITTLE TIGHT.
I--ERR, I MEAN. IT IS A LITTLE, I--
YES.
GOOD LOOK, "MAIN MAN." NICE BABY ARM.
WE'RE TALKIN' AT LEAST AN ADOLESCENT HERE, LADY.
THANK YOU, VIXEN. GOOD TO SEE IT DIDN'T BURN DOWN UP HERE.
YOU SOUND SURPRISED, BRUCE. AND YOU'RE ABSENT ONE LOST SCIENTIST.
PALMER FOUND SOMETHING HE NEEDED DOWN THERE. HE STAYED.
THERE'S A LOT TO TALK ABOUT.
AFTERTHOUGHT HASN'T STOPPED. HE APPEARS AND DISAPPEARS WITHOUT A TRACE.
THE MIGHT BEYOND THE MIRROR IS SUMMONING HERSELF WITH EACH WISH SHE GRANTS.
...THEN SHE'S IN FOR SOME BAD NEWS, MARI...

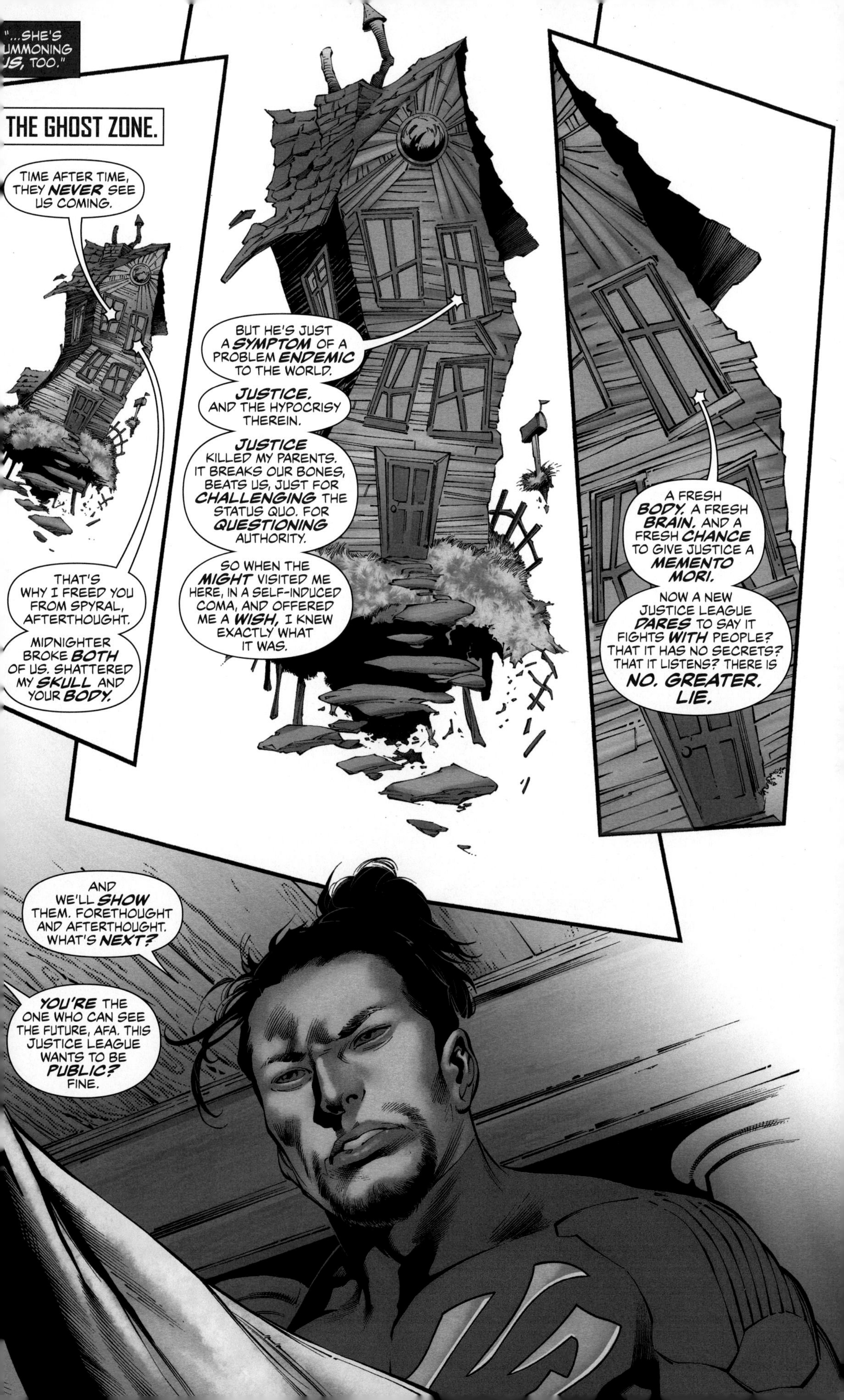
"...SHE'S
UMMONING
US, TOO."
THE GHOST ZONE.
TIME AFTER TIME, THEY NEVER SEE US COMING.
THAT'S WHY I FREED YOU FROM SPYRAL, AFTERTHOUGHT.
MIDNIGHTER BROKE BOTH OF US. SHATTERED MY SKULL AND YOUR BODY.
BUT HE'S JUST A SYMPTOM OF A PROBLEM ENDEMIC TO THE WORLD.
JUSTICE. AND THE HYPOCRISY THEREIN.
JUSTICE KILLED MY PARENTS. IT BREAKS OUR BONES, BEATS US, JUST FOR CHALLENGING THE STATUS QUO. FOR QUESTIONING AUTHORITY.
SO WHEN THE MIGHT VISITED ME HERE, IN A SELF-INDUCED COMA, AND OFFERED ME A WISH, I KNEW EXACTLY WHAT IT WAS.
A FRESH BODY. A FRESH BRAIN. AND A FRESH CHANCE TO GIVE JUSTICE A MEMENTO MORI.
NOW A NEW JUSTICE LEAGUE DARES TO SAY IT FIGHTS WITH PEOPLE? THAT IT HAS NO SECRETS? THAT IT LISTENS? THERE IS NO. GREATER. LIE.
AND WE'LL SHOW THEM. FORETHOUGHT AND AFTERTHOUGHT. WHAT'S NEXT?
YOU'RE THE ONE WHO CAN SEE THE FUTURE, AFA. THIS JUSTICE LEAGUE WANTS TO BE PUBLIC? FINE.

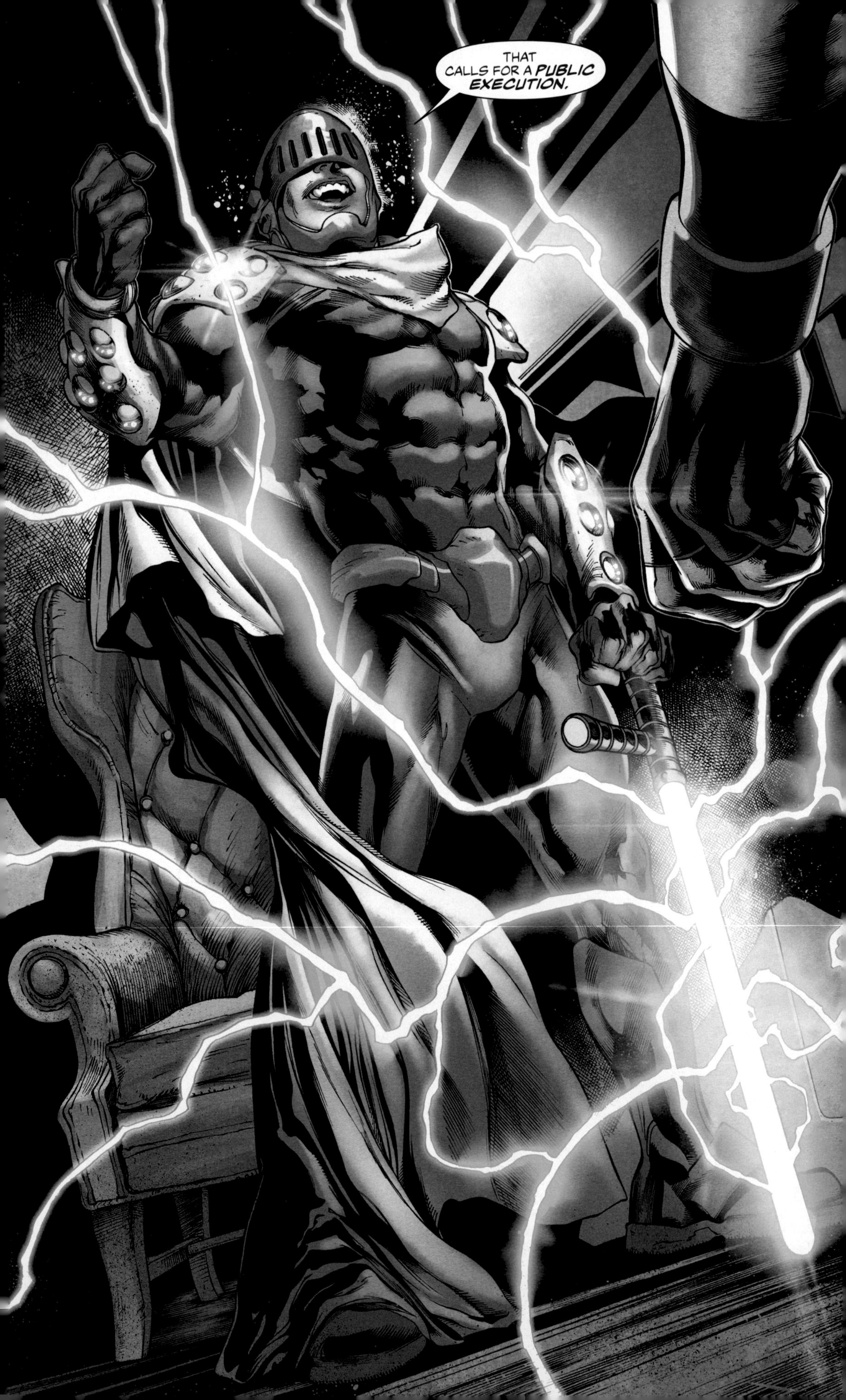
THAT CALLS FOR A PUBLIC EXECUTION.

JUSTICE LEAGUE OF AMERICA

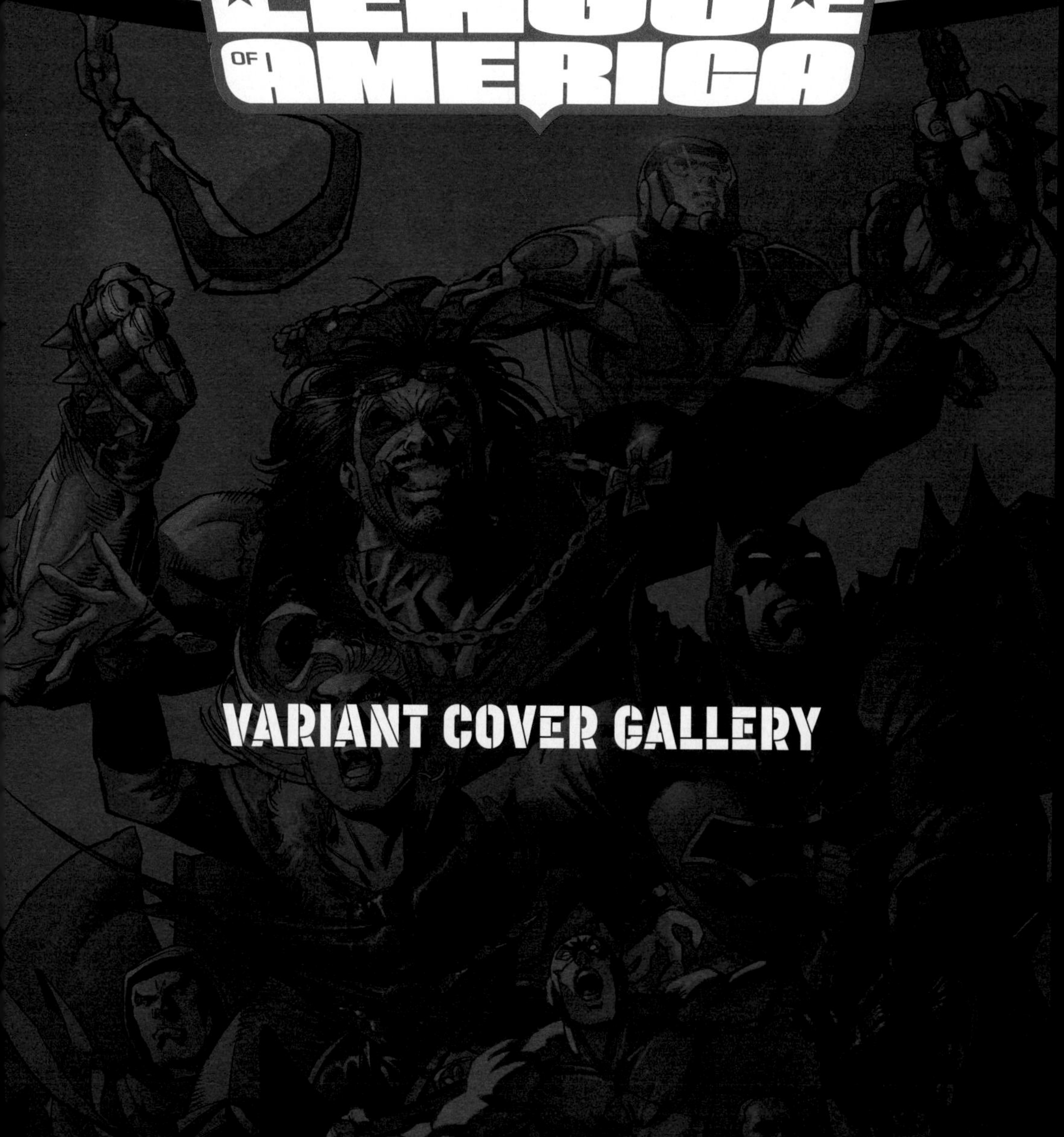

VARIANT COVER GALLERY

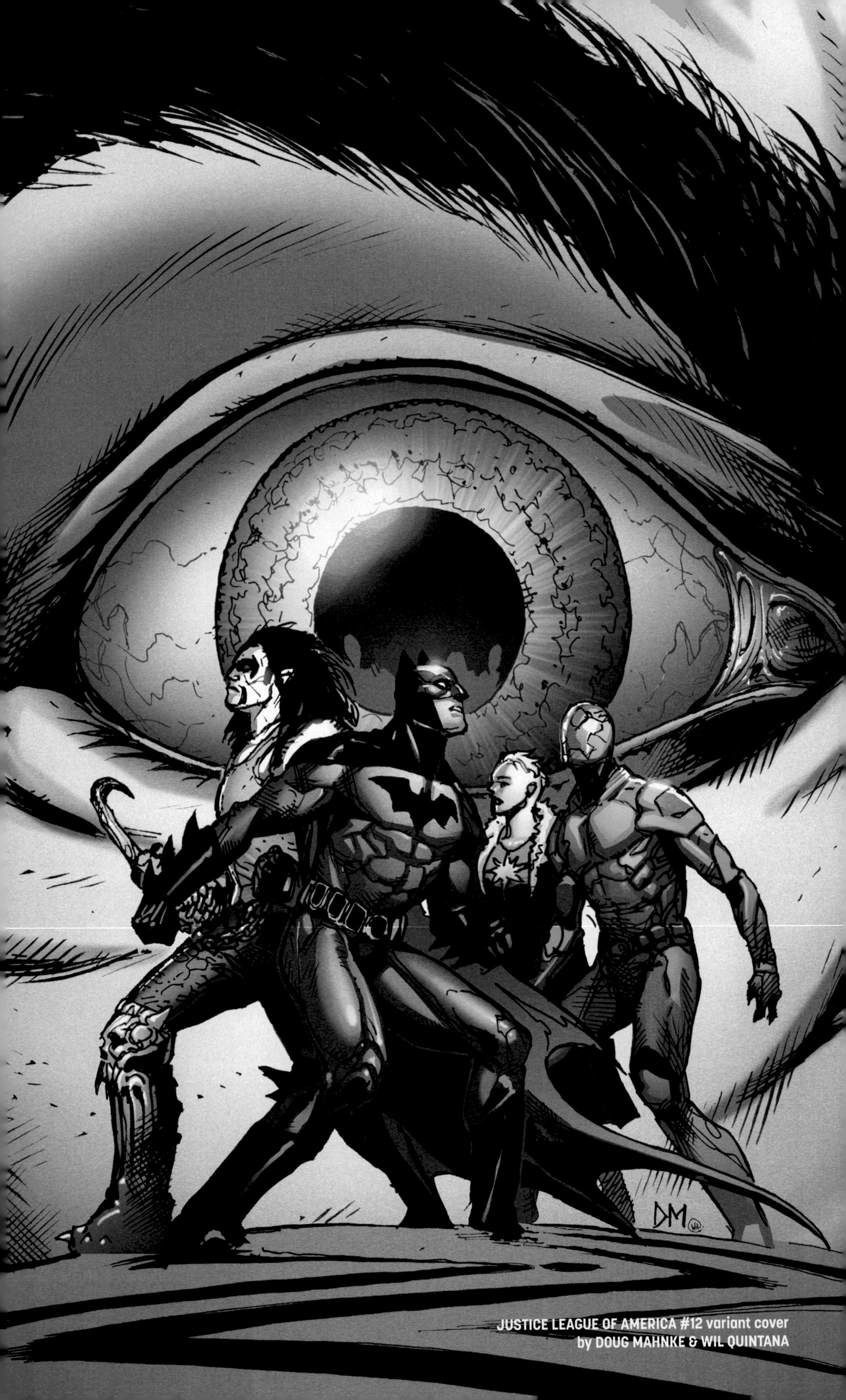

JUSTICE LEAGUE OF AMERICA #12 variant cover
by DOUG MAHNKE & WIL QUINTANA

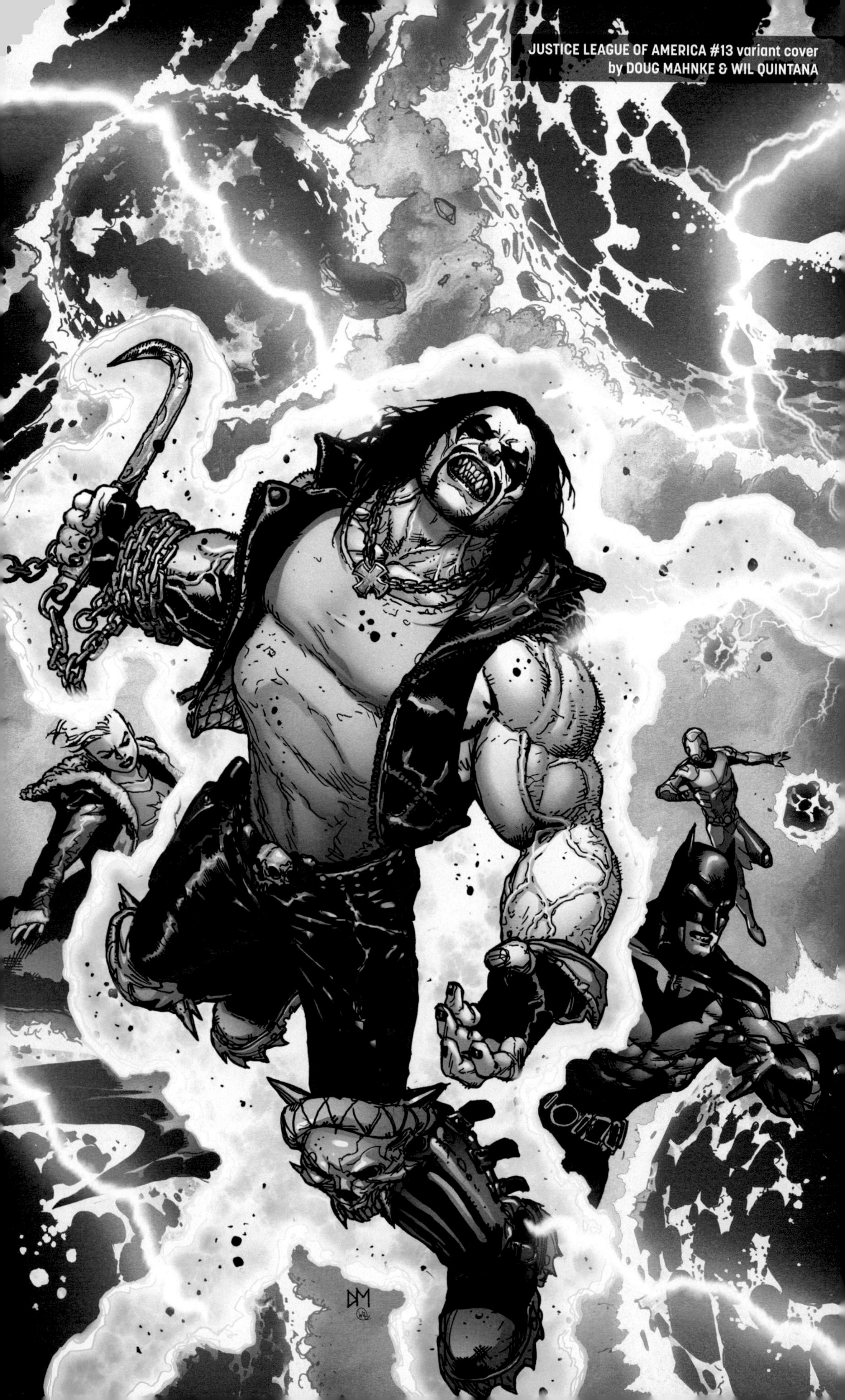

JUSTICE LEAGUE OF AMERICA #13 variant cover
by DOUG MAHNKE & WIL QUINTANA

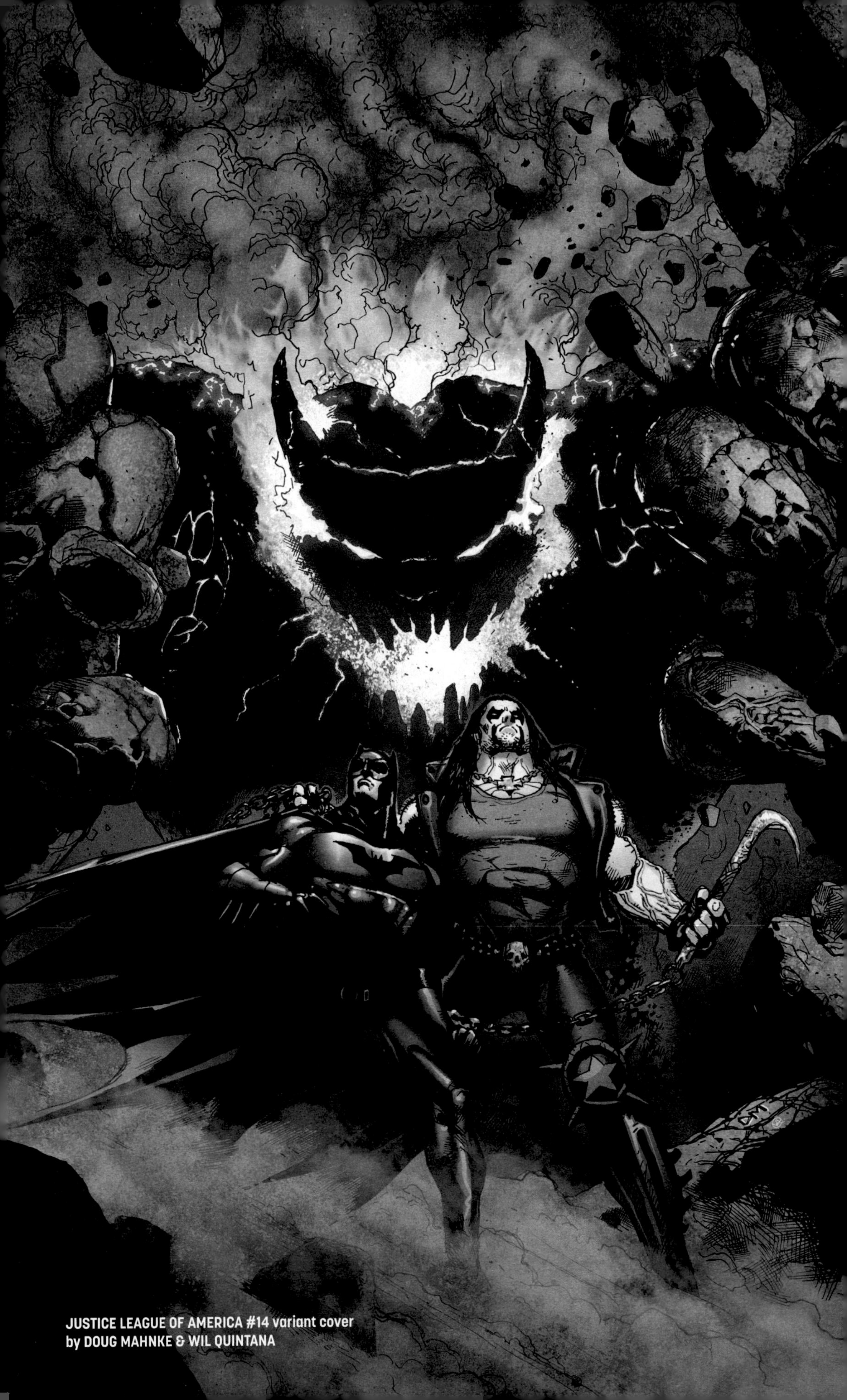

JUSTICE LEAGUE OF AMERICA #14 variant cover
by DOUG MAHNKE & WIL QUINTANA

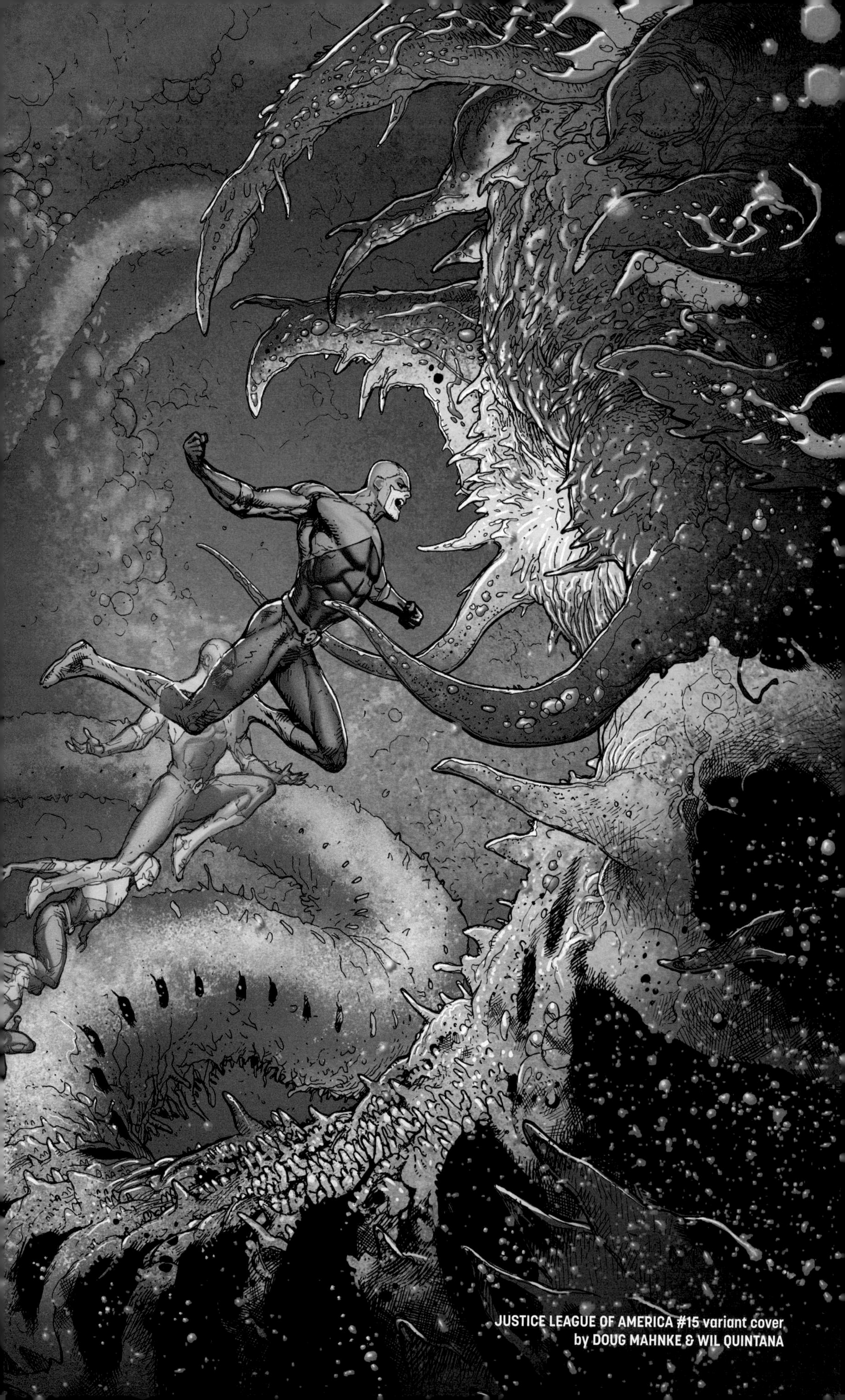

JUSTICE LEAGUE OF AMERICA #15 variant cover
by DOUG MAHNKE & WIL QUINTANA

JUSTICE LEAGUE OF AMERICA #16 variant cover
by DOUG MAHNKE & WIL QUINTANA

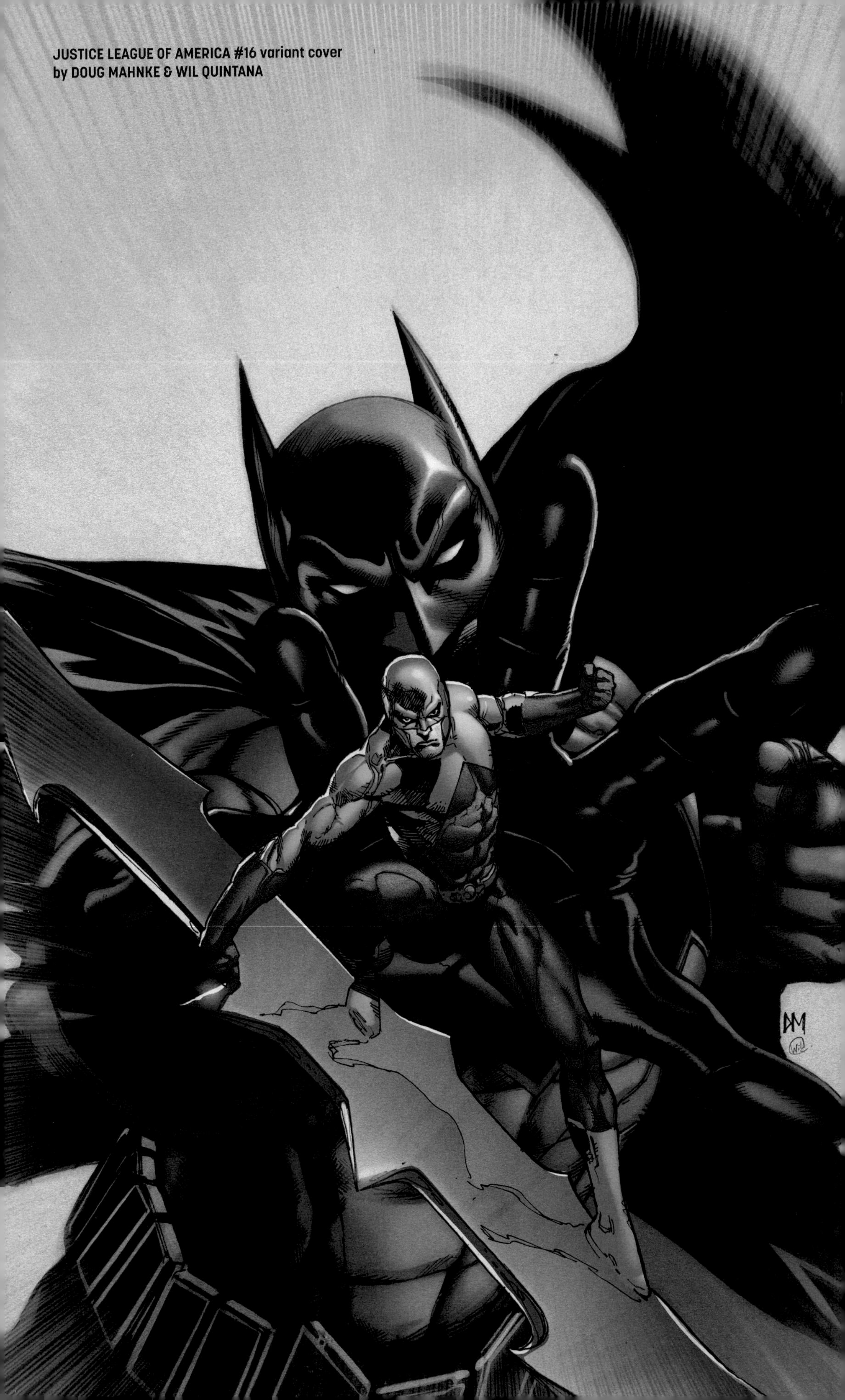

JUSTICE LEAGUE OF AMERICA #17 variant cover
by DOUG MAHNKE & WIL QUINTANA

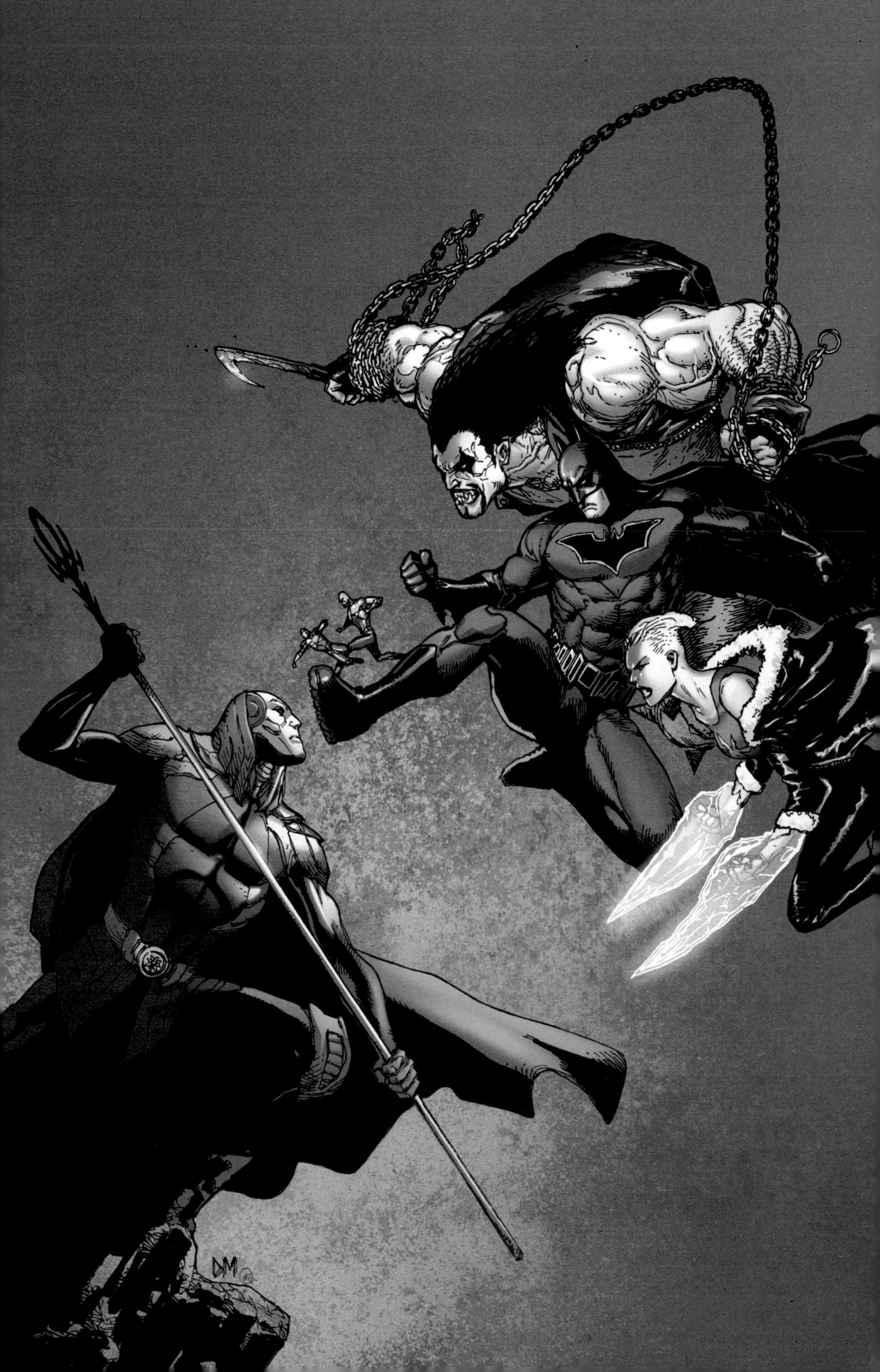

"Some really thrilling artwork that establishes incredible scope and danger."
—IGN

DC UNIVERSE REBIRTH
JUSTICE LEAGUE
VOL. 1: The Extinction Machines

BRYAN HITCH
with TONY S. DANIEL

VOL.1 THE EXTINCTION MACHINES
BRYAN HITCH • TONY S. DANIEL • SANDU FLOREA • TOMEU MOREY

VOL.1 THE IMITATION OF LIFE
JOHN SEMPER JR. • PAUL PELLETIER • WILL CONRAD

**CYBORG VOL. 1:
THE IMITATION OF LIFE**

VOL.1 RAGE PLANET
SAM HUMPHRIES • ROBSON ROCHA • ETHAN VAN SCIVER • ED BENES

**GREEN LANTERNS VOL. 1:
RAGE PLANET**

VOL.1 THE DROWNING
DAN ABNETT • PHILIPPE BRIONES • SCOT EATON • BRAD WALKER

**AQUAMAN VOL. 1:
THE DROWNING**

Get more DC graphic novels wherever comics and books are sold!